The Quality of Madness

Also by Tim Rich

Caught Beneath the Landslide: Manchester City in the 1990s

THE QUALITY OF MADNESS

The Life of Marcelo Bielsa

Tim Rich

Quercus

First published in Great Britain in 2020 by Quercus.
This paperback edition published in 2021 by

Quercus Editions Ltd
Carmelite House
50 Victoria Embankment
London EC4Y 0DZ

An Hachette UK company

A CIP catalogue record for this book is available
from the British Library

MMP ISBN 978 1 52940 501 9
Ebook ISBN 978 1 52941 032 7

10 9 8 7 6 5 4 3

1 – MARTYN HAYHOW/AFP via Getty Images: 2 – Andreas Rentz/Bongarts/Getty Images:
3 – ANTONIO SCORZA/AFP via Getty Images: 4 – AP Photo/Natacha Pisarenko:
5 – Jose CABEZAS/AFP via Getty Images: 6 – AP Photo/Andres Kudacki:
7 – Gabriele Maltinti/Getty Images: 8 – BERTRAND LANGLOIS/AFP via Getty Images:
9 – BORIS HORVAT/AFP via Getty Images: 10 – Cal Sport Media/Alamy Stock Photo:
11, 12, 14 – George Wood/Getty Images: 13, 15, 16 – Alex Dodd – CameraSport via Getty Images

Typeset by CC Book Production
Printed and bound in Great Britain by Clays Ltd, Elcograf S.p.A.

For my brother, Chris

'There is more latitude in the eccentrics. They are always honest and have their own quality of madness. In the final analysis, they will be the saints.'

The actress Margaret Rutherford
talking about her cousin Tony Benn

Contents

PART TWO:
EUROPE

PART THREE:
YORKSHIRE

PART ONE: AMERICA

Prairie Rose

If Buenos Aires is the heart of Argentine football, then Rosario is its soul. Like the north-east of England, its fame lies not in the silverware it has won but in the men it has produced and the passion with which they are supported. The city's development was underpinned not by coal, steel and shipbuilding but by the vast prairie of the Argentine pampas. Rosario dealt in wheat, cattle and horses. Then came football.

The city and its two main teams, Newell's Old Boys and Rosario Central, developed footballers because, unlike the great clubs of Buenos Aires – Boca Juniors, Independiente and River Plate – they could not afford to buy them. Rosario became known in Argentina as 'the Cradle of Football'.

Rubén Gaggioli, a businessman from Rosario who represented Lionel Messi when he went from Newell's to Barcelona as a thirteen-year-old, said: 'It's not like in Spain, where an underage player can have their own car, earn a salary and live well. In Rosario, those kids don't have anything so when they go out on to the pitch, they will lay down their lives to win. They have this essence to become great players. It's not just in the city of Rosario. It's also about its surrounding areas. A lot of Newell's greatest players – Jorge Valdano, Mauricio Pochettino and Gabriel Batistuta – come from the outlying areas. They come from the famous *potrero*. It's something that in Europe practically doesn't exist. The *potrero* is where kids play on the streets on patches of open, uneven ground. This is where these young footballers are created.'

Before Messi, before Tata Martino and Marcelo Bielsa, before Mario Kempes, Ángel di María and César Luis Menotti, Rosario's great claim to fame was as the place where the flag of Argentina was first raised. This was in 1812 and the man who raised it on the bend of the Paraná river was General Manuel Belgrano. At that time there was no country called Argentina, just a vast province of the Spanish Empire called the Viceroyalty of Río de la Plata. It was made up of what is now central Argentina, Uruguay, Paraguay, northern Chile and southern Peru. Its main sources of wealth were its silver mines and the thousands of head of cattle that were exported every year through the port of Buenos Aires. However, by the time the Spanish fleet, under the command of its French allies, was shot to pieces at Trafalgar in 1805, the silver was beginning to run out while British control of the seas meant the cattle stayed where they were.

Then, in 1806–7, began the strange love-hate relationship between Britain and Argentina, when British forces attempted to seize control of the province. They were met with anything the citizens of Buenos Aires could lay their hands on: muskets; boiling water and oil thrown from top-floor windows; artillery directed by regular troops. The British were attacked by African slaves, creoles - those who had lived all their lives in South America. This action is recalled by Argentinians simply as 'the Defence'. In August 1807, the Redcoats surrendered. On his return to England, the commanding officer, Lieutenant-General John Whitelocke, was court-martialled and sacked, essentially for losing to an army of amateurs. Some 1,200 of his soldiers, deserters or prisoners of war, stayed behind to help build the new Argentina.

The fact the citizens of Buenos Aires had beaten the British by themselves and that the Spanish governor, Rafael de Sobremonte, had fled with the city's treasury which he had then managed to lose, had broken the last ties with Madrid. On 27 February 1812, Belgrano unfurled the blue and white flag of Argentina in Rosario. Four years later, Argentina was an independent nation.

Rosario became the booming centre of the country's great wheat and cattle belts. By 1926 nearly half the city's population were immigrants, many from Liguria in north-western Italy. In the words of Juan Álvarez, a Rosarino who became the country's attorney general in 1935, Rosario differed from Santa Fe or Buenos Aires because it had not been founded by the Spanish. It was, he said, 'a self-made city', and it was one with radical politics. Che Guevara was born here. His sport of choice was rugby.

Marcelo Bielsa's great-grandfather was a carpenter from Esperanza, an agricultural town about a hundred miles north of Rosario. He sent his son, Rafael, to Buenos Aires to learn how to become a master furniture maker. Rafael was more interested in books and the law and he enrolled himself in the University of Buenos Aires. In January 1918 Rafael Bielsa graduated with a doctorate in jurisprudence. His thesis sounds remarkably modern – a study into accidents at work and how they were covered by the law. Three years later Rafael was in Rosario, as general secretary of the city council. He worked at the Ministry of Justice, became president of the Rosario bar association, taught literature at the School of Commerce.

By 1949, when he was 60, Rafael Bielsa was one of South America's foremost lawyers. He was dean of the Universidad del Litoral at Santa Fe, professor at the law faculty at the University of Buenos Aires, an honorary professor of the Sorbonne in Paris. His great house in Rosario, by the Parque de la Independencia, housed a library containing more than 3,000 books. He had turned down a position on Argentina's Supreme Court because he was not convinced of the independence of those who would share the tribunal with him.

At this time Argentina was changing radically. It was the time of Juan and Eva Perón, whose programme of sweeping reforms in favour of Argentina's working class, wrapped up with nationalist posturing, appealed to both left and right. Rosario was a fervently Peronist city. In February 1946, when they were campaigning for the presidency, Juan and Eva were mobbed as they arrived at the city's rail station after a six-hour journey from Buenos Aires. In the central square, with swarms of locusts weighing down the night sky and people climbing banana or palm trees for a better view, the cry that was to haunt Argentine politics for generations was first heard. 'Evita.'

The Perons' ideology had no time for intellectuals from the left or the right. Bernardo Houssay, the first Argentine scientist to win the Nobel Prize, was driven from office. Jorge Luis Borges, perhaps the country's greatest writer but a political conservative, was asked to leave his position at the unassuming library where he worked and wrote. He was offered a new job as inspector of poultry and rabbits at the Buenos Aires market. Bielsa was forced out of his position as dean of the Universidad del Litoral. He outlived the Perón dictatorship and began codifying the law of the provinces of Santa Fe and Mendoza. Buildings and streets were named after him; one is in his home town of Esperanza, another in a working-class district of Rosario.

There is another in Buenos Aires, by the Chacarita Cemetery, which contains the grave of Leopoldo Galtieri, who persecuted Rafael Bielsa's grandson and namesake, and the tomb of Alexander Watson Hutton, the Glaswegian who in 1893 founded the Argentine FA.

Marcelo Bielsa's father, also called Rafael but nicknamed 'El Turco' (the Turk) was also a lawyer, although as the journalist and commentator, Román Iucht, recounts in his study of Bielsa, *La Vida por el fútbol*, he was a less driven personality:

El Turco always had a bohemian personality and inherited his father's profession, though he tended to lean politically more to the right. He loved cars and admitted he would have liked to have become a mechanical engineer. He worked in his father's study, although his clients were not of the same standing, they were much more simple cases. For him, the law was a job rather than a vocation. It was his custom that every day at noon he would go to a Basque bar, the Laurak Bat, in the centre of Rosario for a drink with his friends. It was common for him to be taken out of the bar by his children who were tired of waiting for him in the car and had to remind him that there was a family lunch waiting for them. He listened to a lot of music and Marcelo's friends who came to the house in Calle Mitre recalled Frank Sinatra as a permanent soundtrack.

The family lunches to which the Bielsa children dragged their father out of Laurak Bat would have been worth the wait. Their mother, Lidia, was a superb cook. She was also a history teacher and both her passions would form a central part of Marcelo's life. When in the mid-1990s he was in Mexico managing Atlas Guadalajara, his assistant, Ernesto Urrea, recalled: 'He read so much that I think he knew more about Mexican culture than I did. I have also never seen anyone eat as much. He loved the *antojitos* [Mexican street food] that they sold on street corners. When we went to restaurants, he would order every dish on the menu just so he could taste each one.' When he was manager of Chile, Marcelo's favourite restaurant was La Signoria, an unpretentious Italian place in Santiago, where he would order *la torta del nonno*, a chocolate cake filled with pears sautéed in honey.

Lidia Caldera gave her children something more fundamental than a taste for good food. She was from a far more working-class background than her husband, and where the Bielsas lived in Calle Mitre bordered onto a working-class *barrio*. Lidia mixed easily with people from both sides of the tracks and, though her children would go to university, become politicians, architects, manage football teams, write novels and design hotels, they were not snobs. It is one of Marcelo Bielsa's great attributes that despite coming from a moneyed, intellectual family, he would form strong relationships not just with working-class footballers but with those like Carlos Tévez, whose background was dirt-poor.

Marcelo was the middle of three children, all of whom would reach the peak of their chosen careers. In one year, 2003, Rafael would be Argentina's foreign secretary, Marcelo would be managing the nation's football team and the youngest, María Eugenia, a renowned architect, became deputy governor of Santa Fe province, which included their home city of Rosario. It was Rafael, born in February 1953, who followed his grandfather's path most directly. When he was Britain's chancellor of the exchequer in the 1970s, Denis Healey, who was MP for Leeds East, liked to say he was a politician with a hinterland, that he had interests outside the Palace of Westminster. Rafael Bielsa's hinterland included the law, politics and poetry. Despite the humiliation his grandfather had suffered at the hands of Juan Perón, Rafael and his sister, María Eugenia, became supporters of a left-wing nationalist version of Peronism, opposed to both the military junta and socialism. He would write novels and histories, and attempt to negotiate the restoration of direct flights between Buenos Aires and the Falkland Islands with the British foreign secretary, Jack Straw.

As a young man Rafael became attracted to radical politics. In September 1969, when he was sixteen, 30,000 demonstrators, spearheaded by 4,000 students protesting against the military dictatorship of Juan Carlos Onganía, seized control of the centre of Rosario. By mid-afternoon the government controlled a mere six blocks of the city, concentrated on the radio station, the court building and the army and police headquarters. At nine o'clock that night, the crackdown began, led by the Second Army Corps. There were scores of dead. Leopoldo Galtieri, who was to become well known to the Bielsas, took a leading role in the violence. A calm of sorts was restored.

María Eugenia Bielsa was born in 1958, three years after Marcelo, five after Rafael. As with all the Bielsa children, the value of education was drilled into her. 'In my house there was a rule that you had to be a university student,' she recalled in 2004. 'My dad wanted me to become an accountant because I'd earn plenty of money. My mum just wanted me to be a university student.' Her passion was architecture. She studied then lectured in the subject at the University of Rosario and, like Rafael, became involved in the politics of Peronism, which flourished after the downfall of the junta. While he became foreign secretary, she was the deputy governor of the Santa Fe province and in 2019 after the victory of the Peronist presidential candidate, Alberto Fernández, she was once more back in frontline politics, helping to oversee the creation of a Ministry of Housing, a department she headed. It was through María Eugenia that Marcelo met his wife, Laura Bracalenti, a fellow architect, with whom he would have two daughters: Inés, born in 1989, and Mercedes three years later.

Marcelo, was the middle child, born in July 1955. He would have many interests but only one passion, which was to stay with him all his life: football. His attitude at School Number Three, a primary school in the Calle Entre Ríos, in one of Rosario's middle-class districts, would be the same as when he oversaw games at Newell's Old Boys or at the Estadio Monumental in Buenos Aires. If his team was not good enough, he became angry. Cheating of any kind left him furious. In *La Vida por el fútbol*, Román Iucht wrote:

Football was his religion and the mass took place every weekend. Every Friday night, the young Marcelo began his ritual. He would obsessively prepare his kit, putting out his shirt, socks and shorts and polishing his boots. Early on Saturday morning, around eight o'clock, he would go round to his neighbour, Hugo Vitantonio, who lived a few metres away. They would go out into the street and wait for the team to gather. They were all boys from the area, which was a middle-class district. During the week they would be separated by school life. Some, like Bielsa, went to the Normal, others to Juana Manso. On Saturdays, they were reunited by their passion for sport. Their destination would be the Parque de la Independencia or the Corazón de María church, which had a football pitch at the bottom. Another option was to go to the stadium of Central Córdoba, a typical lower-division club, and use the training pitches the first team did not require. The boys felt they were professionals and were playing to become heroes of the game. Their team was called Blue Star.

Mostly, Marcelo played as a defender, though a desire to win would drive him into midfield or even attack. They did not then call him El Loco but El Cabezón, which translates as 'Big Head'.

Pedro Vitantonio was Blue Star's 'manager'. One day, while they were playing on an improvised pitch in the park, a policeman turned up to investigate a complaint that they had damaged a tree. Pedro accepted responsibility and the policeman began to lead him away. Suddenly, both men were surrounded by eleven- and twelve-year-old boys demanding that Pedro be released. Then Marcelo threw himself to the floor, grabbed the policeman around the ankles and was dragged along while demanding his manager be released.

There were other football-related brushes with the law. When a policeman came to answer a complaint about a broken window, the young Bielsa shouted at him to wait until he had taken a corner. That was enough to have him carted off to the station until his father came to get him. Even then, Marcelo would not leave until his ball had been returned to him. Both those stories seem to indicate that Rosario in the 1960s either had very little crime to investigate or an awful lot of policemen.

By 1966, when Argentina had been controversially beaten

by England in the World Cup quarter-finals and labelled 'animals' by Alf Ramsey, Marcelo was ready for secondary school at a time when football was being talked of with a fierce passion. When Antonio Rattín was dismissed at Wembley for dissent, took ten minutes to leave the pitch and sat on the red carpet that had been laid out for the Queen, the reaction in Argentina was ferocious. The team was treated like heroes and declared 'the moral winners of the World Cup'. As he stepped off the plane, Rattín, who was to become a right-wing politician after retirement, was wrapped in the national flag. The newspaper *Crónica* stated that 'Spiritually, England is still the pirate that despoiled the Caribbean and robbed us of the Falklands.' In the British embassy in Buenos Aires, the ambassador, Sir Michael Cresswell, was placed under armed guard for his own protection.

The school Bielsa attended, the Sacred Heart, had been founded in 1900 and was one of the most prestigious in Rosario. Its elegant white colonnaded facade, with a statue of the Virgin Mary on the roof, was a short walk from his grandfather's mansion. 'He didn't like getting dressed in the morning,' Rafael Bielsa recalled. 'He would sleep in his jacket and trousers. They said he was mad but these weren't unusual things to do.'

There was something else a short walk away from his house: the Coloso del Parque, the home of Newell's Old Boys. It was his uncle, Pancho Parola, who introduced Marcelo to the club, forging a bond that would never leave him.

Throughout his life, he would return again and again to his experiences at Newell's as a fan, a player and a manager as an example of how football should be played and lived.

Newell's, like so much in Argentina, had English roots. Isaac Newell had come to Rosario from Kent as a teenager in 1869 and later founded the Anglican Commercial College of Argentina, a school whose coat of arms was red and black. In November 1903 Isaac's son, Claudio, set up a football team which he named after his father, Newell's Old Boys. They kept the school colours. In 1939 both Newell's and its great rivals, Rosario Central, joined the Argentine Football League for its first season. Like Newell's, Rosario Central had been formed by the British, in this case a group of workers for the Central Argentine Railway.

The club was slightly older than Newell's, having been founded in 1889. The origins of their blue and yellow kit are also English, based on the colours Leeds United wore until 1961 when Don Revie decided that the all-white of Real Madrid would suit them better.

The clubs' nicknames date from the 1920s, when – and nobody is very sure of the date – a leper hospital asked the two clubs to play a charity game. Newell's accepted; Rosario refused. Since then, Newell's have been known as Los Leprosos (the Lepers) while Rosario are Las Canallas (the Scoundrels). Fans of Newell's sometimes tell a story that Che Guevara, who supported Rosario Central, worked in a leper colony as an act of penitence. Like many stories it is true but not quite. In their tour of South America on a 500cc Norton – a trip that would later be filmed as *The Motorcycle Diaries* – Guevara and his friend Alberto Granada stopped at several leper colonies, but only because Granada had worked with lepers in Argentina and this was the best way to earn food and money that would keep them on the road. Making amends for Rosario Central had little to do with it.

To gauge the depth of the Newell's–Rosario Central rivalry, it is worth recalling an interview Bielsa's father gave to *El Gráfico* in 1998, the year Marcelo won his third league title in Argentina. 'I never saw Marcelo play nor have I seen him manage,' said El Turco. 'It's not that I don't like football, it's because I am a Central supporter and also because I prefer another type of football, one which has less marking and pressing. We talk about it every time he comes home. He has his point of view and he tells me that he has to train his teams to win.'

When Marcelo Bielsa was growing up, Argentina's football was divided into two championships. The Metropolitano was contested over the first half of the season while the second half was devoted to the Campeonato Nacional. Rosario had been the slightly more successful side. They won the Nacional in 1971 and again in 1973. Newell's had won nothing in their history, and then in June 1974 they came to the last game of the Metropolitano season top of the league. It was played at Rosario Central's ground, the

Gigante de Arroyito. Central needed a win to take the title; Newell's could do it with a draw. With twenty-one minutes remaining, Central were two up. They did not hold on and in the eighty-first minute Mario Zanabria, who would later work with Bielsa in Mexico, scored the equaliser that would give Newell's their first piece of major silverware. By then Bielsa was nearly nineteen and had been with Newell's youth teams for six years. He would break into the first team only briefly in 1976, a year when Argentine politics was careering towards total breakdown. The government, led by Juan Perón's second wife, Isabel, was being assaulted by terrorism from both left and right. The communist Montoneros guerrillas had attached a limpet mine to the new destroyer *Santísima Trinidad* and blown out the bottom of her hull. An attempt by the guerrillas of the People's Revolutionary Army to storm the arsenal at Monte Chingolo outside Buenos Aires was repelled by attacks from helicopter gunships. Inflation reached 700 per cent. The peso was devalued twice. Newspapers openly called for the army to intervene and on 23 March, the chief of staff, General Jorge Videla, launched his coup. Isabel Perón was arrested and the army moved in.

Amid all this, Marcelo Bielsa was attempting to forge a football career.

Football with the Generals

As the economy crashed, as the generals waited, Marcelo Bielsa prepared for the Olympic Games. Argentina may have been falling apart but in football a golden age was beginning to dawn.

César Luis Menotti was from Rosario. He had been a striker for Central, won the Argentine championship with Boca Juniors and played alongside Pelé at Santos. It was, however, as a manager who espoused beautiful, fluid football that he reached the pinnacle of his career. He once said: 'When football is played the right way, like painting, like music, it tends to be something beautiful and, if that idea is not sustained, it vanishes.' In 1973, he had taken Huracán, one of Buenos Aires' smaller clubs, to the league title. The following year, after a clunking, unsophisticated Argentina had been humiliated in the World Cup, swept away by the brilliance of Johan Cruyff in the rain in Gelsenkirchen, Menotti was appointed to repair the damage.

A chain-smoking left-wing intellectual with long hair, Menotti was hardly the dictatorship's ideal of a national team manager, but Argentina was due to stage the World Cup in 1978 and Menotti represented their best chance of winning it. He was untouchable. In January 1976 he contacted Jorge Griffa, Newell's academy manager. Argentina were due to play a qualifying tournament for the Montreal Olympics and Menotti wanted Griffa to send Newell's reserve team to Recife on Brazil's north-east coast. Bielsa was one of those chosen to go.

Bielsa was twenty and played well enough in central defence to be named in the team of the tournament alongside Brazil's Edinho, who would play in three World Cups. Argentina finished third but the following month Bielsa made his debut for Newell's Old Boys in the rain at the Coloso del Parque in a 2–1 defeat to River Plate. One of his closest friends at Newell's was Roberto Agueropolis, a fellow defender who would later play for Panathinaikos. Agueropolis was a year older than Bielsa. He was building a house but with the money Newell's were paying him he could not afford to finish it. Bielsa offered him his salary, telling Agueropolis: 'Take my money and put a roof on your house. Pay me back when you can.' Throughout his career, Marcelo Bielsa would be tough about money. He knew his worth and the contracts, sometimes negotiated by Rafael, would be lucrative. Yet it was money that Bielsa would always spread around. When he heard that his friend from Rosario, José Falabella, was unable to have children, he paid for sessions of artificial insemination and became the godfather to José's daughter.

Bielsa loved being part of Newell's, although his time in the first team would be brief, with a 1–1 draw against San Lorenzo and a 3–1 defeat to Talleres de Córdoba in December. There would be one more game, a 3–1 victory over Esgrima La Plata, but it would not take place for another eighteen months and Bielsa would only come on as a substitute three minutes before the final whistle blew on the match and on his playing career for Newell's Old Boys. In between, he had been offered the opportunity to play in Córdoba, a city that dominates the high sierra to the west of Rosario. Being sent out on loan is one of football's harder assignments. You arrive as a stranger to the loneliness of a hotel room before training among players who in Bielsa's case would have suspected he was not good enough for a club like Newell's. He and three others from the Coloso del Parque had made the 230-mile journey by bus. He was given an apartment on the seventh floor.

He would be playing for Instituto de Córdoba, who were in the regional rather than the national league. His first game saw him share a pitch with the fathers of two footballers whom he would manage with Argentina, Roberto Ayala and

Nicolás Burdisso. Bielsa was becoming increasingly disaffected. Instituto finished eighth out of ten in the Córdoba League and Bielsa was disillusioned by the standard of the football and his own performances. He spent most of his free time learning how to tango or alone on the seventh floor reading. One of his team-mates remarked that for away games the rest of the team stuffed their bags with music cassettes to take with them; Bielsa filled his with books.

'He liked "difficult" conversations,' said Eduardo Anelli, who played for Instituto as a winger. 'He would sometimes stand in front of the manager, saying, "I disagree," and we would look at each other asking ourselves what he meant by that.' Another team-mate, Miguel Olmedo, said: 'Technically, he did not stand out but he was very demanding of himself in training. He always demanded that we worked with more emphasis and once he said we should ask the coach for more physical preparation.'

The head of the junta, Jorge Videla, had a saying for those his men went after. 'They are neither alive nor dead,' he once commented. 'They are disappeared.' In 1977 Rafael disappeared. Marcelo asked to return to Rosario. He arranged for his contract to be terminated and repaid Instituto de Córdoba the money that was still owing on it. To live in Rosario in the late 1970s was to live under the rule of Leopoldo Galtieri, who led the Second Army Corps. He ran everything in the city: his men kicked down doors in the dead of night in search of insurgents. Galtieri had a taste for Johnnie Walker

Black Label scotch and for shedding other people's blood. The grand house where Dr Rafael Bielsa once lived and worked was taken over by the Argentine security services and the library became a room from which telephones were tapped.

One of the properties Galtieri controlled was Quinta de Funes. It was a large ranch – think Southfork in *Dallas* – that lay amid some lush lawns. Inside were people far more vicious than the Ewings. The Quinta de Funes was a terror laboratory to be used against those the army thought bent on destroying the dictatorship. One of their suspects was Rafael, now twenty-two. Rafael had become a committed opponent of the junta, although it was not the hippyish, flowers in your hair kind of opposition that had paralysed the United States as the Vietnam War dragged towards its unwinnable conclusion. His activism was hard, determined, puritanical. 'When I was young and involved in radical politics in the 1970s, drugs were considered a tool of imperialism,' he said. 'We made fun of the hippies because cannabis made them unable to function.' He was arrested, blindfolded and brought to the Quinta de Funes. A man's voice, deep and gravelly, asked why Bielsa had been donating books to a Marxist library. Only several years later, when he went to the Plaza de Mayo in Buenos Aires with 100,000 others to hear Galtieri, now president of Argentina, announce the occupation of the Falklands, did Rafael realise whose voice it had been. Many years later, he would incorporate his experiences at the Quinta de Funes in a novel, which in 2015 was released as a film, *Operation Mexico, A Pact of Love.*

Rafael spent three years in exile in Spain before returning to Argentina in 1980. Two years later came the Falklands War and it says something for the hysteria that gripped the country that Rafael, working as a lawyer in the Ministry of Justice, something of an oxymoron in Galtieri's Argentina, was caught up in it. He decided to volunteer for military service. Interviewed by the *New York Times* in a queue to register, he said: 'After many years, this is the first thing that has brought us together. The soldiers who were killed in the disembarkation were the first martyrs that Argentines have been able to share.' Behind him was an engineer with a far more sanguine view of the invasion. 'This is just a manoeuvre by the military to distract us,' he told the *New York Times* reporter, James Markham. 'The economy is in a mess; the country could explode. Most of the people here are civil servants who think that by going to the Malvinas temporarily they can get double pay. I'm going because I want to make money. If I can be among the first ones there, I can get the first contracts and make a lot.'

Nobody in Buenos Aires, Markham reported, thought there would be a war. The junta was prepared to offer the islanders colour television in time for them to watch the World Cup from Spain. That had been a bauble the junta had dangled before. In 1978, as the nation prepared for its own World Cup, Argentina was presented with colour television for the first time. As for so many people in Argentina, the 1978 World Cup left a deep impression on Marcelo Bielsa, not just because the home side won but also because of the style and drama with which César Menotti's side took the trophy.

Rosario played a central and hugely controversial part in that World Cup. Perhaps because its capacity was slightly greater, perhaps because it was where Mario Kempes, the spearhead of Menotti's attack, played his club football, the Gigante de Arroyito rather than the Coloso del Parque had been chosen to stage the city's games. Argentina played all of its second-group games in Rosario. Whoever topped the group would go to the World Cup final. On his home ground Kempes scored twice against Poland and for good measure punched the ball off the line from Grzegorz Lato. The offence went unpunished. The encounter with Brazil was a turgid goalless draw, notable for the return of Leopoldo Luque to Argentina's attack. Earlier in the tournament, the striker had dislocated his elbow in the 2–1 win over France in the Estadio Monumental. His brother, driving from Santa Fe to Buenos Aires to see him, was burned to death in a car crash on the Pan-American Highway. There were two games left. Brazil's match, against Poland in Mendoza, in the foothills of the Andes, finished an hour and a quarter before Argentina faced Peru at the Arroyito. Brazil won 3–1. Argentina would have to win by four clear goals if they were to meet Holland in the final.

What followed is football's equivalent of the Kennedy assassination, a game alive with conspiracy theories that ranged from vast grain deliveries made from Argentina to Peru to $50 million of trade credit being unfrozen. The Argentine government was even accused of offering their counterparts in Lima use of their torture centres – which to two military dictatorships would have seemed like a cultural exchange.

Before kick-off, Videla, accompanied by Richard Nixon's former secretary of state, Henry Kissinger, who was a fervent football fan, entered the Peruvian dressing room 'to wish the opposition good luck'. 'Were we pressured? Yes, we were pressured,' said José Velásquez, who played in midfield for Peru in what turned into a 6–0 rout that swept Argentina to the final and a storm of ticker tape in the Estadio Monumental. 'What kind of pressure? Pressure that went from the government to the team managers and from the manager to the coaches.' Peru's goalkeeper, Ramón Quiroga, had been born in Rosario and when interviewed by *La Nación* twenty years later he said he felt more Argentine than Peruvian. On the eve of the game, some of Peru's players approached the manager, Marcos Calderón, asking him not to select Quiroga.

The problem for the conspiracy theorists is that only when the final whistle blew in Mendoza seventy-five minutes before kick-off in Rosario did Argentina know the exact score – 4–0 – that would send them through. Not one of

Menotti's players, not even those viscerally opposed to the junta, thought the match was fixed. Just before the World Cup began, soldiers had entered a bowling alley and arrested two of Alberto Tarantini's friends, who were never seen again. At a reception for Argentina's sports stars, the defender plucked up the courage to walk over to Videla and ask the general what had happened to them. Videla replied that he had not been responsible. Tarantini thought Peru had suffered stage fright but no more.

The centre-back, Luis Galván, told Jon Spurling for his book *Death or Glory*:

All of us were used to explosive atmospheres inside Argentine grounds but this was quite unlike anything else. The noise and the colour were special. I glanced up at the dignitaries' section when we ran out. There was Videla and Lacoste (the admiral who was to succeed Videla). They were lords of all they surveyed. Although you try to focus on the game, you realise it is more than a game when the junta is there. Mario Kempes scored after twenty minutes and we went in at half-time 2–0 ahead. It is always the perfect score, I think. You've enough of a lead to be confident in what you do but not enough so you can sit back and relax. In the second half we pulverised Peru. Did I detect anything remotely wrong with Peru's performance? Not for one minute.

By the time the World Cup was lifted in the Monumental, Bielsa was already turning his thoughts towards coaching. The theatre critic Kenneth Tynan once remarked of his relationship with an actor or director that 'a critic is someone who has a map but can't drive'. Jorge Griffa would say something similar about Bielsa: 'He didn't have the ability to be a great player but he had the idea of what one was.' By the time he was twenty-four, Bielsa knew his career as a footballer was unlikely to take him very far but he was already studying his maps. José Luis Danguise, who had gone from Newell's to Córdoba with Bielsa, said: 'He was already sketching out his career as a coach. You would go to his apartment or he would come to mine and on a piece of paper he would demonstrate how Instituto should play. He was far in advance of us in his vision of what football could be.'

Bielsa's last taste of what football was like as a player came in the third division with Argentina de Rosario. 'He was becoming more serious,' recalled one of his team-mates, Luis Martarello, to *Mundo Deportivo*. 'He didn't laugh and he hated jokes, although nobody made them. It seemed like he was preparing for other things.' Initially, the other things included running a newspaper kiosk with Raúl Delpontigo who had been his faithful companion from Newell's to Córdoba and then Argentina Rosario. They would pile their bicycles high with newspapers to take them to the kiosk, although according to Delpontigo Bielsa never quite found the courage to shout out his wares. He did, however, become an expert in sourcing sports magazines from around the world and the kiosk lasted ten years before it was sold. By then, Bielsa had become not just a coach but one of the most exciting and innovative coaches in South America. His first job would be at the University of Buenos Aires.

It was December, midsummer in Argentina, and Aldo Forti, the head coach of the University of Buenos Aires was driving through the city on his way to the doctor's. The traffic was bad and he was running late. At the corner of Scalabrini and Las Heras, the phone rang. He was not inclined to pick it up but the number was Spanish so he took it. 'Mr Aldo Forti? Are you busy?' It was Marcelo Bielsa phoning nearly thirty years after he took over the University of Buenos Aires football team. He was now in charge of Athletic Bilbao. 'I was thinking of my appointment. I wondered if the conversation would take as long as one of his press conferences,' said Forti.

I wanted to write it down, so I would remember it. I didn't have a biro, let alone a piece of paper. I would have written what he said on a brick, a bit of concrete or even on the street itself. He talked mesmerisingly for eight minutes and at the end I said: 'I hope I can remember all of this.'

In Bilbao, Bielsa had been thinking of the past. The University of Buenos Aires had been his first coaching job and he wanted to apologise for not having been in touch for all these years. He had taken up the appointment in 1982, the year his brother went to the Casa Rosada to volunteer to fight, the year the Falklands War saw the grisly grip of the generals come loose, the year Argentina changed forever.

In 1982, Aldo Forti was studying architecture. Soon he would be doing 600 sit-ups a day with Bielsa refusing to end the training session until every exercise was completed to perfection.

He believed everyone should be treated equally but the higher you rose in the squad, the more should be demanded of you. At least, that is what he believed at the age of twenty-seven. There was a guy called Eloy del Val, a real physical specimen, whom he wanted to take down a peg or two. Once, when we were going up the steps to the dressing room, Bielsa took off his watch and his jacket and gave them to the person nearest to him and said: 'Mr Del Val, let us settle this like gentlemen.' There wasn't a fight but it was a sufficient display of strength for him to be able to put this guy on the bench for the next game. He would respond really strongly if one of his players was kicked from behind. He would run on to the pitch to defend his players. Another time, when one of our players was elbowed, Bielsa went looking for the offender after the game. He may have been only three years older than us but he convinced us with the conviction with which the guy talked. There was the professionalism. Under our previous coach, we were playing a semi-final at 10.30, they knocked on the door at ten and the coach was fast asleep. We repeated Bielsa's exercises until they were second nature. Time didn't matter; he didn't say as other coaches would have said: 'They are only students; they are tired.' He demanded. Always. Today it's common to work like Bielsa but in the day he was an innovator. We went from being coached by a man who did not know what time the games started to someone like Bielsa who took us to the training grounds of Argentinos or Boca Juniors reserves.

Miguel Calloni studied agronomics at Buenos Aires. He was twenty-three when Bielsa took over the side.

There was always a distance between us. We never chatted or gossiped, despite the fact we were quite close in age to one another. Nor did he open up to us very much. He was never a mate but I have very good memories of him. He was very full on and really believed in his ideas. There are very few players who speak badly of him after having passed through his hands. As a team we wanted to attack and physically we could really take on the teams we were up against.

He motivated us with the seriousness with which he took things. I don't remember there being a revolt over too much training for example – which you might have expected from students.

Then there came a chance meeting, back in Rosario. Bielsa ran into Eduardo Bermúdez, who had once coached him in the reserve teams at Newell's. He told Bielsa he had taken over as manager of Central Córdoba. There was a job going at the Coloso del Parque. Together, they went over to see Jorge Griffa. 'I want to be a coach,' Bielsa said. 'Perfect. Come and work with me and let's see how far we get.'

The Road to Murphy

It was one o'clock in the morning, midwinter 1987. A white Fiat 147 was lost on the prairie and the occupants stopped at a service station to ask directions. They were driving towards the small town of Murphy, looking for a teenage boy who at that time would almost certainly be asleep. Mauricio Pochettino would get up at five in the morning to go to school, where he was studying agriculture. Once they were back in the car, Marcelo Bielsa and Jorge Griffa set off again. The pair were in the midst of a grand project that would transform Newell's Old Boys into the champions of Argentina. Newell's, like Rosario Central, lacked the wealth of the great clubs of Buenos Aires and Bielsa and Griffa both understood that youth development was the key to their survival.

Once he began work at the Coloso del Parque, Bielsa had

divided up Argentina into blocks of 50 square miles and organised football tournaments in each one. They took the best boys back to Rosario for trials. That evening they had just held a trial at Villa Cañás, a small town three hours' drive south of Rosario. They were having dinner with one of the local coaches when they asked him if there were any boys they might have missed. The coach mentioned Pochettino. They set off straight away.

Murphy lies on Route 33, which runs 468 miles south-east from Rosario to Bahía Blanca on the Atlantic coast, where the flatness of the prairie meets Patagonia and Argentina starts turning into a wild land of glaciers and fjords. Bielsa and Griffa found Pochettino's house and knocked on the door. His mother answered and, not unreasonably given the time, asked her husband, Hector, to come down and talk to these strangers. Their son takes up the story in his autobiography, *Brave New World*:

Bielsa told me that after chatting for five or ten minutes they didn't know what to say or talk about so they decided to ask my father: 'Could we see the boy?' Despite the early hour, my proud parents said yes and they came to my bedroom to take a look. They saw me sleeping and Griffa asked: 'May I see his legs?' My mother pulled the covers off me and they both said: 'He looks like a footballer. Look at those legs.' Although my small bedroom was full of people admiring my legs, I slept like a log and had no idea about it until my old man spilled the beans the following morning.

Murphy could claim to be the very heart of Argentine football. It was named after a sheep farmer from County Wexford, John James Murphy, who in 1844 had bought a passage from Liverpool to Buenos Aires. Once there, he had earned a living digging ditches. 'We live like fighting cocks in this country,' he had written to his brother. Murphy became a hugely successful sheep farmer, who was able to pay the equivalent of £6,000 today for a first-class berth to visit his family in Ireland. In 1883, once the Argentine government had cleared the native Mapuche Indians, he bought 46,000 hectares of land that would one day bear his name. Sheep gave way to wheat and cattle, and families from Piedmont in northern Italy, like the Pochettinos, came to farm.

Murphy produced something else: footballers. As you enter the little town on Route 33, there is a billboard depicting twelve players below which are the words 'Murphy, Ambassadors of Good Football'. That a town of 4,000, so insignificant it was not thought worthy of being officially named until 1966, should have produced a dozen professional footballers, including Paulo Gazzaniga, who joined Pochettino at Tottenham, seems extraordinary. Bielsa and Griffa's journey to Murphy carries echoes of Alex Ferguson pulling up outside Ryan Giggs' house on his fourteenth birthday to sign him for Manchester United in the same year, 1987. Ferguson was driving a gold Mercedes rather than a little white Fiat but there was a similar determination not to allow young talent to escape. There was another similarity, too. Giggs had been training with Manchester City, who had fully expected to sign him. Pochettino had been training with Rosario Central.

One of the first of Murphy's footballers to break through had been David Bisconti, who had joined Rosario Central and whose career later took him to Japan. Bisconti had recommended Central to Pochettino and, after school, he used to take the three-hour bus journey to Rosario, train with Central's youth team, stay the night, train again and then take the bus back down Route 33. Griffa and Bielsa persuaded Pochettino to come with them in January, the month in which he would be able to sign professional forms, for a tournament in Mar del Plata. They converted him from a striker to a defender, which did not stop him scoring a spectacular goal against a Paraguayan team, Olimpia, that won Newell's the final. He signed.

At Newell's, Pochettino said he felt closer to Griffa than to Bielsa but that together they formed a formidable team. 'Griffa was a fearless person who, from the very first time I met him, impressed me with his energy, his gruff imposing voice and his aura of invincibility,' Pochettino said. 'He didn't spin yarns like a poet. On the contrary, he was very direct and his words would get straight through to you, resonating deeply. He acted like he spoke.'

Marcelo Bielsa's relationship with Jorge Griffa was perhaps the strongest and most rewarding of his career. In November 2018, a few months after Bielsa joined Leeds, Newell's opened an accommodation centre for their players, paid for by Bielsa and designed by María Eugenia. It was named after Jorge Griffa, who was the guest of honour for the official opening. Four decades after they began working together, Bielsa paid an emotional tribute, via video link, to a man who had become his mentor:

Every day I would wait until it was 7pm and go to the office Jorge had at the Parque just to listen to him talk. Few things that are said today about sport were not told to me in his own way by Jorge forty years ago, He was a teacher with a capital T. He taught me his unconditional love for football and a decency that has survived in a world full of vices. He had the idea that a job must be done in a professional manner even if you receive nothing in exchange. In other words, we do things in return for nothing just for the pleasure of seeing the results of the efforts we made – just so we can measure what we are capable of.

Griffa was born and grew up on Route 33 in the town of Casilda, famed for producing one of Argentina's most celebrated tango singers, Agustín Magaldi, who in *Evita* is depicted as Eva Duarte's first lover and mentor. Like Bielsa,

Jorge Griffa played as a centre-half though he was a vastly more successful one. He was resilient and tough, especially when it came to finding his way home to Casilda after a game. Sometimes, he would hitch a lift on a milk truck; other times he would sleep in the church where his uncle worked. After five years with Newell's Old Boys, Griffa crossed the Atlantic to join Atlético Madrid. He was part of a team that won La Liga and the Copa del Rey and in 1962, in Stuttgart, the Atlético side overcame Fiorentina to win the Cup-Winners' Cup. Remarkably, he won these trophies while in consistent pain, having torn his cruciate ligaments when he was twenty-one.

I carried on. To have an operation on the cruciate ligaments at that time basically meant having to quit football. Of course, it hurt and I would spend each Monday with ice wrapped on the leg. I would wrap bandages below my knee when I played which prevented me stretching it too much.

After a spell in Barcelona with Espanyol, Griffa returned to Newell's in 1972 to begin overhauling their youth system. His idea, one that would be seized upon and expanded by Marcelo Bielsa, was to actively bring young footballers to the Coloso del Parque rather than just rely on whatever Newell's produced in their own constituency:

To compete with River, Boca, Independiente, San Lorenzo and, at that time, Huracán, we had to come up with an idea. So, I decided to go and look for players instead of waiting for them. The other teams waited for players to emerge while we went to look for them. That is how we made a great team.

Bielsa and Griffa divided Argentina up into seventy zones and subdivided each zone into five. From these 350 zones they thought they might find perhaps three young footballers of interest. In total, they scouted 1,050 players and travelled nearly 3,500 miles, from Misiones near the border with Brazil, laced with jungle, to the Río Negro, which marks the beginning of the wastes of Patagonia. As a journey it was the equal of Che Guevara's as depicted in *The Motorcycle Diaries* and produced rather more in the way of concrete achievements. The Fiat 147 was not a car designed for long distances or many passengers, especially since the handle on the left-hand door was broken. Bielsa did not always travel with Jorge Griffa. Sometimes a friend of Bielsa's father, Oscar Isola, who happily enough was a mechanic, would come with him. Other times it was Luis Milisi, a friend of Bielsa's who sold spare parts. Once when Milisi asked if they could take a detour so he could do a bit of business, Bielsa suggested it would be better if they went their separate ways and drove off.

Often when scouting they trusted their instincts. Once

Argentina's National Youth Team found themselves in the town of Reconquista on their way back to Buenos Aires from Corrientes in the north of the country. They hastily arranged a game against the local team. They lost 2–1. Although Reconquista is a seven-hour bus ride from Rosario, Griffa was watching the striker who scored both goals. 'He didn't look like a footballer,' he noted. 'He was a big lad and, when he shot, the ball could go anywhere. He didn't know how to head the ball properly and nor did he have the physique of a footballer.' He decided to sign him anyway. The boy's name was Gabriel Batistuta. It took considerable persuasion to get him to stay at Newell's. His first passion was horses – after retirement, Batistuta would indulge his love for polo – and his great ambition was to become a doctor. Batistuta's father was a slaughterhouse worker who was determined his son would enjoy a better life than he had done. Griffa persuaded Batistuta that football could offer him as much as medicine.

'I had it in my head that a footballer's career was a risky one,' said Batistuta.

I went back to Reconquista. Newell's gave me twenty days off and I stayed for a month until they came looking for me. Griffa found me and said: 'We have confidence in you and, trust me, you will play in the Primera.' It was enough to convince me and, six months later, I was playing in the Primera. When I signed my first contract, I thought I might make a living from football. It was at Newell's that my mindset totally changed. I fell in love with football.'

Initially, it was hard. 'When I arrived at Newell's, I was fat, it was as simple as that,' he said. Bielsa told Batistuta to get rid of the *alfajores*, which are very sweet biscuits covered in chocolate. 'He also taught me to train in the rain and I hated him for it. We were a group of dreamers and the greatest dreamer was Bielsa. He dreamed about being Arrigo Sacchi whom he constantly watched winning European Cups with AC Milan. He wanted that to be us – a group of street kids to become heroes.'

Batistuta made his debut in 1988 but it was only when he moved to Boca Juniors two years later that Gabriel Batistuta began turning into the striker who was to become known as 'Batigol'. He played only sixteen times for Newell's before heading south, first to River Plate, where he failed to make a mark, and then to the Bombonera to win the title with Boca. 'Griffa and Bielsa wanted to create their own team at Newell's and make them champions,' he recalled.

They did it and I missed out on it. It hurt a lot not to have stayed at Newell's. I felt that by leaving I was betraying the ideas of Bielsa and Griffa and even my own team-mates. When they were successful, I told myself: 'I can't go back.' I was too proud but it worked out well for me at Boca. I was lucky.

Bielsa's youth teams played in games organised around Rosario. Among his players were Fernando Gamboa, Eduardo Berizzo and Darío Franco, who would all win the Primera under Bielsa's management. They were impeccably drilled. In the book *Life in Red and Black*, Martín Prieto describes watching them play against a minor club, Deportivo Armenio, and seeing the team change shape on the pitch 'like an umbrella opening and closing'. While Griffa and Bielsa were laying the foundations, Newell's was undergoing an extraordinary transformation under José Yudica, one of the forgotten greats of Argentine football. When in 1988 he took Newell's to the first national title in their history, he also became the first manager in Argentina to win titles with three different clubs, having taken Quilmes to their only title in 1981 and four years later winning the championship with Argentinos Juniors, whom for good measure he made Copa Libertadores champions. However, for a man born in Rosario and who had joined Newell's as a midfielder in 1959, it was winning the Primera at the Coloso del Parque that kindled the warmest memories. 'It happened to me in a way that perhaps it does not happen to anyone else,' he said. 'To be a fan of the club, to be a player who becomes a manager that makes that club champions – it is like one of those films that is never forgotten.' There was almost a spectacular sequel. He took Newell's to the final of the Copa Libertadores, where they would face Nacional of Uruguay. The first leg was played not at the Coloso del

Parque but at Central's ground, the Gigante de Arroyito, which had a bigger capacity. Newell's won, 1–0, but in the return in front of 75,000 at the Centenario in Montevideo, they were overwhelmed.

In 1990, Yudica made a decision that would change Bielsa's life. He took up an offer to manage Deportivo Cali, where he had won the Colombian league as a player. There was a vacancy at the Coloso del Parque – one that Marcelo Bielsa was ideally placed to fill. The move to Cali marked the beginning of the decline of Yudica's coaching career, which never really recovered from a day in 1992, when he was managing Argentinos Juniors once more. Argentine football had long been infected by groups of organised fans, known as the *barras bravas,* who dealt in violence and intimidation. Suddenly, there was a disturbance at the training ground; the *barras bravas* were at the gates. Their target was Yudica's son, who was working as his assistant. Yudica rushed towards them, holding a gun which he fired into the air. He saved his boy from a beating but at the cost of his job.

Newell's carajo!

It was the eve of the final game of the season. Newell's were at home to San Lorenzo, a club that had precisely nothing to play for. If Newell's won, they would be champions. If they failed and River Plate overcame Vélez Sarsfield, the glory would be denied them. The team spent the night at the Military Aviation College in Funes, not far from where Rafael had been imprisoned by Leopoldo Galtieri. Marcelo Bielsa demanded total concentration, even from himself. 'My wife is pregnant and there are complications,' he told his players. 'I have told her that in an emergency she can call her parents or her sisters but not me. If one of you needs a telephone for a situation more urgent than that, then you can use it.'

Newell's drew with San Lorenzo. In Buenos Aires, River Plate and Vélez still had six minutes to run. There, too, the scores were level. The Newell's players waited by the touchline. Transistor radios were pressed to as many ears as the speakers would allow. For Bielsa, the tension was too much. He had left the stadium and was now outside on a training pitch behind one of the stands. A helicopter clattering overhead meant he could barely hear. All he could see through the wooden slats of the stand were the legs of the Newell's fans. He noticed none of them was moving from their seats and nobody was shouting. 'Inside of me I was asking them to please say something,' he recalled afterwards. 'Then one fan turned around and recognised me. He gave me the score with hand signals. Then there was this huge roar and I ran inside and everyone started hugging me.'

River Plate had drawn. Newell's were champions. By the time Bielsa returned to the touchline, wearing a grey, sweat-stained shirt, some of the crowd were on the pitch, some were still behind the fences. His players hoisted their manager up onto their shoulders and as he clutched a Newell's shirt in one hand, he began screaming 'Newell's *carajo!*' ('fucking Newell's!') over and over again. It was the kind of language he would normally never use but it expressed the sheer relief, the utter unbridled joy of it all. He had taken his club – one that was thought more in danger of sliding out of the Primera than winning it – to the summit in his opening season. With his first throw of the dice, he had rolled a six.

A few months before, Marcelo Bielsa had been sitting in an office in Rosario's Calle Mitre, not far from where he grew up. He was thirty-four and was being interviewed for the job of managing Newell's Old Boys. His champions had been Jorge Griffa and one of his old friends, Carlos Altieri, who was a director of the club. 'He is capable, he's a hard worker and he's from Newell's, what more do you want?' had been Altieri's campaign message. The team was starting to falter and, with limited money, the need was to push young players forward and nobody knew the young players at Newell's like Marcelo Bielsa.

There were alternatives. Reinaldo Merlo, who had played more than 500 games for River Plate, had been given a shot at managing at the Monumental. Although he had been dismissed, his successor, Daniel Passarella, had given Merlo great credit for building a team that he would take to the title. There was Humberto Zuccarelli at nearby Union Santa Fe. Neither, surely, would have interviewed as well as Marcelo Bielsa. One of those in attendance was Raúl Oliveros, the club treasurer. Bielsa preached sacrifice and humility at a club that financially and in playing terms was on the slide since its exploits in the Libertadores. The policy of having the pre-match *concentración* in high-class hotels, like the Presidente in central Rosario, would cease. 'He's a phenomenon,' said Oliveros to Altieri. 'It has to be him.'

In England, Bielsa would have faced two hurdles. He had not really played the game and he was posh. A man with Roy Hodgson's playing career and Frank Lampard's private education, complete with A grade at Latin, would run the risk of being portrayed as Jacob Rees-Mogg in a tracksuit. In Argentina, this seems to have been far less of an issue. The sports journalist Esteban Bekerman says Bielsa's background was seldom if ever mentioned. Mauricio Pochettino remarked that in Argentina almost everyone refers to themselves as 'middle-class'. In Murphy his father, who had left school at twelve, worked 100 hectares of land by himself. They had an outside bathroom. He told Mauricio he was middle-class.

However, Bielsa's use of language was a problem. Bielsa speaks a clear, precise Spanish using idioms he felt some of his players would not understand. He sometimes used a thesaurus before giving team talks, to put his words into a simpler language. When addressing footballers, he would use the formal *usted* rather than *tú*. The best way to imagine it in English would be if he were to address his players as 'Mr Shearer' or 'Mr Gerrard'.

There were times when words would not do. Sometimes, to make his point, Bielsa would draw on the boots or studs of a player where he wanted the ball to be played. 'I come from a very modest background,' the defender Fernando Gamboa remarked in *La Vida por el fútbol*. 'When he started to do his drawing on my studs, I couldn't believe it. When he was doing it, I stopped listening because all I could think about was how he was ruining my boots.'

The tactics used by Bielsa were different from those Argentine football had been used to. The impact of the two World Cup victories in 1978 and 1986 had divided coaching in Argentina into two camps. There were those who followed César Menotti's ideas that the very essence of football meant taking risks, and the football of Carlos Bilardo which held that, no matter how you got it, the result was everything. Bielsa claimed to be following a 'middle way' that combined the best of both. 'It's really not true to say that every coach in Argentina either followed Menotti or Bilardo,' said Esteban Bekerman.

The idea came about because we football journalists in Argentina like to put everyone in boxes. At the time, Bielsa's ideas seemed new. He was obsessive about training, repetitions and educating his footballers about the game. He also said something which I dis-agree with. He said in Argentina we like our football played quickly, that we have no patience with a con-tinual passing game. If you study the history of football in Argentina, we have always liked players with very good passing ability who move the ball around. José Pékerman (who took Argentina to the 2006 World Cup) was much more typical of Argentinian football than Bielsa. Bielsa and his disciples like Gabriel Heinze, when he took over at Vélez Sarsfield, and Mauricio Pochettino at Tottenham, play too quickly for our taste.

It is more difficult to make good decisions if you have too much speed. He had that passion for football that is so evident in Rosario, you see it in Bielsa, in Lionel Messi and Jorge Valdano. Bielsa wanted football with no customs posts. He wanted the ball passed quickly from defence to midfield with a lot of speed and a lot of running. Some people try to put Pep Guardiola and Marcelo Bielsa on the same level. They are not the same, they are very different. The way Guardiola's teams play is very South American, very Argentinian. They pass the ball a lot, there is a lot of time on the ball, a lot of tiki-taka if you like. If you watch Gabriel Heinze's teams at Vélez, they are very similar to Bielsa's – they don't have a midfield. Heinze is very interested in defence and attack, which is very honest because football is essentially about defence and attack. The Newell's team he [Bielsa] built will always be remembered as one of the greatest teams Argentina saw in the 1990s but it will not be remembered as more than that because they didn't win anything internationally. They did not win the Copa Libertadores; they didn't win an Intercontinental Cup. There was a price to be paid for being so single-minded and being so well known for how you play, and that is that every single team that played against Argentina in the 2002 World Cup when Marcelo Bielsa was manager knew exactly how they would play. There would be no Plan B.

Mauricio Pochettino observed that the greatest difference between himself and Bielsa as a coach was that he was less obsessed with the opposition than his mentor had been.

Cutting back on the Hotel Presidente meant the young team trained, ate and slept at the Funes Military Aviation College, which had been built in 1979. For relaxation, it offered a table-tennis table, a pool table and a video recorder which allowed the squad to watch occasional films together. Those who had won the title with José Yudica were surprised to be swapping the Presidente for something altogether more spartan. When the goalkeeper, Norberto Scoponi, asked why Bielsa wasn't staying with the players, he replied: 'I am not staying with you because I am working for you.' He meant he would be alone studying the game to come. At noon on Sunday – match day in Argentina – Carlos Altieri would pick him up and drive him to the college. On the journey, Bielsa would go through what he thought would happen and go into the strengths and weaknesses of the opposition. 'He anticipated everything,' said Altieri. 'He would tell me what was going to happen and it usually did. If the result was different, then it was something I would always remember. It was at that time I realised he was a genius.'

Bielsa was not only ahead of his time in training methods but also in the use of video tapes. Even when he was running the Newell's youth teams, he would have a video cassette playing on the bus showing the match they had just played. When he became first-team manager, the videos became more frequent. Cristian Domizzi, who would play for him at Newell's and in Mexico with Atlas Guadalajara, recalled:

> I remember one day when he brought us some video cassettes of Jari Litmanen. He wanted me to observe his movements. I was astonished because I had no idea who he was. Later, the guy became a phenomenon at Ajax but when Bielsa gave me these videos, he was still in Finland and nobody knew him. I couldn't believe it. Only Bielsa could have got hold of that film.

His first game as a first-team manager came on 19 August 1990. Newell's were at home to Platense from Buenos Aires' northern suburbs, on the shores of the River Plate. A volley from Gerardo Martino gave Newell's a 1–0 win.

The Sundays came and went: a draw with Argentinos Juniors, a last-minute win over Huracán. They were not convincing. Román Iucht, who observed Newell's from the press box, wrote of mutterings that Newell's had exchanged a Ferrari for a Ford Model T. In Rosario, as in Newcastle or at Tottenham, style mattered. It was about how you played as well as what you won, and Newell's were spluttering to their victories.

The senior players – Gerardo Martino, Scoponi and the midfielder Juan Manuel Llop – were unconvinced by Bielsa's methods. 'We saw Marcelo as someone who had come to impose a new style of play upon us that we were not used to and that we were supposed to support unconditionally,' said Llop. Martino had been at Newell's for nearly a decade when Bielsa took over. He was an elegant, imperious midfielder, aged twenty-seven when Bielsa arrived, but it was a reflection on the youth of the squad and of Martino's position within it that he was called 'Tata' or 'Daddy'. 'If Gerardo had disapproved of the project, he could have wrecked it,' Bielsa remarked. 'It caused him to be distracted but his attitude was an example for the boys. They would have thought to themselves: "If Tata Martino is doing it, then why shouldn't we?" He was always willing, always friendly, always a gentleman.' Martino did not think his boss especially mad. 'He is called El Loco because the thinkers in football are usually called "El Loco,"' he said, looking back years later.

He is definitely not crazy. He has charisma and that's important but charisma alone is not enough. He is also very intellectual and has left a mark wherever he has gone. He is a coach that footballers want to play for and, if you are a journalist, he is someone you want to talk to. He has left a footprint wherever he has been.

Martino describes himself as a 'disciple of Bielsa' and would go on to manage Paraguay to a World Cup quarter-final and take over at Barcelona and Argentina. Martino admitted that, although his teams play very differently, he is still influenced by what he heard on the training pitches at Newell's or in the dressing rooms at the Coloso del Parque. In one respect, Gerardo Martino and Marcelo Bielsa would prove to be similar. Although Bielsa managed Argentina for six years and Chile for four, at club level he has not stayed in one place for very long. Neither has Martino, although at Barcelona he was not given a choice about his departure. 'It is very rare that coaches stay as long as an Arsène Wenger or an Alex Ferguson because once players start to hear the same message every day it becomes routine, and that's when you need to make a change,' he said. 'Coaches also have their own goals so when you feel like you have accomplished a lot at one place, then you start to think about other challenges.'

Bielsa worked with Martino, and allowed his game to meld into what he was attempting to do with the rest of the squad. 'We were closer at the end of the season than we were at the beginning,' said Martino, and by the finish, Newell's were everything Marcelo Bielsa wanted them to be. Almost. It was the derby where everything changed. Gerardo Martino said that Rosario Central versus Newell's Old Boys compared to Barcelona against Real Madrid for raw passion. 'The problem was always getting out alive.'

The day before they went to the Gigante de Arroyito to face Central, Fernando Gamboa, Newell's young defender who was not yet twenty, had difficulty sleeping during the post-training siesta. He went out into the corridor where there was a Pacman video machine. He began to play. Into the corridor strode Bielsa.

'How are you? Are you ready to play?'

'I am desperate to play, gaffer.'

'Can I ask you a question?'

'Yes, gaffer, ask away.'

'Tell me, Fernando, what would you give to win tomorrow's game?'

'Everything, gaffer. You know me.'

'But what is everything?'

'Tomorrow is life itself, it's as simple as that.'

'I think you can give more than that.'

'More? I don't think I understand you.'

'You have to give more than this.'

'Gaffer, I will play each ball as if it's my last.'

'No, I am thinking of something else. We have five fingers on each hand. If I guarantee now that we will win the derby, would you cut off a finger?'

'But, gaffer, if we win five derbies, I am not going to have a hand left.'

'It seems to me that you haven't understood a damn thing what all this is about.'

The following evening, a Monday night, Gamboa scored Newell's first goal, a diving header from point-blank range. There would be six more goals. The three scored by Rosario Central came from free kicks or penalties put away by David Bisconti, Central's own boy from Murphy. The ones scored by Newell's were altogether more adventurous: a one-two on the edge of the box, finished lethally by Julio Zamora, whom Bielsa had brought back to Newell's from River Plate; then the kind of goal that would become synonymous with Bielsa's teams, a surging, muscular run by Ariel Boldrini that took him to the very edge of a byline that was festooned with ticker tape and paper rolls, followed by a pull-back for Cristian Ruffini to drive home.

Once Bisconti had scored Central's second with a free kick that was as good as his first, Newell's broke away. There were only two men in Central's half, Newell's Lorenzo Sáez and the goalkeeper, Alejandro Lanari. Sáez chipped him from twenty-five yards. There was time for Bisconti to complete his hat-trick with a penalty but as he tried to drag the ball out of the net from Scoponi's grasp, it triggered a brawl. The full-time whistle went: Newell's had won one of the great Rosario derbies, 4–3. 'There is no title that is worth more than victory in the derby,' Bielsa said afterwards. It would not be long before he would have the title as well. He did not ask Gamboa for his finger.

Liberator

Winning his first title with Newell's Old Boys was the happiest moment of Marcelo Bielsa's coaching career. He would never forget it. Even when he was at the summit of his profession, driving a fabulous Argentina side imperiously through qualification to the World Cup, he would still say. 'My happiest moments were at Newell's.' His squad recognised they had been part of something extraordinary. As Mauricio Pochettino put it: 'Bielsa gave the team a different way of playing from everyone else. The variety of our tactics changed the conventional structure of our domestic football. The lads could play in defence or they could go into the middle of the pitch or out to the wings.'

It was a form of total football, the kind of tactics that stated that no player was necessarily fixed to a single position, the vision which had seemed so utterly revolutionary when deployed by Holland in the 1974 World Cup. They were tactics Bielsa would employ throughout his career, especially when it came to using midfielders in defence. The key to Bielsa's tactics is moving the ball from defence to attack as swiftly as possible and midfielders who could defend were able to pass the ball more swiftly and more accurately than traditional full or centre-backs.

Gary Medel would be used as a defender for Chile as would Javi Martínez at Athletic Bilbao. When Bielsa was at Leeds, Ezgjan Alioski was often shifted from a winger to a full-back. An attacking full-back, combined with a winger, placed as wide as possible on the flanks, would often create a two-against-one against the opposition full-back. Martínez, one of the few to be coached by both Marcelo Bielsa and Pep Guardiola, concluded that, although their methods may have been different, they both 'saw football differently'.

Unlike in 1988 when Newell's had won the title over thirty-eight matches, the season in Argentina was divided into two. There was the Apertura and then another nineteen games that made up the Clausura. At the end of it all, the winners of the Apertura would face the winners of the Clausura to determine who could call themselves champions of Argentina. In the Clausura that followed their title, Newell's performed flatly and finished eighth, a dozen points behind the winners, Boca Juniors. In the following Apertura, in 1991, they fared even worse, finishing third bottom.

When reflecting on why there should have been such a discrepancy, Juan Manuel Llop noted: 'We had two poor seasons because of the level that was demanded of us to win the championship. We had a small squad, too. The players were from the youth system and Marcelo was extremely demanding. That, along with the pressure of challenging for the title, made a certain easing off inevitable.'

Llop's comments were the first sign of an accusation that was to be made against Bielsa throughout his career, particularly in Bilbao and Marseille but also at Leeds. He would train his players so hard that towards the end of the season they would lose momentum because of sheer exhaustion. It became known as Bielsa Burnout. This was an accusation Bielsa has little time for. He pointed out that in his first season at Leeds his team created more chances, ran more yards and made more tackles than any other team. However, when interviewed by the author Jonathan Wilson for his history of football in Argentina, *Angels with Dirty Faces*, Llop argued that at Newell's there was mental as well as physical exhaustion.

It's not just physical tiredness but mental and emotional tiredness because the competition level is so high that it's difficult to keep up with it after a period of time. Not all human beings are the same or think the same or react in the same way. Bielsa's style, his training sessions demand continuity and it's difficult.

Throughout his career, Bielsa has relied on small, tight, disciplined squads. It can foster an intense team spirit but the cost of injury is obvious. Bielsa also put his trust in young footballers. For his study, *Perfectionism and Burnout in Junior Soccer Players*, Andrew Hill, a lecturer in sports and exercise science at Leeds University, studied 167 footballers in eight professional football academies or centres of excellence. A quarter experienced some symptoms of burnout. Dr Hill concluded: 'Players who reported perceived pressures from others, a fear of making mistakes and other external pressures were at the most risk from burnout. Non-perfectionists and players who displayed perfectionism driven by their own high standards were significantly less vulnerable.' In a study of 12,000 sports injuries in American children as young as twelve, Dr Mininder Kocher, an orthopaedic surgeon at the Boston Children's Hospital, warned against 'intensive and repetitive training'.

Given that Marcelo Bielsa's methods were all about instilling perfectionism in others, largely through intensive and repetitive training, this might be taken as damning evidence. Except that Dr Hill was writing in 2014 when Bielsa was managing Olympique de Marseille rather than Leeds United and that Dr Kocher is unlikely ever to have heard of Marcelo Bielsa. They were researching generally and in Dr Kocher's case not specifically about football. As sport becomes more intense and as what are known as 'marginal gains' are ever more intensively mined, the casualty list will grow longer. One of the standout documentaries of 2019 was *The Edge,* an investigation into how England became the best cricket team in the world. England, who since 1987 had lost nine of the previous ten Ashes series, endured an intense training regime that culminated with them beating Australia home and away. By 2011, they were number one in the world. The real poignancy of the film comes when the players count the cost. Andy Flower, the coach who among other things set up a boot camp in a Bavarian forest to drive his team still harder, wonders about the cost to his family. The wicketkeeper, Matt Prior, asks himself if he is any longer a good person because his life had become so wrapped up in the business of winning. Jonathan Trott, the Warwickshire batsman whose Test career was cut short by depression, suffered more than anyone. At the end of *The Edge* he breaks down in tears.

There is not that sense when Bielsa's players are interviewed. Almost without exception, they will talk of how he has made them see football differently, how he has improved their game, even the way they think. In the words of Gabriel Batistuta: 'He took street kids and made them into heroes.' Bielsa Burnout does not explain how Newell's recovered to win a second title in 1992 or come within a penalty shoot-out of becoming champions of South America. If burnout and exhaustion was the major factor, then once Bielsa had left his post and a less intense training method was reapplied, results should start to swing back into line. Instead, the opposite happened. After Bielsa left Rosario, Newell's were twice almost relegated. Marseille were never the force they had been in his one season at the Stade Vélodrome. Only at Athletic Bilbao was it true, and it was in Bilbao that the strongest protests were made about the price of Bielsa's drive for glory.

There were good reasons why the Clausura should have been such a disappointment. Newell's' young team knew that whatever happened over those nineteen games, they would be in the play-off for the Argentine championship in July. This was one of the great weaknesses of the Primera – if you had won the Apertura and lost the first few games of the Clausura there was little motivation to press on, particularly for a young side like Newell's. There were specific reasons, too. Gerardo Martino, one of the fulcrums of the side, had left to spend a season in La Liga, playing for Tenerife. That also drained the side of momentum.

There were still some highpoints. In April came the Rosario derby, this time at the Coloso del Parque. Central were demolished, 4–0. Mauricio Pochettino scored the opening goal and ran to the fences to celebrate with the fans. 'As you would expect, we were gods in Rosario that evening,' he said. He invited some players back to his flat for beer and pizza and then off to a nightclub called Arrow, an unpretentious place not far from the Paraná waterfront. There he met Karina, who was studying to be a chemist. She liked sport but it was rugby rather than football. Despite this, she became his wife.

In July 1991 came the play-off with Boca Juniors to decide the overall winners of the Primera. Newell's won the first leg, 1–0, playing not at the Colaso del Parque but at Central's ground, the Gigante de Arroyito. A header from the twenty-one-year-old Eduardo Berizzo gave Newell's an edge but the return would be a daunting proposition. Boca were the biggest club in Argentina. They had not lost a game in the Clausura and were managed by Óscar Tabárez, one of the great South American coaches, a man whom Bielsa admired to the extent that he would provide a foreword for the biography of a man who took Uruguay to four World Cups. He was called El Maestro (the Teacher), which he had been after his retirement as a player and before he went into management. Like Bielsa, Tabárez was fascinated by literature and politics and named his daughter, Tania, after Che Guevara's last girlfriend. He would make less of an impact in Europe than Bielsa – there was one especially disastrous spell at AC Milan – but Tabárez's record as an international manager was superior. 'El Maestro Tabárez is a faithful representative of what it is to be Uruguayan or at least of the values that we Argentines attribute to our neighbours,' Bielsa wrote. 'He is balanced, he has common sense, sincerity, modesty.'

There was nothing modest about the setting for the championship decider on 9 July 1991. There were 55,000 in Boca's stadium, the Bombonera, a ground where the championship had not been in a decade, hungry to see the cycle smashed. The Copa América, staged in Chile, began before the cumbersome process of deciding the champions of Argentina was finished. Newell's were without Fernando Gamboa. Boca Juniors lost the spearhead of their attack, Batistuta, and paid the greater price. Argentina won the 1991 Copa América and Batistuta was the tournament's highest scorer. He earned a transfer to Fiorentina, where he would turn from a very good striker into a great one.

The teams emerged to a blizzard of ticker tape pouring down from the stands. Newell's had been strengthened by the return of Gerardo Martino from Tenerife. In this kind of atmosphere, they would need Tata. In the event, Martino did not last the first half before he was taken off injured. Bielsa was so infuriated by the tackle that he got himself sent off and was forced to pass messages to the touchline via the faithful Carlos Altieri. In Batistuta's place was Gerardo Reinoso, who had made the heretical transfer from River Plate. He would play three games for Boca and score one goal. Nine minutes from time, on a pitch that resembled a mudflat, Reinoso scored his goal. The final was now level.

The match, angry and brutal, went into extra time. Each side had a man sent off. Then a season was decided on penalty kicks. Norberto Scoponi saved the first two Boca penalties; the fourth was missed. Newell's Old Boys were undisputed champions of Argentina.

The party was soon over. The hangover was fierce. The 1991 Apertura was a disaster. Of their nineteen matches,

Newell's won three and had eight players sent off. Only the bottom club, Quilmes, won fewer. For the only occasion in Bielsa's time at Newell's the derby was lost to Rosario Central. 'I die after each defeat,' Bielsa said at the time. 'The week that follows is hell.' In the last few months of 1991, he would die frequently. In February 1992 came a game after which he would long for death itself.

Newell's Old Boys were in the Copa Libertadores, the South American equivelant of the Champions League. The group stage saw them paired with teams from Argentina and Chile. The first group game was at home to San Lorenzo. They lost, 6–0. It mattered not that San Lorenzo's goals were beautifully taken, a twenty-five-yard free kick from José Ponce, a first-time volley on the run from Alberto Acosta, who would finish with a hat-trick. It mattered not that Acosta, whose career would take him to France, Chile and Japan, remarked that he never had and never would play as well as that February night at the Coloso del Parque. The score was damning.

There are ways to react to humiliation. In February 1999, after losing 8–1 at home to Manchester United, the Nottingham Forest manager, Ron Atkinson, declared that he hoped the fans had enjoyed 'a nine-goal thriller'. Atkinson saw no reason to torture himself over the result. Nottingham Forest were in an advanced stage of disintegration while Manchester United would win the Treble. These things happened. It is safe to say that Marcelo Bielsa was not Ron Atkinson. He did not accept that these things happened.

'When the mistakes are of such a grotesque magnitude, the conclusion has to be that the manager is responsible.'

He was not the only one who thought that. Soon the *barras bravas* were at the door of his home in Rosario. There were about twenty of them, demanding he come out and face them. Bielsa came out holding a hand grenade. 'If you don't go now,' he told them, 'I will pull the pin.' The *barras bravas* dispersed.

In an interview with *Kaiser* magazine one fan said: 'The madness sparkled in his eyes. Nobody could look at Bielsa, only at the grenade in his hand. We imagined he would face us with a shotgun, not a grenade.' This was 1992, the year his predecessor at Newell's, José Yudica, had advanced on the *barras bravas* of Argentinos Juniors with a loaded pistol. However, to have a hand grenade in your home where you live with your young family was of a different magnitude. It is hard to believe the grenade was real. What the incident achieved was to make his nickname stick. He would be forever El Loco.

The next match was a league fixture in Santa Fe, against Unión. Bielsa hid himself away in the Conquistador Hotel in the city, leaving the preparations to others.

I shut myself in my room. I turned off the light, closed the curtains and realised the true meaning of an expression we sometimes use lightly: 'I want to die.' I burst into tears. I could not understand what was happening around me. I suffered as a professional and I suffered as a fan. For three months our daughter was held between life and death. Now she is fine. Does it make any sense that I want the earth to swallow me over the result of a football match?

The results of the football matches became better, beginning with a goalless draw at Santa Fe. It was the start of a run of twenty-six matches which Newell's would not lose. 'I remember Bielsa talking to us individually and to the collective, making changes and slowly turning around the situation,' Mauricio Pochettino recalled. When he turned the light on in his room at the Santa Fe Conquistador and began working again, his methods were not doubted or changed. They were implemented more fiercely. When in October 2019, managing Tottenham, he began sifting through the wreckage of a 7–2 home defeat by Bayern Munich, Pochettino remembered how Bielsa had responded to disaster.

Newell's would play the first three matches of their Copa Libertadores campaign at home. The Chilean clubs, Coquimbo Unido and Colo-Colo – who had won the Libertadores the previous season - were beaten comfortably. Amid all this the Rosario derby was won.

They flew to Santiago to face Universidad Católica; like all of Newell's group games in Chile, this one was drawn. Qualification for the knockout phases of the Libertadores was not difficult. There were five teams in each group. Four went through but Newell's went through in first place. Given the way they had begun it had been quite a turnaround. In the 1992 Clausura they were still unbeaten. In their opening five matches, Newell's did not concede so much as a goal.

The Libertadores was now in its knockout stage. In the round of sixteen, Newell's overcame the Uruguayan champions, Defensor Sporting, whose modest stadium by the River Plate was considered too small for the occasion. The game was moved to the Centenario in Montevideo. It was remembered for Defensor's equaliser. There were six minutes remaining and Josemir Lujambio was hemmed in by two Newell's defenders. Lujambio had his back to goal, took the ball down on his chest, flicked it up with his boot and volleyed it over his own head, past Nolberto Scoponi and into the net. Lujambio was twenty and this was a goal full of the arrogance and bravery of youth.

Newell's won the return by a single goal to set up a quarter-final with San Lorenzo, the club that three months before had so humiliated Bielsa in his own stadium. San Lorenzo were from Boedo in the south of Buenos Aires, a *barrio* where the naked realities of working-class life were lightened by a passion for the tango and literature. According to the tango that bears its name, Boedo is a place of street-corner poets.

There was nothing lyrical about San Lorenzo's treatment when they returned to the Coloso del Parque. It would have been poetic had they been beaten by six. They lost 4–0, three headed goals and a volley from close range from

Pochettino, who had scored the first. The return leg was rendered irrelevant, although not long afterwards one of their most fervent fans, Jorge Bergoglio, would have the compensation of being consecrated as a bishop, the first step on his journey to becoming Pope Francis.

The semi-finals pitched Newell's against América de Cali, the most powerful football club in Colombia, the bastion of Cali's working classes. Since 1982 they had won seven Colombian titles and they were underpinned by a river of cocaine money from the Cali Cartel, led by the Hernández brothers, Gilberto and Miguel. In the words of their striker, Willington Ortiz, the domestic titles were the merest bagatelle to the Hernández brothers. 'The league titles didn't compensate. The team was put together to win the Libertadores.' The aim was to do it before Atlético Nacional, a club run by Pablo Escobar's Medellín Cartel.

América de Cali reached three successive Libertadores finals and lost them all. In 1989, Atlético Nacional beat the Paraguayan side, Olimpia, to bring the cup to Colombia for the first time. Escobar was photographed with the trophy as he prepared to board his private jet. Inside América's stadium, the Pascual Guerrero, the need to win the Libertadores had now become acute.

The first leg at the Coloso del Parque was a grinding, remorseless affair. In the tenth minute América broke through as Antony de Ávila drove the ball into the roof of Scoponi's net. Seven years before, the final of the Copa Libertadores between América de Cali and Argentinos Juniors had been settled on penalties. De Ávila, who stood 5'3" and was nicknamed the Smurf, had been the only one not to score. He was deeply motivated. On the touchline, Bielsa showed his dissatisfaction with the looseness of it all. In the seventy-seventh minute, Alfredo Mendoza equalised to give Newell's something to cling on to in Colombia.

It is 3,810 miles from Rosario to Cali, roughly the distance between London and the Afghan border. Even by that measure, getting to the second leg of the semi-final was a tortuous business. Newell's flew first to Jujuy in the mountainous north-west of Argentina, then to Guayaquil in Ecuador and thence to Bogotá. Finally, they made it to the open bowl of the Pascual Guerrero. Overlooking the stadium and seemingly overlooking most of the city was the Cristo de Cali, an 85-foot-high statue of Jesus. As he practised taking a penalty, Pochettino recalls looking up at it. If it came to it, he would be ready. It came to penalties. Lots of penalties.

The bus ride to the stadium was almost as tortuous. The bus was far too small for the squad, some of whom had to stand as it crawled through the city. Then the driver turned into a street that was full of funeral homes and workshops that made coffins. When they reached the stadium, they were a target for every kind of missile – especially Mendoza, who had once played for América's city rivals, Deportivo Cali. 'It was like a jungle where you cannot see the threat – or the stones,' said Pochettino. 'There was this big plastic tunnel for you to walk out through and it went nearly to the middle of the pitch. Eduardo Berizzo received a battery on his head and it cut him. We had to wait, go inside and get him stitched up before playing a semi-final.'

Talking of Liverpool's captain, Tommy Smith, Bill Shankly once remarked, 'He wasn't born, he was quarried,' and there was something of that in Berizzo. He was physically imposing and a born leader. He would organise Bielsa's defence at both Newell's Old Boys and Atlas Guadalajara and be his assistant at Chile. Bielsa called him 'the best person I have ever met in football'. In these final stages of the Libertadores, Berizzo was a granite rock.

'No-one believed in us,' said Pochettino. 'Cali were the favourites and it was all prepared for them. I remember that semi-final because we were so brave, although we parked the bus after we scored early and tried to play counter-attack. We defended all the time and they equalised in the eighty-ninth minute.' Pochettino, who told the story as Tottenham prepared for their Champions League semi-final against Ajax, neglected to mention that it was he who scored Newell's goal. As they trained on the pitch, Bielsa gathered his squad together and told them to practise free kicks and corners. Given the circumstances, he predicted this might be Newell's best route to a goal.

It took him four minutes to be proved correct. Julio Zamora sent a high free kick into América's area and Pochettino, his marker clinging to him, rose and fell and headed it home. Newell's began a furious defence. Berizzo was struck again, this time by a volley of coins wrapped up in tape. There were two clearances off the line. Both teams were reduced to ten men and in the last moments, Newell's conceded a penalty and, when Jorge da Silva converted it, the Pascual Guerrero erupted not with a roar but with a screech. Once extra time was ploughed through, there followed the most extraordinary shoot-out in the history of the Copa Libertadores, one that Marcelo Bielsa, having been sent off, watched from the mouth of the tunnel.

There were twenty-six penalties in all. Pochettino, who took Newell's seventh penalty, sent his in the vague direction of the Cristo de Cali. Cristian Domizzi struck the bar. After each miss, América failed to score the penalty that would have sent them to the final. Both goalkeepers hit the target. Eduardo Berizzo, showing his habitual resilience, scored both the penalties he was required to take. Then Nolberto Scoponi leapt to his left to push Orlando Maturana's kick onto the post. Finally, it was over. One spectator had died of a heart attack and ten others had been taken to hospital and treated for cardiac arrests.

'A display of courage' was how Bielsa described it, and Berizzo was the first man he embraced. Back at the hotel, they drank champagne and ate and talked until dawn, although since dawn was not that far off when Scoponi made his final save, this was not quite as decadent as it sounds.

A month later, in another hotel, the Novotel by the vast

Morumbi Stadium in São Paulo, Marcelo Bielsa would sit down and watch another match and then watch it again. It made no difference. Newell's Old Boys had lost the final of the Copa Libertadores. There had been another penalty shoot-out in another virulently hostile stadium. This time there had been no heroics. They were playing São Paulo, one of the great Brazilian teams, a side that boasted Cafu, Leonardo and Raí. Given the way Brazilian football has been plundered to feed Europe's Champions League, there will probably not be another club side like them in South America. In the Intercontinental Cup, they would face the Barcelona managed by Johan Cruyff, the one that in Catalonia they referred to as 'the Dream Team'. São Paulo would win. Two years later they would beat AC Milan, managed by Fabio Capello.

That would have pleased São Paulo's Telê Santana, a manager as revolutionary as Cruyff or Bielsa. In 1982 he had created the beautiful but brittle Brazilian team that had mesmerised the World Cup and which is still talked of in the same breath as the Hungarians of 1954 and the Dutch of 1974 as the greatest side not to win the tournament. Unlike the others, however, Brazil did not even reach the final.

Because of its greater capacity, the Gigante de Arroyito, rather than the Coloso del Parque, was used to stage the first leg of the final. Newell's, as they always did in the Rosario derby, took the away dressing room. The game was settled by a handball. The penalty was converted by the magnificent Eduardo Berizzo into a goal stuffed with toilet rolls and ticker tape. Perhaps Newell's should have won by more. Mauricio Pochettino sent a header wide in the second half but it was a not a night of clear-cut chances.

Everything would be decided in the Morumbi. In Rosario, there had been toilet rolls and ticker tape. Here fireworks twirled down from the stands, smoke poured upwards and vast banners waved. Inside the away dressing room the music from a Rosario folk rock band, Vilma Palma and the Vampires, had died away and Bielsa, who had talked to every player individually, now made his speech. 'Outside, there are 80,000 but in here there is a team of men determined to go out and win. Win the cup and you will be able to walk through the streets of Rosario with your heads held high for the rest of your lives. Go out there and win.'

Frankly, it appeared their ambitions stretched no further than going out there and drawing. São Paulo, too, were dreadful. A contest between the two best club sides in South America stretched for three hours and did not feature a worthwhile shot on target. For sixty-five minutes it seemed Newell's would hold. Then came a reckless, needless tackle from Fernando Gamboa and Raí sent Scoponi the wrong way. The final dribbled away to a shoot-out. With Newell's first penalty, Berizzo struck the post. Mendoza sent his over the bar and Gamboa's was saved. Telê Santana, who had seen his Brazil side knocked out of the 1986 World Cup in Mexico in such a shoot-out, watched impassively before raising his arms wearily above his head as the crowds flooded the pitch.

Break for the Border

'He would be ideal for you,' César Luis Menotti told the president of Atlas Guadalajara, Fernando Acosta. 'Though to tell the truth, he is a little crazy.'

Becoming the sporting director of the second club in Mexico's second biggest city was not a crazy decision but it was a strange, left-field move. Marcelo Bielsa had made Newell's Old Boys twice champions of Argentina. They had come within a penalty shoot-out of becoming champions of South America against one of the greatest club sides the continent would produce. The obvious next move would have been to go to one of the giant clubs of Buenos Aires – Boca Juniors, River Plate or Independiente. Perhaps Spain, maybe Italy. Yet Bielsa seemed exhausted by the years that had just passed and appeared frustrated by Argentine domestic football. He remarked he felt 'empty'. This was not an unusual feeling for a manager, even one who had enjoyed considerable success. When Ottmar Hitzfeld resigned as manager of Bayern Munich after two Champions League finals, he used the same word. He felt 'empty'.

The pain of defeat in the final of the Libertadores refused to subside. In an interview afterwards he confessed:

It had taken a huge effort to only lose 1–0 to a club like São Paulo, these are the kinds of things you have to suffer and for me it is terrible. It is no use saying now that the cup is less important than when we planned to win it. This squad has an unquestionable courage. Nobody can say Newell's were boring. These lads live for each metre of ground, for each pass. It is a team where you are pushed to the limits, not where you are comfortable. Now we must show the maturity to win the championship because that is also going to define us. It is done. I am shattered but I believe that the great defeats lead to the next triumphs.

Perhaps because it was overshadowed by the drama of the Copa Libertadores and perhaps because they won it rather more easily, winning the 1992 Clausura lacked the sheer emotional punch of the first title. Newell's had lost only once, 1–0 at Estudiantes, on their return from the tortuous and draining Libertadores semi-final against América de Cali. They had sealed the title with a game to spare in a goalless draw at home to Argentinos Juniors. In Liniers, the railhead for the country's vast meat industry, Vélez Sarsfield had failed to overcome Gimnasia La Plata. They were done.

They celebrated the title in the Pan y Manteca restaurant in Rosario, long a stronghold for Newell's fans. Bielsa's final game as manager of Newell's Old Boys came on 5 July 1992, a 1–1 draw at Platense's modest stadium. Then he was gone.

Bielsa's resignation from Newell's has echoes of Kenny Dalglish's departure from Anfield in February 1991. Liverpool were top of the league but the pressures were overwhelming Dalglish. He felt he could not relax, could not escape the stress. There was the constant pain of the Hillsborough dead. He was adored unquestioningly at Anfield but beyond the Shankly Gates, he was not so sure. He probably needed an extended holiday. Instead, he walked out, although Dalglish hankered ever afterwards to come back home. When he did, nearly twenty years later, it was a mistake.

Marcelo Bielsa could not boast Kenny Dalglish's playing career but like Dalglish at Liverpool he was admired beyond measure. They named a stand at Anfield after Dalglish; they named the stadium after Bielsa. He had only been managing Newell's for less than three years but he had been part of the club for a decade and had worked like nobody else in football. He needed a sabbatical. In a way this is what Mexico offered. He would not be front of stage at Atlas. He would be observing from the wings, overseeing the club's youth policy, its development, its overall strategy. 'I went to Mexico because I needed to iron out some exaggerated aspects of my character. It was in Mexico that I became a more reflective person,' he said.

Acosta had first met Bielsa in Rosario while he was managing Newell's. They had talked. Atlas were interested in a Brazilian footballer; naturally Bielsa had a video of him. A relationship was formed. Then Acosta made his approach. There were attractions. Guadalajara was Mexico's cultural and artistic centre; Atlas played in the same red and black as Newell's. Atlas, which had been founded by a group of friends who played football at Ampleforth College in Yorkshire, had a reputation for fluid football and for developing young players. They also possessed something else which was to attract Bielsa to clubs across the globe – passionate fans. The supporters were known as La Fiel or 'the Faithful' and their faith had been sorely stretched. Atlas Guadalajara's only league title had come in 1951.

Atlas shared the stadium, the Jalisco, with CD Guadalajara. It was here that Bobby Moore and Pelé embraced in the 1970 World Cup. It was here that Gordon Banks made the save that would become immortal. It was at the Jalisco that the France of Platini and the Brazil of Socrates played out their epic quarter-final in 1986. It was this stadium that Marcelo Bielsa could be seen walking around as he composed himself for his press conferences. He was coming to a city and a club in trauma. A few months before Bielsa formally joined Atlas, the area around the Jalisco Stadium, five square miles of the city, had been destroyed by underground explosions. New water pipes made of zinc-coated iron had been built too close to steel gasoline pipelines. Underground humidity began to cause a reaction and slowly the gasoline pipes began to corrode, leaking their contents into the soil. On 19 April 1992 residents in Calle Gante reported the stench of gasoline and white plumes of smoke coming from the sewers. Investigators were called but advised it was not necessary to evacuate the Atlas district, which was then convulsed by eight enormous explosions in under an hour. Only then was Atlas evacuated. Officially, the dead numbered 252 but unofficial estimates put the casualties at more than a thousand with up to 600 missing and 15,000 homeless. The cost of the damage was thought to be $1 billion.

By then, Atlas's sporting director, Francisco Ibarra, had contacted Bielsa, who considered the offer for two months. He travelled to Mexico and helped out at several training sessions without revealing to the players who he was. He was accompanied by Carlos Altieri, whom Bielsa had asked to judge the level of the team. Neither of them was convinced by what they saw. Bielsa has, however, always been convinced of his own worth. While he hesitated, Atlas offered him more money, although Bielsa's concerns were not primarily financial. Altieri recalled:

He had to make a decision and although the payments in his contract were important, he told me it was not the money that decided him whether to lead this team or not. He said he would pay the hotel bill before telling the directors he would not be taking charge of the first team. However, Ibarra had already announced his arrival to the press. Bielsa was able to get exactly what he wanted: a physio, a first-team coach and substantial revisions to his contract.

Bielsa wanted Mario Zanabria to manage the first team. Zanabria had been a midfielder with Newell's and won the Copa Libertadores twice with Boca Juniors. He was at his in-laws' in Santa Fe when Bielsa called offering him the job. Bielsa said he had to know the answer in half an hour. Zanabria asked for a little more time but the following day was on his way to Mexico. On the plane he met Professor Esteban Gesto, a physical conditioning specialist, who would work with Uruguay's greatest manager, Óscar Tabárez, in two World Cups. 'Marcelo Bielsa was also a teacher,' Gesto said, referring to Tabárez's nickname El Maestro (the Teacher). 'We had shared tasks at Guadalajara and I admired him for the way he explained what is failure and what is not failure. Football was everything to him and those who were not prepared for it had a short life.'

Mario Zanabria's time in Guadalajara was shorter than he expected. The Mexican league, the Primera División, was divided into four groups. The top two from each went into a knockout contest. Atlas did not make it out of their group and it was small consolation that none of the other Guadalajara clubs did either.

Bielsa designed a system to screen a potential 20,000 footballers a year. It was a similar process to the one he had organised at Newell's. Tournaments were held across the country and fifteen players were selected from each one. When, in the 2006 World Cup, Mexico played Argentina in Leipzig, eight of the starting eleven were players who had been discovered by Marcelo Bielsa. 'The work he organised was impressive: fast, effective and efficient,' said Acosta. 'He organised a player-recruitment network that still exists across ninety-two towns and cities in Mexico.'

Bielsa enjoyed his time away from the limelight. Arsène Wenger, who had gone to Japan exhausted by the continual struggle at Monaco to wrest the title from Marseille, once remarked that Nagoya had taught him the 'value of solitude'. Similarly, Bielsa said that Mexico had 'made me more reflective'. 'I understood that football was not life.'

'He changed when he went to Guadalajara,' said Carlos Altieri. 'He took up golf and lived in a luxurious apartment. He was very calm during the games and was sent sweets, newspapers and magazines from home.' Relaxation only went so far, though, as his assistant Ernesto Urrea pointed out: 'He arrived with a catalogue of 300 training exercises and left with more than 500. His wife is a trained architect; she drew them up and Marcelo filmed them in action to show the other coaches at Atlas. He is a creative mind and one of the smartest people I have ever met.' Not long after his arrival in Guadalajara, his in-laws arrived for a visit. One of Atlas's directors, Samuel Alvo, suggested he should take his family to Puerto Vallarta, one of the jewels of Mexico's Pacific coast. Much as Saint Tropez had been made famous by Brigitte Bardot, Puerto Vallarta, a small fishing village, had been 'discovered' by Richard Burton and Elizabeth Taylor. Burton had filmed Tennessee Williams's play *The Night of the Iguana* here. They had built a house, Casa Kimberly, and the world had followed.

Bielsa did not enjoy the beaches; he was preoccupied by a forthcoming friendly with Puebla. As Alvo related:

> They had barely arrived at the hotel when Marcelo asked for two video recorders and shut himself in his room to watch Puebla's last ten matches on videos which he had packed in his suitcase. He put his father-in-law to work, taking notes on the videos as he watched them. He only saw the sea from the balcony of his room and his feet did not touch the sand.

After a single season, Zanabria was dispensed with and Bielsa was asked to manage the first team. This he did, reluctantly. He employed products of his youth team: Jared Borgetti in attack, Pável Pardo in midfield, Oswaldo Sánchez in goal. He brought in those he had known at Newell's: midfielder Ricardo Lunari and defenders Eduardo Berizzo and Cristian Domizzi. Lunari was playing for Universidad Católica in Chile.

I got a phone call at one in the morning: 'Ricardo, it's Marcelo Bielsa. I want you to come and join me in Guadalajara.'

'Of course, coach. I would love to come.'

'Great, let's see if the clubs can come to some agreement.'

He called me the next morning. 'Ricardo, I want you to know that your club wants $1 million for you and you know you are not worth $1 million, don't you?' I said, 'Coach, I know I am not worth a million dollars.' Bielsa said: 'I know. I am sorry but there can be no deal.'

Fifteen minutes later, a director of my club calls me to say that Atlas have paid $1 million and I am going to Mexico. I went to Mexico and from the airport they took me straight to the training ground, not because I had to start training but because Marcelo Bielsa wanted to talk to me. He sat down with me, looked me in the eye and said: 'I want you to know; I want you to be convinced that you are not worth a million dollars.' I said: 'Coach, I know I am not worth that.' He said, 'Right, now go and train.'

There were many who appreciated Bielsa's methods and there were some who did not. 'The first thing Bielsa transmits is fear,' said the midfielder Rodolfo Navarro, who was a teenager when Bielsa began coaching Atlas.

During his first days there, he spoke to us with his eyes looking down at the ground. The only time he spoke to us was when we had made a mistake. The immense levels of his demands were obvious. Within several months we had done 500 different exercises. Bielsa's methods are outside the normal sporting practice. Physically, it's intense but it is also mentally exhausting because you are faced with a permanent new way of working.

A few could not take it at all. Martín Ubaldi, who had been signed from Independiente, approached a member of Bielsa's staff, Ricardo Rentería, by the training ground fence. 'He said he could not take it any more. These sessions were killing him.' Jared Borgetti, who would become Mexico's record goalscorer, had a different view of his manager's methods: 'Bielsa was a warlord. When I arrived in Guadalajara, I knew nothing about football. He taught me a lot about how to see the game, how to analyse it. He is very demanding, a perfectionist. It is wrong to say he taught me to play; it went much deeper than that.'

Atlas finished second in their group and made the play-offs for the first time in twelve years. In the quarter-final, they faced Santos Laguna, a club based in Torreón in northern Mexico. Atlas scored after a dozen minutes in the first leg at the Jalisco but there were no more goals and the second leg was lost, 3–1. However, by the start of the 1994–5 season, Bielsa appeared exhausted. Atlas did not begin well and after twenty-two matches, of which only seven had been won, he resigned. His final game was on 28 January, a win over Gallos Blancos, settled by a Borgetti goal. It was not enough to keep Bielsa at the Jalisco.

The foundations he had laid were firm ones. Borgetti, Pável Pardo – who was to win 148 international caps – and Oswaldo Sánchez would become the bedrock of the Mexico team in two World Cups. In 1999 Atlas Guadalajara reached the Primera División final, losing to Toluca only on penalties. Most of their players had been coached by Bielsa. 'Unfortunately, Bielsa did not get to harvest all his work,' was how Fernando Acosta remembered him.

Bielsa did not immediately return to Argentina but remained in Mexico, perfecting his golf, a game he preferred to play alone. Four-balls were not in his nature. He was thus available for the biggest job in Mexican club football.

Club América were disliked for their success, their heavy spending and their willingness to bring in foreign talent. In the 1980s they had dominated Mexican football but the decade that followed had been a barren one. Seen from the directors' box at the Azteca Stadium, Leo Beenhakker appeared a good bet to break the logjam. The Dutchman had managed Real Madrid to three La Liga titles and taken Saudi Arabia to the knockout stages of the 1994 World Cup. In April 1995, with Club América top of the league and certain to qualify for the play-offs with sixty-three points from thirty-one matches and a goal difference of +38, Beenhakker received a call at 7.30 in the morning at his home in the elegant city of Cuernavaca, the centre of the Mexican film industry. The voice on the other end of the line told him he was fired. Club América had been in financial dispute with their defender, Joaquín del Olmo. The president, Emilio Diez Barroso, had told Beenhakker not to select him. Not only had Del Olmo played in the last game against Puebla, he had been sent off.

Bielsa was approached by Barroso to take over and, after watching videos of every one of Club América's games from the past two seasons, he accepted. He inherited a side eminently capable of winning the Primera División, with an attack led by the Cameroon striker, François Omam-Biyik, and Cuauhtémoc Blanco, who could claim to be the greatest striker Mexico produced. There was also Luis García Postigo, whose goals had beaten Ireland in Florida's shattering summer heat during the 1994 World Cup. Maurizio Gaudino was one of the stranger additions to Bielsa's squad. A graceful midfielder who had won the Bundesliga with Stuttgart, he had been arrested over a car theft scandal. Expensive cars had been stolen to order, sold in eastern Europe and then claims would be made on the insurance. His club, Eintracht Frankfurt, considered Gaudino something of an embarrassment and he was loaned out first to Manchester City, where he became a cult hero, and then to Club América. He found the sessions under Bielsa in Mexico City at the El Nido training centre rather different from those organised by Brian Horton at Platt Lane: 'The pitch was divided into four corners and you were not allowed to leave your corner,' he said in an interview with the German magazine *Rund*.

A session lasted two hours and everything was filmed, which for its time was very unusual. Bielsa loved the high pressing game and to keep it up we did sprint training on Tuesdays. We would run on a volcano at 3,500 metres altitude [11,500 feet]. We did it for one and a half hours with weights. I had a lot of red blood cells after that. I found him mad but in a positive way. We had the impression that he never slept.

Not a lot of Club América's players enjoyed running on top of a volcano with weights strapped to them. There seems to have been an increasing tension over Bielsa's training methods. Bielsa himself was becoming increasingly frustrated with the media demands placed upon him by Club América, which was owned by Televisa, the largest broadcaster in the Spanish-speaking world. After three straight defeats, he was sacked. It was his first sacking, the first failure of his managerial career. Dismissal was not to become part of his career as it did for Claudio Ranieri, who was to see the words 'by mutual consent' used in Spanish, Italian, French, English and Greek. Usually, Bielsa went on his own terms. Now he returned to Guadalajara, took up his old position as Atlas's sporting director and successfully sued Club América for compensation.

In June he flew to England to watch Euro 96. There he would study train timetables to ensure that, if there were two games played on the same day, he could watch them both. On the plane with him was Jorge Valdano, a man who like Bielsa grew up at Newell's Old Boys and who considered the way you played football to be more significant than whether you won. As a player, Valdano had won the biggest prize football had to offer, the World Cup, and he had managed Real Madrid to La Liga. It was on this flight that Bielsa turned to Valdano and said: 'After you have lost a game do you ever think about killing yourself?'

The Meat Market

Raúl Gámez counts as one of the more extraordinary men Marcelo Bielsa has worked for. He is a passionate fan of Vélez Sarsfield, portrayed as a hooligan turned president, who saw one of Buenos Aires' lesser-known clubs become world champions. Gámez is tough, wiry and supremely fit. He looks a decade younger than his seventy-five years. He grew up amid the *barras bravas,* groups of fans who mobilised themselves 'to defend the honour of their club'. Their usual method was violence. 'We fought with clean fists, without weapons or alcohol,' is how Gámez describes that time. A confrontation with police earned him a six-month sentence. Long after Bielsa had left Vélez, Gámez was the victim of a kidnapping which he foiled by throwing himself from a speeding car. He was a man not to be messed with.

Gámez smiles when reminded of the day he encountered

his English counterparts. It was June 1986, with Argentina facing England in the Azteca Stadium. In a profile of Gámez in *These Football Times,* the journalist Christopher Weir comments on him trading blows with 'what looks like the cast of a Shane Meadows drama'.

'I punched people but I was also punched,' he said thirty-three years later. 'It was a mistake to get involved but there was a lot of tension between the Argentine and English fans because of the Malvinas, and it's wrong to say that everyone involved was a hooligan. People got caught up in it. It just took over and kicked off inside the stadium and outside it.' At least Gámez could celebrate an Argentinian victory and one of the greatest goals ever seen at a World Cup. 'I have seen goals as good as the one Diego Maradona scored against England,' he said. 'But I have never seen a goal like that in such an important match. Messi can score those kinds of goals but it is rare for him to do it when the pressure is really on.'

The *barras bravas* were a powerful force who exerted considerable pressure and in 1992 Vélez appointed Gámez as vice-president in charge of football operations. In the boardroom of Vélez's ground, El Fortín (the Little Fort), he admitted to 'thinking differently' from the way he had done on the terraces. Within two years, Vélez had beaten AC Milan to win the Intercontinental Cup. In 1996, Gámez was elected for the first of what would be three terms as president.

Almost immediately after taking charge of Vélez's football operations, Gámez pushed for Bielsa to become manager. By then, Bielsa was in Mexico working as Atlas Guadalajara's sporting director. He told Gámez that his daughters were still young and he was against the idea of moving them. There was plenty about the club that would have appealed to Marcelo Bielsa. Vélez were not one of the giants of Argentine football. They were based in Liniers, on the western outskirts of the capital and close to the railheads that brought the cattle in from the pampas. It was the centre of the country's meat industry.

Despite its name, the Little Fort was not that little: some 300,000 had jammed into it for a Queen concert over two nights in February 1981. Vélez were also passionately supported – 50,000 would march through the streets of Liniers to El Fortín to celebrate the club's centenary. They also possessed an extraordinary collection of young players.

In 1992, Newell's under Bielsa had reached the final of the Copa Libertadores with seven home-grown footballers. Two years later, Vélez had done the same. They even faced the same team in the final, São Paulo. The difference was that Vélez won. During the interval at the second leg at the Morumbi, Gámez had punched the referee's door down, raging about perceived injustices. His players held their nerve to win on penalties.

When Bielsa turned him down, Gámez appointed Carlos Bianchi, the club's greatest goalscorer, to take charge. It seemed the sort of thing a fan would do, like appointing Alan Shearer to manage Newcastle or Thierry Henry to take charge of Monaco, except that unlike those two exercises in sentimentality, this worked spectacularly. The Intercontinental Cup final that pitched the winners of the Copa Libertadores against the European champions tended to matter more in South America than across the Atlantic. However, by any standards Vélez's 2–0 victory over the Milan side that had destroyed Barcelona in the 1994 European Cup final had an impact well beyond the National Stadium in Tokyo. Bianchi departed to take charge of Roma, a move that ended disastrously when he attempted to offload the young Francesco Totti to Sampdoria. By 1997, Gámez was ready to make another move for Bielsa, who had ended his five-year exile in Mexico. 'I began doing what a journalist would do,' Gámez said.

I went around asking as many people as I could find what their opinions were of Marcelo Bielsa. When I spoke to him, we had a lot of conversations. The passion of the fans really appealed to him as well as the fact that we were not one of Buenos Aires' really big clubs. What made the negotiations easier was that we had come looking for him. We wanted that same dedication he had shown at Newell's. We wanted to give him the space to work and we were pretty committed.

The other candidate beside Bielsa was Carlos Bilardo. The man who had taken his country to two World Cup finals had made a not especially successful return to Boca Juniors, working once more with Diego Maradona. Their careers that had flared so brightly together would fade together.

Bielsa was appointed in August 1997. Esteban Bekerman is a journalist who now runs the Entre Tiempos bookshop in the arty San Telmo district of Buenos Aires. The shop is filled with back copies of *El Gráfico* and adorned with photographs of Argentine footballers from the golden years of the 1940s. At his presentation, Bekerman offered Bielsa a copy of his book on Vélez Sarsfield and would do the same to Bielsa's disciple, Gabriel Heinze, when he took over the club twenty years later. 'The press manager at Vélez was an old journalist called Eduardo Rafael, who worked for *El Gráfico*,' Bekerman recalled.

He had covered the Estudiantes team that had beaten Manchester United to win the Intercontinental Cup in 1968. Rafael was a journalist at a time when journalists travelled with and mixed with the players they reported on. He had a fantastic memory and had great stories to tell. Bielsa took him to one side and they talked about that Estudiantes team for three hours. He was taking over a team that had won everything under a man like Carlos Bianchi who was not obsessed by tactics. He used to say that the only thing he knew about tactics was that if the right back was in an offensive position, the left back should be playing in a defensive position.

Bianchi led through force of personality. He led because he was perhaps the greatest footballer ever to play for Vélez Sarsfield. His was basic, no-nonsense stuff. A director, quoted in Jonathan Wilson's study of Argentine football, *Angels with Dirty Faces*, said that Bianchi told his players 'to put the toilet in the bathroom and the oven in the kitchen'. Bielsa was never much of a player and his method was all about making footballers rediscover their role on the pitch. He did not necessarily want his oven in the kitchen. They had won everything playing one way and now they were asked to rip up what they knew. In Esteban Bekerman's words, 'They went on strike.'

The results were dreadful. Only Christian Bassedas, a midfielder who would disappear without trace at Newcastle, seemed to understand Bielsa's methods. Bassedas may have been part of the side that had beaten Milan in Tokyo but he would seldom play better than he did now. It was partly through his efforts that Vélez clambered as high as fourth in the 1997 Apertura. In November, Bielsa gave an interview to *La Nación*. It turned out to be one of the last interviews he would grant. The stresses upon him seemed obvious. He talked about the effect defeat had on him. It was a subject

Bielsa always seemed happier to discuss: he seemed more comfortable with it than success.

> The things I like to do seem to cost more. For example, when I lose, I have less desire to play sport or to go out to eat. I find it more difficult to talk to my wife and less entitled to play with my daughters. I feel less deserving of happiness. However, if you call me an obsessive, someone who cannot live with himself when he loses, it's a lie. I don't think of football as life or death.

He understood what was wrong at El Fortín. The players wanted the success they had enjoyed under Bianchi and could not understand why Bielsa did not use Bianchi's methods to get it. 'The successful player is rooted in the events that brought him success,' Bielsa said.

> Here, without letting go of my habits, I try to consider their needs and create a common bond. In this game there is nearness and distance, rejections and assimilations. Everything bad that happens at Vélez is my responsibility. The worst thing that can happen to a manager is indifference. A manager cannot accept that. A team can be bad but not indifferent. Conviction is a basic element of being a manager. If I am not convinced, then I don't convince anyone else, and

if I don't talk with a sparkle in my voice, I don't get people around me and I don't get support for a project that demands blood.

One of the men who drew most blood from Bielsa was Vélez Sarsfield's goalkeeper, José Luis Chilavert. One of the first things Bielsa told his squad was that the past counted for little; everyone at El Fortín would be treated equally. For the man who would count himself as the greatest goalkeeper South America had produced, the past counted for quite a lot. In the penalty shoot-out in São Paulo that had won the Copa Libertadores Chilavert had saved the first spot-kick and scored Vélez's second. In both legs he had played superbly. He was not equal to anyone, let alone Pablo Cavallero, his twenty-four-year-old understudy, who was one of the club's youth-team products and who under Bielsa would become Argentina's first-choice keeper. 'Bielsa is an obsessive guy, he wants the players not to fail; to be machines,' Chilavert recalled. 'I told him machines also fail.' Later, Raúl Cardozo, a defender who had been at the club for more than a decade, told Bielsa he preferred Bianchi's management style. Bielsa exploded, called his players 'cowards'. Chilavert struck back:

I told him: 'There are no cowards here. This team has won everything and you haven't.' He replied: 'You don't belong in this squad any more, get outside.' I told Bielsa exactly what I thought of him and he said I would regret it. I was training by myself for a month. Pablo Cavallero was in goal and we were losing games by a landslide. One day we sat together in a room and had it out.

Then the squad found itself flying to Jujuy in Argentina's far north-west, where the vast plateau of the Altiplano can rise to 15,000 feet. There was turbulence; the plane began to buck and yaw. Bielsa was sitting on one side of the aisle, Chilavert on the other. The manager stretched across and touched his goalkeeper's shoulder.

'Chilavert, are you happy?'
'Yes.'
'How happy are you?'
'I live well. I have my wife, my daughter.'
'How much money do you spend on your holidays?'
'I don't know; about $30,000 I suppose.'
'Don't do that. It is a slap in the face of the people.'
'So, you're another socialist who drives a Mercedes Benz. Why don't you give the $800,000 you earn to the deserving poor?'
'But Chilavert, you don't have to depend on money to live.'
'Marcelo, until I was seven, we stole food that was meant for the mice just to have something to eat.

I know both sides; that of the poor and that of the privileged. In Paraguay I washed myself on the patio with cold water taken from the cistern because we had no water heaters. That's why, when they talk about footballers being lucky, I say people only see us when we have made it. They don't see the effort we have put in just to get here.'

The plane landed. Their relationship improved to the extent that years later Chilavert would say that Marcelo Bielsa might not have been the best manager he played under but he was the man who understood him the most. In 2002, when Bielsa was at his lowest point, after Sweden had eliminated Argentina from the World Cup, Chilavert commented: 'A manager can do nothing if a Swede hits a free kick at the near post and Pablo Cavallero does not react.' It was perfect Chilavert. He had backed someone he had grown to like, made a point and had a go at another goalkeeper.

'It wasn't just Chilavert, there were a lot of people who found Marcelo Bielsa difficult,' said Raúl Gámez.

Bielsa was a man who thought all day long about what he was going to do and who could be very demanding. It was a totally different relationship from the one the players had with Bianchi. They had known him for a very long time, they were friends. You cannot really be friends with Bielsa, though I absolutely respected him. I once asked him why he didn't come to me with the problems he had with the players. Bielsa replied that, if he had done, I would have heard only one side of the story, his side. The players began to understand his methods and in the second season he won the championship. I think that, given what he had endured, winning that title was one of his biggest achievements. I didn't try to influence him. We would have dinner but never at each other's house or in a restaurant. It would be at the *concentración* before a game. We would talk about our families, life and football but never the specifics of the Vélez team or who would play. He wanted his own space for that. We would also talk when walking around the training pitches but he would walk fast and it was very hard to keep up.

They all sometimes found it hard to keep up. Bielsa would put a mattress down at the back of a van and lie there with a video recorder watching games while one of his backroom staff drove him back to Rosario. 'I don't think it's quite right to call him El Loco,' said Gámez. 'He wasn't mad at Vélez. When we give that nickname it can refer to someone who is passionate, obsessive about something, and Marcelo Bielsa was certainly that. He was a rebel, definitely. I have never met a coach like him. He was unique.'

Martín Posse, one of Vélez's leading strikers, invited

his manager to his wedding. It was the evening after a victory over Boca Juniors. Bielsa turned up with a video of Posse's performance for the groom to study. Posse would have better wedding presents. Nevertheless, Posse, like almost everyone else at El Fortín, regards Bielsa as the man who got the most out of him, the man who made him the player he was meant to be. It was Posse who scored the goal that won Vélez Sarsfield the 1998 Clausura, which vindicated all of Bielsa's methods. 'It took us a whole season to understand what he wanted, to convince us what was good for the team.'

Posse had made his debut for Vélez when he was sixteen. Within a year he had won the Argentine title and the Copa Libertadores. 'I didn't ever mark anyone. I thought it was a waste of time. As a forward I thought you were only meant to attack. Bielsa showed me how to get stuck into defenders and from pre-season I knew Vélez would be up for the title.' They were top after three games, having lost only once, but with two matches remaining there was still a chance Vélez Sarsfield might be caught. Gimnasia La Plata and another Buenos Aires club, Lanús, were three and four points behind them. The final match at El Fortín pitched Vélez against Huracán, the club where Luis César Menotti had made his name in the early 1970s. Lanús travelled to far Jujuy while Gimnasia were at the Coloso del Parque facing Newell's.

Vélez won, 1–0. The goal came in the first half, a header

from Posse that drifted over the goalkeeper, who back-pedalled and fell to the turf. Posse tore off his shirt, waved it above his head and ran. Vélez were so superior that it seemed inconceivable this would not decide the champion-ship. When the final whistle went, champions were what Vélez Sarsfield were. In Rosario, Newell's had done precisely what Bielsa would have wanted them to do and beaten Gimnasia La Plata. In Jujuy there had been a goalless stale-mate. Posse was lifted high upon his team-mates' shoulders as the team began its slow parade around El Fortín. Ariel de la Fuente, the third-choice goalkeeper behind Chilavert and Caballero, was twenty years old. Bielsa had chosen this game for his debut. De La Fuente celebrated by stripping down to his underpants and giving the rest of his kit away to the supporters, pushing the shirt and shorts through the wire that separated them. When he was interviewed afterwards, Bielsa, wearing a grey long-sleeved T-shirt, seemed utterly calm. He dedicated the title to his brother. Later he would tell Rafael that he was not so sure he was right to have dedicated it to him.

There was every reason to stay. There would be another crack at the Libertadores with a team that was in sync with his methods. He and Raúl Gámez were not exactly friends but there was a strong bond between the two. However, Gámez knew that Europe exerted a strong pull. The trickle of leading players across the Atlantic had become a stream and then a flow. Bielsa had become frustrated that fewer and fewer Argentine footballers chose to play in Argentina. By 2019 there would be 1,800 Argentine footballers plying their trade abroad. In the World Cup summer of 1998 came an offer to join them. It was from Espanyol, the second club in Barcelona, one that would never realistically escape the shadow of the Nou Camp but one that would open up new horizons. 'Of course, I wanted him to stay but he had only signed a one-year contract,' said Gámez.

> He left Vélez with some strong foundations with good young players. We lost the quarter-finals of the Libertadores and after that the economics of the club started to suffer. I would have had him back but I think if he returns to Argentina, the only club he will go to is Newell's. In a perfect world, I would appoint Marcelo Bielsa for ten years, leave him alone and see what happens.

Spain was a natural first step for any Argentine wanting to play in Europe. Menotti had coached the young, carefree Diego Maradona at Barcelona, Carlos Bilardo had taken charge of the older, bulkier, more suspicious one at Sevilla. Alfredo di Stéfano had won five European Cups with Real Madrid, Jorge Griffa had spent a decade with Atlético Madrid. Both, incidentally, finished their careers at Espanyol. The club was based in Sarrià, one of the wealthier areas of the Catalan capital. It had two distinct features. It was the first Spanish club to have been entirely founded by Spaniards and had competed longer in La Liga than anyone else without winning it. Their last trophy had been the Copa del Rey in 1940. In 1988, they had reached the final of the Uefa Cup and somehow managed to squander a 3–0 first-leg lead to Bayer Leverkusen and then lose on penalties. Nevertheless, the club was stable. They had been promoted back to La Liga in 1994 and in subsequent seasons Espanyol's lowest position had been twelfth. They had also completed the tricky move from their old ground in Sarrià to Barcelona's Olympic Stadium on Montjuïc.

In June 1998, Bielsa was announced as Espanyol's new manager. When the press met him at El Prat airport, his first request was if anyone knew where the nearest internet cafe was. He acted quickly. There was one player he knew well. Mauricio Pochettino had moved to Espanyol four years before. Martín Posse accompanied Bielsa from Vélez Sarsfield. So, too, did Claudio Vivas, who had failed to make it as a goalkeeper at Newell's but had been offered a job on Bielsa's coaching staff at twenty-two. Vivas had followed Bielsa to Guadalajara and then to Vélez. There would be jobs for him with Argentina and at Athletic Bilbao. Naturally, Luis Bonini, his faithful, demanding conditioning coach crossed the Atlantic with them. His impact on Pochettino was immediate. Training would begin at the Sant Cugat High Performance Centre at 7.45am, followed by breakfast and a ninety-minute gym session. Bielsa would come in after lunch to begin work. His first session reduced Pochettino to tears.

'Our encounter was crucial for me as he woke me up from a period of lethargy,' he related. 'I was seemingly asleep, hibernating. I was too much in my comfort zone. I was lost but did not know it.' The first task was the Intertoto Cup, a deeply unloved competition that allowed clubs that had not qualified for European football by merit to enter a tournament with the slightly dubious prize of a place in the Uefa Cup. Rather more importantly, it gave people football matches to bet on, although given that the 1998 model was being run in competition with the World Cup in France, punters would have enough outlets for their money.

Bielsa was not much interested in the Intertoto and fielded what was essentially a second team for the competition. His focus was on the training ground. Double sessions were introduced, the Friday massage sessions scrapped. On 4 July, Espanyol played their first game under Bielsa. It was against Boby Brno, one of the Czech Republic's lesser-known teams who played in the country's biggest stadium, the 50,000-seat Za Lužánkami. It is a safe bet that most of those seats were empty, although those who did come saw Espanyol win, 5–3.

On the same day in Marseille there was a rather more important match that would decide Marcelo Bielsa's future before his time at Espanyol had properly begun. It was Argentina vs. Holland in the quarter-finals of the World

Cup, a match where every seat was taken, a match decided by one sublime moment: the long ball from Frank de Boer, taken down by the tip of Dennis Bergkamp's boot with his first touch, past Roberto Ayala with his second and into the goal with his third. The defeat marked the end of Daniel Passarella's rule as Argentina manager. During his time in charge, Passarella had waged war on long hair, jewellery and homosexuality. Argentina's FA may have thought it time for a more sophisticated approach. José Pékerman, the AFA's new sporting director, phoned Bielsa and asked if they could meet. On 15 August they went for dinner at the Princess Sofía Hotel, not far from the Nou Camp. Bielsa assumed Pékerman wanted to discuss Pochettino or Posse. Instead, he was offered the biggest football job Argentina had to give.

The timing was completely off. He had yet to manage Espanyol in a meaningful match and Marcelo Bielsa, the son and grandson of lawyers, was a man who loathed the thought of breaking a contract. Fortuitously, his contract contained a clause that stipulated he could leave if he were approached to manage *la selección*. It was a clause Espanyol's president, Daniel Llibre, seemed to accept. His board was less certain. Fernando Molinos, the club's managing director, noted that the contract actually stated that, if Argentina came calling, Bielsa could 'ask for' it to be terminated. It did not stipulate Espanyol had to accept the request. The trading began.

In Room 619 in the Hesperia Hotel, Bielsa wrestled with the problems of organising Espanyol's pre-season, which climaxed with a 1–0 win over Juventus, and trying to ensure he did not miss out on the greatest opportunity of his life. The season opened with a 2–1 victory over Tenerife.

Espanyol offered a compromise. Bielsa could leave by Christmas Eve, when La Liga paused for its winter break, or when the club had found a replacement, whichever was the sooner. Bielsa flew back to Buenos Aires. The meeting with Pékerman, the president of the AFA, Julio Grondona, and Hugo Tocalli, who headed Argentina's youth programme, was scheduled for 10.30am at Argentina's training ground at Ezeiza, not far from the airport, on 8 September. Bielsa arrived an hour early.

By the afternoon, he had been given the keys to the kingdom.

The Smell of Blood

Not long after he had reached the summit of his ambitions and become manager of Argentina, Marcelo Bielsa gave an address to pupils at his old school, the Sacred Heart College in Rosario. Its subject was failure. 'Success distorts, relaxes and tricks us,' he said. 'Failure is formative and brings us closer to our own convictions. The moments in my life when I have grown the most have been during the failures. The moments in which I have become a worse person have been in success.' When Bielsa stood up to speak, it was tempting to ask what he knew of failure. He had not made it as a professional footballer but had probably guessed he would not, and he had at least played for Newell's. As a manager he had taken Newell's, the club he adored, to two league titles and the final of the Copa Libertadores. After four years in Mexico, he had returned to Argentina and won it again with Vélez Sarsfield. Argentina had begun their qualification campaign for the World Cup in Japan and South Korea at a giddying pace. He was forty-five years old. He had the kind of acquaintance with failure that you might have with the man behind the counter at the corner shop. You would know his name, perhaps whether he was married; other than that, nothing. By the time the World Cup was done, Marcelo Bielsa would have the kind of relationship with failure where one finishes the other's sentences.

Despite his success at club level, Bielsa's appointment was not universally welcomed. His critics argued he had neither played for the national team nor managed one of the country's two great clubs, Boca Juniors or River Plate. Only towards the end of a spectacular qualifying campaign did fans begin chanting his name. By the time the squad set off for the Far East, he was spoken of in messianic terms. There was something divinely ordained about the loss of his goalkeeper. Carlos Roa had been one of the successes of the 1998 World Cup. He had saved David Batty's penalty to eliminate England and was seen by Manchester United as Peter Schmeichel's long-term successor. However, Roa was a Seventh-Day Adventist who believed that the new millennium would usher in Armageddon. In June 1999, after helping Real Mallorca finish third and winning the Zamora Trophy as La Liga's best keeper, Roa gave away everything he owned and retreated to Villa de Soto, a small town in the mountainous interior of Argentina, to await the End of Days.

When the apocalypse was unavoidably delayed, Roa returned to Real Mallorca, who he said never questioned him about where he had been. They were, however, flummoxed by his request that he should no longer work Saturdays.

The prospect of Bielsa having to work for Espanyol while preparing Argentina for the Copa América did not materialise. The win against Tenerife was the only victory they achieved under him. Unsurprisingly, given the squad knew he would be going, Bielsa's grip loosened the moment his appointment as Argentina manager was announced. Games at Real Mallorca and Deportivo La Coruña were lost, and after a 2–1 reverse at Valladolid, just before the derby with Barcelona, Espanyol announced he would be replaced by another Argentine, Miguel Brindisi.

The club finished seventh in La Liga. The following year, under the charge of Paco Flores, who had played for Espanyol, been their assistant manager and run their youth teams, they beat Atlético Madrid to win the Copa del Rey. It was their first trophy for sixty years. Bielsa called his backroom team from Barcelona to the training complex at Ezeiza. Román Iucht describes the scenes in Bielsa's office in *La Vida por el fútbol*: 'It was transformed into a bunker at permanent boiling point in which people worked to the limit of exhaustion. Hundreds of videos which in time would grow into thousands were piled on to the shelves and gave the place the air of a laboratory.'

Lists were drawn up of every Argentine professional

footballer eligible for *la selección*. Bielsa's first squad, when it was announced was, however, a conservative choice. He would be radical with the media. From now on there would be no exclusive interviews, no players paid to write ghosted columns or give their views to television or radio channels. The first tournament was the 1999 Copa América. It was staged in Paraguay, although the nation's most famous footballer, Luis Chilavert, refused to take part, arguing that Paraguay had better things to spend its money on.

Bielsa, too, had to deal with absences. Juan Sebastián Verón and Roberto Sensini made their excuses and neither Gabriel Batistuta nor Hernán Crespo made it to Paraguay. In their place, Argentina's attack was led by the tall striker from Boca Juniors, Martín Palermo. Kily González and Juan Román Riquelme would lend support in forward roles. Argentina found themselves in a tough group, alongside Colombia and Uruguay. Bielsa's first competitive match as an international manager was, however, one of his more straightforward assignments. Ecuador were beaten 3–1. Palermo made the first goal, drawing away defenders as Riquelme delivered his free kick to allow Diego Simeone to head home. Palermo then scored twice more.

Colombia had beaten Uruguay and the second game would decide which of them topped the group. What unfolded was a match in which the referee, Ubaldo Aquino, awarded five penalties. Four of them were missed. Three of them by Martín Palermo.

The first ten minutes contained two penalties. Palermo took the first but aimed slightly too high and struck the crossbar. For Colombia, Ivan Córdoba made no such error. After the restart, Hámilton Ricard, one of the more improbable members of Middlesbrough's attack, was pushed in the back by Roberto Ayala. Ricard took the penalty himself and saw it saved. Argentina were awarded another penalty to bring the game level. The players looked to the bench for Bielsa's guidance. The manager indicated Palermo should take it. He did, with precisely the same result, a struck crossbar, the striker's head thrown back in anguish.

The last fifteen minutes were the stuff of bad dreams. Javier Zanetti was sent off, Colombia scored twice more and Argentina were awarded another penalty. This time Bielsa was determined Palermo should not take it but his instructions did not arrive in time. This time the penalty was saved, although Palermo displayed resignation, rather than frustration. Bielsa called him an 'egoist'.

The defeat by Colombia ensured Argentina would face Brazil in the quarter-finals at Ciudad del Este, an industrial border town. They were facing perhaps the last great team Brazil have produced, the one that took part in three successive World Cup finals and but for Ronaldo's breakdown on the eve of the 1998 final in Paris might well have won all three. They would win this tournament, too. Just as they would do in the final against Uruguay, Rivaldo and Ronaldo scored. A goal down, Argentina were awarded another penalty. This time Roberto Ayala took it. The kick was saved by Dida, though Palermo still carried the can for the idiocy against Colombia. He would not play for the national team again for more than a decade.

The qualifiers for the 2002 World Cup in Japan and South Korea beckoned. For Argentina, getting there was usually a formality. The only time they had failed to qualify had been for the 1970 tournament in Mexico, the one in which the magic and genius of Brazilian football was fixed forever in the firmament. Then only three South American sides qualified for a sixteen-team World Cup. Argentina found themselves in a qualifying group of three along with Bolivia and Peru. Having lost both their opening games, Argentine officials bribed the referee, Sergio Chechelev, to ensure that Bolivia won their fixture against Peru to even things up. They did, although Argentina still finished bottom of their group.

For the 2002 tournament, all ten South American teams would play each other, four would qualify automatically and the fifth would go into a play-off. There was never the slightest doubt Argentina would falter. They qualified in first place: twelve points clear of Ecuador in second. The early games set the tone. Chile were thrashed 4–1 in Buenos Aires, Venezuela were beaten 4–0 away and Bolivia were overcome at the Monumental. It was, however, the fourth game which saw Bielsa impose his authority on his team. It was June 2000 against Colombia in Bogotá. Argentina had a history with Colombia that needed addressing, and it went deeper than all those missed penalties in Paraguay. In September 1993, Colombia had played Argentina at the Monumental in Buenos Aires. Argentina had never lost a World Cup qualifier at home. Diego Maradona gave his pre-match verdict. 'Argentina are up here,' he said, before pointing to a spot six inches lower. 'Colombia are down there.' Colombia won, 5–0. After Faustino Asprilla had chipped Sergio Goycochea for the fourth, which he celebrated with a forward roll and a sign of the cross, Colombia's assistant manager, Bolillo Gómez, turned to the head coach, Francisco Maturana, and said: 'Now we're fucked.' What he meant was that back in Colombia this victory would unleash a wave of national hysteria of the kind that Bielsa would have to deal with nine years later.

Colombia should have staged the 1986 World Cup but gang violence, guerrilla warfare and corruption had made it impossible. Now here was a chance to win the World Cup they had been humiliatingly unable to stage. Pelé declared them favourites. Everyone wanted a piece of the team, especially those close to the drug lord Pablo Escobar, who had gone to the same school in Medellín as Maturana. Members of the Colombia squad were taken, blindfolded, to a farmhouse near Cali and told how much money they could make if results went well.

Naturally, once in America, they froze and shut themselves off in their rooms to avoid journalists. They were the first team to be eliminated. Andrés Escobar, who had scored an own goal against the United States in Pasadena, defied his manager's warnings that the squad should delay its return 'until things cooled down'. In a car park outside a bar in Medellín, Escobar was shot dead.

In the dressing room at the El Campín stadium, Bielsa delivered one of his most memorable speeches.

> You know that in a street fight most of the time you beat each other to a bloody mess but, boys, there are two ways of looking at this. There are those who see blood, recoil and run away from it and there are those who want more and seek it out. I can tell you that out on that pitch and in the stands, there is the smell of blood.

Argentina sought it out. Gabriel Batistuta and Hernán Crespo scored. A curse of sorts had been broken. Bielsa may have earned a reputation for highly technical team talks but his players enjoyed it when he used language like this. Bielsa often made use of a thesaurus. His education stretched way beyond that of most of his players. He had accumulated vastly more information than could ever be imparted in a team meeting, let alone in the ten minutes in the dressing room during the interval. He realised he needed to use simple, precise language. 'He could be very good and not just with tactics,' Juan Sebastián Verón recalled.

'We would get off the bench and want to rip into our opponents. He would talk about the people who followed you, where you came from, your family, that outside on that pitch you would come across somebody who wanted to take something from you.'

Argentina would lose only once in qualification for the World Cup – to Brazil in São Paulo. Colombia were brushed aside, 3–0 in the Monumental. Brazil were beaten in Buenos Aires but perhaps the most significant result was a 3–3 draw against Bolivia in La Paz. Because it stands nearly 12,000 feet above sea level, the Hernando Siles Stadium is a forbidding place to jog around, let alone play football for an hour and a half. After Argentina fought out a 1–1 draw there in 2013, Lionel Messi vomited on the pitch while Ángel Di María had to be given oxygen.

In April 2001, Bielsa's men were 3–1 down with two minutes remaining. No Argentina side had ever won here. Qualification for the World Cup was assured; there was every excuse for winding down and accepting an insignificant defeat. Instead, in the final two minutes, first Juan Pablo Sorín and then Crespo scored. In the dressing room afterwards, members of the team were lying on the floor, bathed in sweat and exhaustion. Roberto Ayala was lying on a stretcher. Bielsa came in, flabbergasted by what had happened, although in the press conference he had been much more reserved. 'What a crazy result, what a crazy result,' he said over and over again.

As his first World Cup approached, Bielsa was determined to leave as little to fortune as possible. No team had more talent and no team would prepare better. At his home in Máximo Paz, a small town deep in the pampas, Bielsa watched endless hours of video of every opponent he might face in the Far East. Every match was divided into five-minute segments in which their play was analysed and notes were made with marker pens. When the team arrived in Japan, two members of staff were employed solely for video analysis. The team's luggage included a crate containing 2,000 DVDs.

However, there was one thing Bielsa could not control, one thing that would upset every calculation and put Argentina's footballers under the kind of pressure their counterparts in Colombia might have recognised. It was not threats and promises from cocaine lords. It was the Argentine economy. With its endless grasslands filled with cattle and wheat, Argentina is the Texas of the southern hemisphere. On the eve of the First World War it was one of the ten wealthiest countries on the planet. However, by the time the debris of the Falklands War was being cleared away to expose years of corruption and mismanagement, Argentina was sickening badly. Under the six years of the junta, foreign debt had trebled to $45 billion. Civilian politicians proved just as unsuccessful at leading Argentina as the military. By 1989, inflation was approaching 5,000 per cent. The Argentine peso was a currency nobody wanted to be paid in. It was then that Argentina's central bank came up with a solution. If Argentina was really the Texas of the southern hemisphere, why not take up the currency they used in Texas? The peso was linked to the dollar at a rate of one to one. Inflation was squeezed out of the system. Contracts, savings accounts, pension funds were all listed in dollars.

When Bielsa returned to Argentina after four years away in Mexico, he found a country transformed. In six years, the economy had grown 36 per cent. It may not have been one of the ten wealthiest countries on the planet but it was the wealthiest country in Latin America. However, by the time Bielsa became manager of Argentina, things were starting to go wrong again. As the Clinton administration took the American economy out of recession, the value of the dollar soared. So did the value of the peso. It meant Argentina's exports – its wine, its beef, its wheat – were suddenly very expensive, especially when Brazil devalued its currency. The Argentine economy began grinding to a halt. This on its own, would not have dragged Argentina under had the government of Carlos Menem not indulged in a vast spending spree in order to smooth his attempt to win an unprecedented and constitutionally illegal third term as president. With his long sideburns and ice-white smile, Menem looked like Neil Diamond. Like the singer he enjoyed dressing up for the cameras, not in rhinestone jumpsuits but in gaucho costumes. He was a good ol' boy who liked to spread money around to encourage people to do favours for him. In November 2018 he was finally convicted of embezzlement at the age of eighty-eight.

The word 'economics' derives from the Greek words for 'the laws of a house'. By the time Menem stepped down, in 1999, debt was everywhere in Argentina's house. It was under the floorboards, it was in the eves, down in the cellar. By January 2002, Argentina's foreign debt totalled $155 billion. The whole structure was creaking. There was no alternative. The peso had to be decoupled from the dollar and left to float. It floated like a rock floats off a cliff. Those who had their contracts paid in dollars now found them paid in pesos, which were now worth a fraction of the old currency. They included Marcelo Bielsa. When he signed his contract in 1998, it was worth $70,000 a month. When the AFA began paying him in pesos, Bielsa found himself earning a third of what he had before. When he set out for the World Cup, Bielsa had not been paid at all for nearly a year and was owed an additional $490,000 in unpaid bonuses.

Argentina's government mirrored its football association. It could not service even the interest on its foreign debt. The default, when it came, was the largest in the history of economics. The average Argentine worker saw his salary halved and if he were in work, he could count himself fortunate. Almost one in every four was unemployed and entitled to $3.94 a day in benefits. One tactic the government had used to finance its spending was to ask pension funds to swap their dollar reserves for government bonds in pesos. Those who had pensions now found them backed not by the mighty greenback but by scraps of paper that grew more worthless by the day. Banks began to fail. Withdrawals were limited to $1,000 a month. Those banks that survived found themselves attacked or besieged. As Michael Smith, who managed HSBC's Argentine subsidiary, remarked: 'We are slightly less popular than serial killers.'

The nationalist upsurge in Colombia before the 1994 World Cup was said to be greater than at any time since the country went to war with Peru six decades before. Something similar now happened to Argentina. From Mendoza in the north to Ushuaia on the edge of the storm-swept Southern Ocean, a nation convinced itself that they would win the World Cup because they had nothing else to hope for. In a poll released shortly before the squad left Buenos Aires for the Far East, 76 per cent of Argentinians thought they would return with the trophy. They had reached the World Cup with some stunning performances. The quality was unquestionable – Batistuta, Verón, Ayala, Pochettino, Simeone, Crespo, Ortega. Bielsa was a magician.

Their traditional rivals seemed in disarray. The Germans, ripped apart and humiliated by England in Munich, had scraped through. Brazil had endured the worst qualification campaign in its history, one that had seen them get through four managers in two years. The latest incumbent, Big Phil

Scolari, was, compared to Bielsa, dull and unimaginative. Holland, the team that had beaten them so hurtfully in the quarter-finals in Marseille four years before, had not even qualified. Yes, there would be England, but Argentina had knocked England out of two of their last three World Cups. Unusually, for a manager of a World Cup team, particularly one of the favourites, Bielsa had not attended the draw in the Korean city of Busan. He was never a man for a junket and his presence would have seemed mildly pointless. 'It would have contributed nothing,' he said. 'You can't suggest any tactics, give instructions or evaluate. You can only accept the luck of the draw.'

Their luck was dreadful. Argentina's spectacular route to the tournament had brought them nothing. In the group stages, Brazil would be in with Turkey, Costa Rica and China. Germany's first game would see them thrash Saudi Arabia, 8–0. Argentina's group, however, had them pitched in with Nigeria, who had won Olympic gold in Atlanta six years before. There was Sweden, who had not lost a game in qualification, and there was England. However, as he spoke to the media at Argentina's training base at Ezeiza, Bielsa carried a sheen of confidence. 'We have been handed matches that make life worth living,' he said. 'England will be a hell of a game. Who wouldn't want to be involved with that? Nigeria is also a challenge. It is what we dream of all our lives and now here it is.'

As he relaxed by his swimming pool in Rome, preparing

to join the Argentina squad, Gabriel Batistuta was not so sure. He understood what poverty was, but he did not buy into the idea that Bielsa was leading a national crusade to bring back the World Cup to a stricken nation. The son of a slaughterhouse worker, as a boy he would scour the streets of the provincial town of Reconquista looking for bottle tops he could exchange for a few coins. When he was at Fiorentina, a club where they built a statue to him, where they refused to take his money whenever he entered one of the modest side-street restaurants he liked to visit, Batistuta would remember the bottle tops to keep himself grounded. 'I don't think we are going to solve the country's problems by winning the World Cup. Absolutely not,' he told Marcela Mora y Araujo, one of the country's leading football journalists.

All we can hope to do is bring them a little joy but we won't find them a job. For the younger players the pressure might be too much. I hope not. I am sure we will talk about the economy but my view is this. We cannot go out on to the pitch to solve the Argentine crisis.

Then he added: 'And after what we did to England four years ago, they will want revenge.'

Before the serious business began, Bielsa decided he needed a break. He called up his old friend Carlos Altieri and suggested they go to Europe and watch some Champions League games. Altieri said he worked in a bank and it would be difficult to drop everything and fly off to watch some football, but Bielsa was insistent. At 7am a car pulled up outside Altieri's house in Rosario for the drive to Ezeiza airport and the Champions League. There was a driver in the front; Bielsa was in the back. His first words were: 'I don't feel well. I feel fat.' Altieri suggested he should go a health farm in nearby Puiggari, run by Seventh-Day Adventists, which specialised in detoxification programmes, hydrotherapy and vegetarian food. Bielsa often went there when he needed to confront the stresses of his life head on. There was a long pause and then Bielsa said, 'Don't get mad at me.' They went to the clinic.

No More Maradonas

Argentina had won two World Cups, once under César Luis Menotti, the man for whom fluid attacking football had been everything, the man who had said that if you cannot take a risk there is no point playing the game. The other triumph had come under Carlos Bilardo, a man who had sought to eliminate risk altogether but who had possessed the greatest sporting talent the country would ever produce, Diego Maradona. Although he always remarked that his policy had been to steer a middle course between Menotti and Bilardo, the squad that Bielsa assembled in Japan was closer to that of 1978 than 1986. Argentina's triumph in their own World Cup had been scarred by the circumstances that surrounded it: the most vicious military dictatorship in the country's history promising 'a World Cup of peace', the dubious 6–0 crushing of Peru in Rosario that allowed them to leapfrog Brazil into the final. However, Menotti had assembled a fabulous side. Had Johan Cruyff chosen to come to Argentina – and he stayed away for personal rather than political reasons – Holland might have had a team to match them. However, Kempes, Luque, Ardiles, Tarantini and Fillol were the spine of a brilliant team. The boys of 1986 were dragged to the final against West Germany in perhaps the most compelling display by a single player in any World Cup.

Sixteen years later, Bielsa had assembled a side that was as good, perhaps better than Menotti's. There was no single outstanding player and perhaps that suited Bielsa. Before the squad departed for Japan, the manager remarked that this time Argentina would succeed through a team effort, rather than relying on individual brilliance. 'There are no more Maradonas,' he said. Bielsa's most left-field decision was to bring a friend of Maradona's, Claudio Caniggia, back into the fold. Caniggia was thirty-five and with Glasgow Rangers when Bielsa called. He had taken part in the 1990 World Cup final but fallen foul of Daniel Passarella's campaign against long hair. In the event, Caniggia did not play a minute of the World Cup, although he was shown a red card on the bench during the final game against Sweden. Afterwards, he showed no bitterness towards Bielsa, describing him as a phenomenon of hard work. Had Argentina progressed further in the tournament, there might have been an opportunity for Caniggia to have come on and show enough glimpses of his flair to turn a game; but they did not.

Bielsa chose three friendlies against teams that would mimic the opponents they would encounter in Japan. February 2002 saw a 1–1 draw with Wales in Cardiff. The following month in Switzerland, Argentina drew 2–2 with Cameroon, while a goal from Juan Pablo Sorín gave them a 1–0 win over Germany in Stuttgart. The team looked impressive but there were faint cracks in its structure, most notably surrounding Juan Sebastián Verón. The previous year, he had been signed by Manchester United from Lazio for £28 million. It was the biggest transfer in the history of the biggest club in the world. For the first time Sir Alex Ferguson would do without two strikers. Verón would control the midfield, Ruud van Nistelrooy would spearhead the attack. It did not work. Paul Scholes was pushed further forward, which meant him playing with his back to goal, which did not suit his game. Verón and Scholes often went for the same ball, and got in each other's way. Scholes was a hero at Old Trafford, one of the Class of 92. Verón was from Argentina. Manchester United finished third in 2002, their worst performance for eleven years. Arsenal won the title at Old Trafford, United were knocked out of the Champions League by Bayer Leverkusen. In the words of his captain, Roy Keane, 'Seba became the scapegoat for our season.' His manager felt the same. At one of his press conferences, Ferguson turned on the journalists who had condemned Verón, called them 'fucking idiots' and swept their tape recorders off the table.

If Verón's form had been poor, his fitness was questionable. He had sustained a calf injury playing for Manchester United in the Champions League against Deportivo La Coruña, the same opponents against whom David Beckham had broken his foot. He had returned to Rome for treatment but when he travelled to Japan for the World Cup the problem still harried him. It was not something he was prepared to share with his manager. The team doctor, Donato Villani, told Verón that his calf was simply strained. Verón said Bielsa knew only that he was 'physically not quite right'. After the opening game against Nigeria, Verón complained of 'rottweilers in my legs'.

Their training base was in Hirono, two hours north of Tokyo. It had been the official training centre for the Japanese national side, who had moved into more modern premises for their World Cup.

Sometimes, the tensions and expectations surrounding Argentina leaked out. Bobby Ghosh, the international editor of *Time*, recalled a visit to Hirono in which Verón and Juan Pablo Sorín tackled each other in training. Both men fell to the ground in a tangle. The shaven-headed Verón leapt up, pointed to Sorín, who had flowing locks, and accused him of 'stealing my hair'.

'The players all laughed but Bielsa wasn't amused,' Ghosh wrote. 'He ordered Verón and Sorín off the pitch, screaming that if they couldn't be serious, they didn't deserve to be on his team. Verón shrugged it off, knowing the manager couldn't possibly follow through with the threat but Sorín looked genuinely worried. Both men left the field, leaving the remaining players in a sour mood.' Ghosh made a note of the aftermath: 'Bielsa paced along the sidelines, glaring at the carefully manicured grass like some demented botanist.'

The first opportunity to put all the training, all the theories into practice came on 2 June at the Kashima Stadium, home to Japan's most successful football team, the Antlers. The result was a routine 1–0 win against Nigeria but it was Bielsa's team-sheet that provoked most comment. Argentina's two principal strikers both played in Rome: Gabriel Batistuta for Roma and Hernán Crespo for Lazio. Batistuta was thirty-three, five years older than Crespo, and although Roma had finished second and missed out on the Scudetto by only a point, Batistuta had not played well. Bielsa had decided Batistuta and Crespo could not play together. He chose Batistuta.

There were good reasons for the choice. Batistuta had scored more World Cup goals in two tournaments than Maradona had in three. He had scored against Nigeria in the 1994 tournament, the match in Dallas that ended with a smiling nurse walking over to Diego Maradona and asking if he would not mind coming for a drugs test. The results would shock Argentina like nothing since the radio announcement that Eva Perón had 'entered mortality'.

There were reasons other than goals for preferring Batistuta. Andrei Kanchelskis, who played with Batistuta at

Fiorentina, remarked that although the striker was quiet and unusually modest for a centre-forward, he had an aura, an authority about him. He was a leader. Bielsa never seems to have been a manager for gut instinct when everything could be analysed and pared down to a scientific conclusion but for this, the most important month of his managerial life, he seems to have made an exception. In the Kashima Stadium, Batistuta headed home Verón's corner. The hunch was proved correct.

Batistuta would start against England, the game that doomed Argentina's World Cup. He would make no impact whatsoever. It had been thirty-six years since Alf Ramsey called Argentina 'animals' at Wembley. It was twenty since the Falklands War, sixteen since Maradona's acts of larceny and brilliance knocked England out of the World Cup in Mexico. It was four years since the breathless brilliance of Saint-Étienne, which had seen the outstanding match of the 1998 World Cup climax in Argentina's victory on penalties. That was the night David Beckham was sent off for aiming a sly kick at Diego Simeone, who reacted like a veteran actor. Elimination in the first knockout stage may have been England's worst performance at a World Cup since 1958 but the manner of their defeat meant they were lauded as heroes, flown back on Concorde from their base on the French Atlantic coast.

An exception was made for Beckham. As an Essex boy who chose Manchester United, he was especially disliked by

West Ham fans. Near Upton Park, effigies of him were hung from lampposts. Some were set on fire. In the four years that followed Beckham had become impossibly famous. When he toured the Far East with Real Madrid the following summer, it was claimed that 'Beckham' was the most recognised foreign word in Japan after 'Coca-Cola'. The veteran journalist Brian Glanville wrote that David and his wife, Victoria, 'lived lives of monumental vulgarity' while praising his skills as a footballer. It was his last-minute free kick, against Greece at Old Trafford, that had sent England through to the World Cup. Bielsa rated Beckham highly, voting for him in the 2001 World Player of the Year awards. Then in the twenty-first minute of Manchester United's 3–2 win over Deportivo La Coruña in the Champions League quarter-finals, Aldo Duscher, an Argentine midfielder who had begun his career at Newell's Old Boys, launched into a reckless two-footed lunge.

Beckham was replaced by Ole Gunnar Solskjær, whose two goals would prove the difference between victory and defeat. Beckham, with Victoria and their three-year-old son Brooklyn in the ambulance, was taken to hospital. It was announced he had a broken foot. Soon England would have a word that would become almost as well-known as 'Coca-Cola'. That word was 'metatarsal'. Although England's most dangerous player was Michael Owen, whose speed had ripped through Argentina's defence four years before and who had just been voted European Footballer of the Year, the nation convinced itself that unless Beckham were fit, England had no chance in Japan.

The Sun published a life-sized picture of Beckham's foot and asked its readers to pray over it. The psychic Uri Geller appeared on breakfast television urging viewers to 'touch your television screens and think of Beckham's foot'. 'Send him healing energies, visualise the bone knitting together. Unleash your healing powers, send your energy to the foot,' Geller said. It must have worked because Beckham led out England to face Argentina in the futuristic Sapporo Dome.

A contest between Marcelo Bielsa and Sven-Göran Eriksson might seem one between a method actor and someone who does light comedy: Marlon Brando up against Terry Thomas. However, Eriksson was often under-estimated in the way that Bielsa was over-estimated. With Lazio and Manchester City he would take on Sir Alex Ferguson three times and win every match. Eriksson used a gentle touch. 'It wasn't rocket science, just sensible decisions about team selection and simple but effective communications,' Gary Neville recalled. 'He gave us the sense that everything was under control; that if we held our nerve, everything would turn out fine.'

Sometimes the touch would be too light. At half-time in the quarter-finals against Brazil, when they reached the dressing rooms in Shizuoka just after Ronaldinho's equaliser, Gareth Southgate complained that when they 'needed Winston Churchill, we got Iain Duncan Smith'. In

Sapporo, managing a team without the injured Neville or Steven Gerrard, it proved perfect. In Saint-Étienne in 1998, there had been thousands of Argentina fans in the stands, chanting and singing more than an hour before kick-off, waving their scarves rhythmically above their heads. They exuded power and menace. Now virtually the only voices inside the Sapporo Dome were English, the stands plastered with the Cross of St George. The economic crash had made it impossible for any but the wealthiest Argentinians to make the 11,000-mile journey.

Still Bielsa was confident. The performance against Nigeria had been encouraging: 'Winning always brings peace,' he said. 'There was nothing in the match against Nigeria that particularly worried me.' Pablo Aimar, who had reached two Champions League finals as part of Valencia's midfield, was more emotional. 'If we win, people in my hometown, Río Cuarto, will be dancing on the roofs of their houses. Our people are suffering a lot and football isn't going to solve their problems but we want them to be happy for a couple of hours at least.'

The hour and a half in Sapporo was not happy. It was tense, frustrating and awful. The defensive pairing of Sol Campbell and Rio Ferdinand was probably the best of the tournament. Nicky Butt held them off in midfield. Owen's pace seemed lethal. He had already struck the foot of the post when he tried to go past Mauricio Pochettino. He went down. Pierluigi Collina gave a penalty. It was a dive.

'Don't believe English football is always about fair play,'
Pochettino recalled years later. 'Owen jumped as if he was
in a swimming pool.' Pochettino knew how to dive. With
Newell's Old Boys under Bielsa, diving convincingly had
been part of the training regime.

'Pochettino did touch me, clipped my knee,' Owen said,
confirming Pochettino's story.

> It wasn't enough to put me down but the reason I did
> go down was because, earlier in the game, someone did
> foul me in the area. I told the referee it was a penalty
> and Collina said: 'Michael, you know you have to go
> down to win a penalty.' So, I thought: 'The next time
> I'm touched, I'll go down.'

The penalty fell to Beckham. Here, then, was his shot
at redemption. For the World Cup, Bielsa had dropped
Germán Burgos, who had been Argentina's keeper for
the Copa América and throughout qualification, for Pablo
Cavallero, who had been his goalkeeper at Vélez Sarsfield.
As the England captain prepared himself, Cavallero indicated where he thought Beckham would place the ball.
He hit it straight in the middle of the goal. He struck it
so hard, Cavallero barely moved, except to drop down on
one knee. When the final whistle went there was anger
and resentment among Bielsa's men. Batistuta refused
to swap shirts. As the England bus prepared to drive

away, some Argentina players banged on the windows, swearing, promising revenge.

Now, however, Argentina needed a win. In Kobe, Sweden had beaten Nigeria, 2-1. They were top of the group with four points, the same number as England. Argentina had three, Nigeria were already eliminated. For the final group game, in Miyagi, which stands amid Japan's tracts of rice fields, Bielsa needed a win against Sweden or a draw, coupled with an improbably big Nigerian victory over England. The omens were not good. The day before had seen France, the defending champions and joint favourites with Argentina, knocked out of the World Cup without scoring a goal.

As they had against England, Argentina had plenty of the ball without doing very much with it. Just before the hour, Sweden were awarded a free kick. It was taken by Anders Svensson, who was then at Southampton. When he began his career at Elfsborg, Svensson evoked comparisons with Beckham, partly because of his looks but also because of his ability with a dead ball. Now, he proved it. His shot curled over the wall and, though Cavallero got a glove to the ball, all he could do was push it into the corner of the net.

Argentina had half an hour to save themselves. Bielsa threw on Verón and Kily González. Finally, far too late, Crespo replaced Batistuta, who remarked afterwards that the goal had appeared to become smaller with every minute that passed. It encapsulated the chief criticism made against Marcelo Bielsa as a tactician, the lack of a Plan B. Gary

Lineker used to say that Johan Cruyff was the most sophisticated coach he had ever worked for but, if Barcelona needed a goal with five minutes left, Cruyff would order the ball to be pumped forward. In contrast, as the journalist Esteban Bekerman pointed out, 'Everyone knew how Argentina would play because Bielsa's teams only play one way.'

With two minutes remaining, Ortega won a penalty which he took himself. It was a dreadful kick that Magnus Hedman palmed away, although Crespo struck home the loose ball. The pressure was unbearable. In the fast-dying moments, Argentina had a free kick that Verón stepped up to take. He looked round to see Bielsa almost on the pitch screaming at him: 'Hit it hard, hit it in the box, look at where the centre-backs are.' Verón needed these few seconds to think. He did not need to be told the obvious. He gestured at Bielsa to get back to the dugout, which was caught on camera, and then delivered an aimless free kick. The whistle blew.

In Argentina, in La Plata, among those who thought Juan Sebastián Verón a mercenary for signing for Manchester United, the gesture was further proof he was not bothered about winning for Argentina. 'I never want to see that picture again,' he said. 'I only told Bielsa to go back a few paces. Nothing more than that.' In Buenos Aires it was 5.30 in the morning. Crespo cried. Verón slumped to the turf. 'I am absolutely devastated. This is the worst moment of my life,' he said afterwards. 'We had hoped to give the World Cup as a present to the people of Argentina.' The crusade had ended as far from the Jerusalem of a World Cup final as it was possible to imagine. 'It was the saddest thing seeing Bielsa crying,' said Verón, watching his manager banging his head against the lockers.

In the dressing room there were some at the back, some lying down, some trying to draw strength from somewhere. I shook their hands one by one. I don't remember what I said, nor do I want to remember. Bielsa could not speak. He was crying with his assistants, Claudio Vivas and Lucho [Javier] Torrente. He wasn't able to talk to us for a long time. His words were short, his sentences brief. He said he felt a very great disappointment and we all started crying.

Germán Burgos, the keeper who had helped take Argentina to the World Cup and then been spurned by Bielsa, got up. He ought to have turned on Bielsa, given him a mouthful. Instead, he gave him a hug. 'You cannot imagine the anger of someone who has played in all the qualifiers and has then been discarded for the World Cup,' said Diego Simeone. 'Yet he stood up and took the manager in his arms. We were all crying but nobody turned on him. That shows the nobility of the man.'

They returned to the hotel, where a buffet had been laid on. Few felt like eating. They talked until the small hours. Bielsa did not join them. 'To see his suffering and frustration, walking the hotel corridors alone, broke your soul,' said Caniggia. In the morning they were desperate to leave, to get out of this World Cup. Bielsa declined to give a farewell press conference, which most managers at a World Cup use to sum up the campaign. Instead, he went for a run.

The training centre they were leaving would suffer a strange fate. In March 2011, an earthquake would rip through north-eastern Japan and destroy the Fukushima nuclear plant. The Hirono training centre was turned into a supply base for the rescue operation and stayed closed for seven more years. Oblivious to superstition, Argentina chose it as their base for the Rugby World Cup in 2019. They, too, went out at the group stages, but that was rather more expected.

In June 2002, the country's footballers took the train to Tokyo's Haneda Airport for a flight to Frankfurt. Some would stay in Europe; others would travel back to Buenos Aires. According to Verón, all were united in the determination not to watch another game in this tournament, which saved them from watching Cafu, the captain of the Brazil side that had stumbled and spluttered its way through qualification, lift the World Cup into the night skies above Yokohama. As Verón said: 'We wanted nothing more to do with football.'

Olympia

Every great defeat requires a victim, and as the Argentina team's plane took off from Haneda, there were two likely blood sacrifices on board: Marcelo Bielsa and Juan Sebastián Verón. Bielsa flew straight back to Buenos Aires and into a press conference. He talked for forty minutes. He was asked why Gabriel Batistuta and Hernán Crespo had not played together. He replied that it had been impossible, they had never practised it. He did not seek to divert the blame for what had happened in Japan. 'I had excellent material to work with and I cannot ignore the fact that the person who had to put it together was me. Of course, you should reproach me for it.' Back home, he was doorstepped by a journalist from *Olé*. He asked to be left in peace.

Even at home in La Plata, the capital of Buenos Aires province with its grid-patterned streets lined with linden trees, Verón found peace impossible to find. In La Plata, the Veróns were royalty. His father, Juan Ramón Verón, had played for La Plata's biggest club, Estudiantes. In one golden year, 1968, he had scored the decisive goal against Palmeiras to win Estudiantes the Copa Libertadores and five months later, at Old Trafford, he had headed the goal against Manchester United that won them the Intercontinental Cup and allowed La Plata to think of itself as the home of world champions. Although he had made the goal for Gabriel Batistuta against Nigeria, Verón had not played well. He had been substituted against England – some said he had deliberately underperformed to please Manchester United. Then, when he came on in the critical game against Sweden, Verón had been filmed telling Bielsa to calm down and then delivered that hopelessly indifferent free kick.

When Verón returned home it was to find that his mother, Cecilia, no longer watched the sports channels and the radio was tuned into the music stations rather than the phone-ins. In the streets, Cecilia could feel the looks, almost hear the whispers. Her son was being called a traitor. They no longer delighted in the fact he played for Manchester United. He was earning a fortune while here the economy had crashed. He was a mercenary now. They were no longer royalty; their subjects had risen up, their crown had fallen. Verón's younger brother, Iani, was sixteen. He had grown up secure in the knowledge of what family he had been born into. Their dining room had been turned into a shrine to his father and brother. There were shirts, trophies, newspapers and photographs. He said he would give his life to be able to play one minute for Estudiantes. Now none of this counted for anything. School was suddenly an unpleasant place to be. There were fights.

The notion that Verón would have played poorly in Sapporo to curry favour with Sir Alex Ferguson, a Glaswegian who regarded England's FA with almost total contempt, was laughable to anyone with even a passing interest in Manchester United. That it was believed, even in the streets of La Plata, even in Verón's own *barrio*, was an indication of how deep the madness was running.

In 2010, the year after he had mirrored his father by winning the Copa Libertadores with Estudiantes, Verón gave an interview to Marcela Mora y Araujo for the *Guardian*. The Veróns were royalty once more in La Plata and he could be more reflective.

We were carrying too many problems, particularly physical ones. I wasn't fit and neither was the team. El Cholo [Diego Simeone] had arrived just fit, [Nelson] Vivas was injured and there were at least four or five others who weren't fit in the squad. Whether you like it or not, the structure of a squad comes under pressure when you have played so many matches together with very few changes and suddenly you find yourself in a situation where five or six players are out of shape.

Our results reflected this. With Bielsa we had an idea from which we never deviated, no matter who the opponents were. We were all very convinced about what we were doing. Before the match against England, he announced the line-up a day early. I remember I'd been testing myself the day before because I wasn't feeling up to scratch and was practising with Bielsa and seeing how I was and he asked me if I were up to it. I wanted to play so badly I said: 'yes'. And then the match turned out to be completely different.

The Argentine press was convinced Bielsa's dismissal was imminent. His contract was up and the headline in *El Gráfico* was 'The War for the Succession', which pitched José Pékerman against Carlos Bianchi. 'Bielsa hasn't said goodbye but he has already gone,' the article related. 'He cannot carry on because his relationship with [the AFA president] Julio Grondona has passed the point of no return.'

There were echoes of the last time Argentina had fallen at the first hurdle in a World Cup. In Chile in 1962 Argentina had won their opening game 1–0, drawn their final match and lost the one in the middle to England. Back then they had lost not in the gleaming silvery surrounds of the Sapporo Dome, but in what the journalist Brian Glanville called 'seedy broken-down Rancagua at the stadium of the Braden Copper Company'. Then, as now, Brazil had emerged as world champions. There was, however, one essential difference. Then, there had been no expectations of Argentina. Before the 1962 World Cup, Pelé had given an interview to *El Gráfico* in which he portrayed Argentina as slow, unfit and tactically outdated. Forty years later, many observers thought Bielsa's Argentina to be the best team in the world.

Bielsa survived. When their performance was coolly analysed, Argentina had been unfortunate. They had conceded only two goals and none at all from open play. Their form in qualification had seemed irresistible. That counted for something. The wrecked Argentine economy also strengthened Bielsa's position. Things were so bad that Grondona was suggesting it would not be possible for the AFA to pay for every player to be flown back from Europe for internationals. Whoever took over the squad would have to accept a pay cut. This Bielsa was prepared to do. Crucially, he retained the support of his players. Shortly after his return, Verón gave an interview in which he said: 'If we did not win, it was because of the players. The manager had nothing to do with it. Now the press are inventing fights between me and Diego Simeone. For four years we were the best team in the world and now they cannot even look at us.' The headline was: 'If I had thought about it more, I would never have gone to the World Cup.' Bielsa read it and asked to see him. His opening question was: 'Is this true, Verón?'

Bianchi went to Boca Juniors, where he would win the Copa Libertadores and for the second time in his career beat

AC Milan to win the Intercontinental Cup. Bielsa returned to Máximo Paz to plot and ponder. He had been given time, perhaps unexpected time. In two years, there would be the Copa América. It was a competition that had long frustrated Argentine football. Between 1921 and 1959 they had won it a dozen times but, in the decades afterwards, there had been just two triumphs. To bring the trophy home to Buenos Aires would be absolution of sorts for the lost World Cup.

For the 2004 tournament in Peru, Bielsa would trust in young players – Andrés D'Alessandro, Javier Mascherano, Carlos Tévez – around a core of experienced footballers he had taken to Japan two years before. 'For us it was a difficult mixture,' said D'Alessandro. 'For this group of kids to start playing alongside Ayala, Zanetti and Kily González was hard. To get to the technical level to be able to play for *la selección* and be part of a team is something you don't do overnight. However, by the time we arrived at the Copa América we felt we were a unit.'

Argentina began in swaggering fashion. In Chiclayo, a few miles from Peru's Pacific shore, Ecuador were destroyed, 6–1. Javier Saviola struck a hat-trick. The middle game, against Mexico, had faint echoes of Japan. It was lost 1–0, and in a tougher competition, a World Cup, it might have been fatal. However, in the Copa América it was possible to qualify in third place. Two late goals from Ayala and Luciano Figueroa gave Argentina a 4–2 win over Uruguay. Winning the group, as Mexico had done, proved no kind of advantage. They would meet Brazil, whose defeat to Paraguay had pushed them down to second in Group C. Carlos Alberto Parreira's side won 4–0.

Argentina's passage to the semi-finals was nothing like as straightforward – they would face the hosts, Peru. It was a grinding, difficult contest. There was tight marking, little space. Mascherano was suspended. In his place was Fabricio Coloccini, who had moved to AC Milan as a seventeen-year-old and in the next five years was to play one game for the club. To make matters worse, Ayala was dismissed. For the only time in the competition, Argentina had to cling on.

What they clung to was a goal from the twenty-year-old Carlos Tévez, who had come off the bench to score from a free kick. Given their vastly differing backgrounds, the relationship between Bielsa and Tévez was a surprising, touching one. Tévez had been brought up, like many of Buenos Aires' poor, on a vast housing project that – like so much designed with concrete in the late 1960s – looked nothing like the architects' drawings. The thirty-nine tower blocks called 'the Army of the Andes' by the designers – but Fuerte Apache (Fort Apache) by those who lived in them – were created to replace the slums and shanty towns in the west of Buenos Aires. On the eve of the 1978 World Cup, people were moved en masse into the new buildings to enable the junta to present Buenos Aires as a model city. Fuerte Apache was designed to house 22,000. Twenty years after the World Cup when Tévez, raised by his aunt and uncle, was fourteen, it was home to 80,000, overwhelmed by drugs, crime and killings that averaged out at one a day. It was a place from which you dreamed of escape.

In 2003, Tévez had been part of a Boca Juniors side that had won the Copa Libertadores but now, in Peru, he would take flight. He adored playing for Bielsa, whom he thought the best coach he had ever had. 'How hard did he make us run?' Tévez laughed before the television cameras in 2007 as Bielsa, now in charge of Chile, prepared to face the Argentina side he had done so much to shape. 'He was the best I have had; he was the manager who made me into an international footballer. All the games I played for him were special because he gave me so much confidence. If I know he is happy, then I'm happy, too.'

The team moved to Lima, the capital, where they crushed Colombia, 3–0, in the semi-finals. Tévez scored the opener. Then came the final, then came Brazil. They were world champions. In Japan, Big Phil Scolari's side had beaten Germany in the final to take the prize that had seemed predestined for Bielsa's Argentina. Scolari, who had studied Bielsa's tactics to help him win the World Cup, was now managing Portugal and was recovering from losing the final of Euro 2004 to Greece in Lisbon.

The man in charge was Carlos Alberto Parreira, who had taken Brazil to the 1994 World Cup. Their performances had been desperately uneven – big wins over Mexico and Costa

Rica, defeat to Paraguay and a penalty shoot-out required to overcome Uruguay in the semi-finals. Momentum was with Argentina and remained with them until stoppage time. Three minutes from the end, with the scores levelled at 1–1, Agustín Delgado rifled in a volley from the edge of the area. Bielsa, down on his haunches, punched the air downwards. Earlier in the year, Delgado, who was to describe Bielsa as 'beautifully mad', had scored the winner for Boca Juniors against River Plate in the final of the Copa Libertadores. That was how to settle a rivalry. The one between Argentina and Brazil was on a different level. The twenty-three-year-old from Rosario must have thought he had settled this one too.

With stoppage time there would be six minutes remaining, six minutes in which Brazil appeared beaten. Tévez taunts the Brazilians with his ball play, draws fouls, eats up time until – ninety seconds into stoppage time – Bielsa withdraws him for Ramón Quiroga. The National Stadium in Lima is a typical South American arena, with vast open stands above which stand huge floodlight pylons of steel and concrete gazing down onto a mottled winter pitch. In the stands, the Argentine fans were standing, waving flags and displaying banners. One declared: 'Bielsa = Brains'. Then, with almost the final kick of the game, the ball bounces in Argentina's area. There are perhaps four blue and white shirts around Adriano as he spins and shoots past Roberto Abbondanzieri, known to everyone as El Pato or 'the Duck', for the equaliser. The entire Brazilian bench, save for Parreira, who has experienced bigger finals, dash onto the pitch. There is a confrontation in the centre circle between the two teams but there is no time to restart. The game will be settled on penalties.

Andrés d'Alessandro's first kick is saved by Júlio César, diving to his right. Gabriel Heinze shoots over the bar. Brazil do not miss and when Juan dos Santos scores the fourth it is done. The aftermath is like that of so many penalty shoot-outs. Kily González is in tears, Javier Saviola goes over to console D'Alessandro and Mascherano, the Duck is flat on his back, staring up at the leaden skies. Bielsa walks blankly around handing out consolations and hugs. In the wake of the defeat, *El Gráfico* published an editorial on where Argentine football and Bielsa now stood. 'Bielsa appeared less rigid in his tactics and, as a result, the team was more flexible. It seemed more harmonious and less like it was playing to a series of pre-arranged diagrams . . . there was more freshness, more patience, more football.' But then the newspaper turned to what even Bielsa had said was the most important thing about the tournament. That it had to be won.

The great opportunity to win has been wasted, especially for Bielsa who will always be the most questioned and least loved of managers. Although he has no reason for self-reproach, his heart must ache at not having won his first title to rebuild his self-esteem. The Copa América is the poor sister of the European Championship and, although it is the oldest continental championship in the world, it has been devalued by the absence of big stars. However, it would have helped Bielsa a lot to win it. It is clear that the national manager is not a charismatic figure, someone who is adept at marketing themselves and it is true that there are many who believe Carlos Bianchi is the best coach in the country. The cup would have allowed Bielsa to be seen in another way because much of society only admires those who get results. Sad but true.

It was a measured analysis of where Bielsa stood, although the phrase that he was the 'most questioned and least loved of managers' did not apply where it really mattered, inside the Argentina dressing room. There he was loved and very rarely questioned. The banners that had been carried to Lima that bore his name also suggested he was admired by those who paid to watch *la selección*. However, to the wider public, who would watch the final in the bars and living rooms of Buenos Aires, Rosario and beyond, Bielsa must have appeared difficult to understand. The press conferences with eyes cast downwards, the refusal to offer cheap soundbites, the studied absence of glamour in the world's most glamorous sport did make him difficult to love for the journalists required to follow him.

The defeat did not leave Bielsa easily. 'I have seen Adriano's equaliser fifty times and I have come to the conclusion that there are things only God can reveal,' he said. Brazil's first equaliser, which came on the edge of half-time, a free kick that Luisão headed past Abbondanzieri to cancel out Kily González's opening penalty, also clung to him.

More than two years later, just after the 2006 World Cup, which had seen Argentina eliminated by Germany in a penalty shoot-out, El Pato was training with Getafe, just south of Madrid. In the quarter-final in Berlin's Olympic Stadium, Abbondanzieri had been injured against Germany and substituted. In much the same way as Juan Sebastián Verón had been turned into the irrational scapegoat for Argentina's elimination in the previous World Cup, there were some who felt El Pato should have had the guts to stay on the pitch and save the penalties, although how he would have done so when injured was harder to say. Bielsa had written to say how sorry he was that El Pato had been forced to put up with this ignorant abuse. 'It was a grand gesture,' Abbondanzieri recalled. 'In the letter he went on to ask me about Brazil's first equaliser in the final of the Copa América when he was manager. "Why did you put three players in the wall, instead of four?"'

There was no time for the hurt to linger. Seventeen days after the final of the Copa América, Bielsa and with him most of the team that had lost in Lima were gathering in Athens, preparing for the Olympic Games. Olympic gold mattered to Argentina. They had come close twice and the losses had stung. In 1928 in Amsterdam, Argentina had played three games to reach the final, in which they scored twenty-three goals – eleven against the United States and six against Belgium and Egypt. They faced Uruguay in the final. Two years before the birth of the World Cup, it was portrayed as a World Cup final. There were a quarter of a million requests for tickets. When a year later the venue for the first World Cup was decided, it was Uruguay, the home of the Olympic champions, who were asked to host it.

The 1996 final was a contest between two extraordinary teams. Argentina fielded Zanetti, Sensini, Crespo, Ortega and Simeone. Against them was the Nigeria of Babayaro, Okocha, Ikpeba, Taribo West and Daniel Amokachi. In the semi-final, Nigeria had come from 3–1 down to beat Brazil. The gold medal match took place in Athens. Not Athens, Greece, but Athens, Georgia, in front of a crowd of 86,000 in the Sanford Arena. With sixteen minutes remaining, Argentina were leading 2–1. Then Amokachi, who had just left Everton after failing to justify the £3 million fee that had taken him to Goodison Park, equalised. When Emmanuel Amuneke, who appeared palpably offside, headed home the winner, Nigeria had snatched gold.

The team that Bielsa took with him to the original Athens was as powerful and probably more driven. It had been a little over two weeks since the final of the Copa América. Some players, like Gabriel Heinze, who had missed his penalty in Lima, were fiercely motivated. In June, Manchester United had signed Heinze from Paris St Germain. Sir Alex Ferguson came to recognise the ruthless streak in his full-back: 'He would kick his own granny but he was an absolute winner who could also play centre-back.' Ferguson assumed Heinze would be available for Manchester United's opening game of the season, against Chelsea at Stamford Bridge. Heinze informed Ferguson he would not be playing for United for at least another month. He said: 'I told the coach of Manchester United that if he wanted me to tear up his contract, I would but that I would still be going to the Olympics. Playing in the shirt of Argentina is the most important thing. It is a shirt that transcends everything else. It is a shirt I would always have a weakness for.' His first game for Manchester United was not until 11 September. It was as well Heinze scored in a 2–2 draw against Bolton. He was voted United's player of what was an admittedly underwhelming season.

For Bielsa, the Olympics would be a perfect tournament. Argentina won the gold medal with a flurry of beautifully executed performances. In Carlos Tévez, they possessed the tournament's leading striker. Defensively, they did not concede so much as a goal. Bielsa appreciated the amateur veneer that hung over the Olympics. 'Amateur' was a word he used often, not in the context of 'enthusiastically shambolic' but in the manner of someone whose main motivation to play sport was the love of it. 'To be here is a luxury,' he said at the start of the tournament. 'It is an unforgettable experience and, although I am ignorant of the culture of the Olympic Games, it would sadden me if I were to come here and not see anything of them. I'd love to watch the athletics, the swimming and the hockey.' Bielsa appeared to have been more relaxed than at his other tournaments. His daughters played hockey and Bielsa sought out the women's hockey team, Las Leonas (the Lionesses), and struck up a friendship with their coach, Sergio Vigil. It was one of Bielsa's few regrets in Athens that he was unable to watch the Lionesses, who were world champions, win their bronze medal against China.

There would be something else that was to link them. When in April 2019 Bielsa ordered his Leeds United team to concede a goal against Aston Villa, the press in Argentina sought out Vigil. In 2002, in a game against Germany, he had persuaded the judge to overturn a disallowed goal, a decision that would give the Germans victory. 'Every action Bielsa has taken during his career has been done with honour,' he told *Clarín*. 'The most important thing in life is to be able to choose who you want to be while pursuing your goal. Bielsa's actions show that the true art of winning is not losing your true self when you lose or when you win.'

The Argentine FA had not wanted their players to stay in the Olympic Village, which stood in the shadows of Mount Parnitha, whose green, forested slopes were said to be the lungs of Athens. 'We were used to hotels, our own bathroom and our own room,' said Kily González, who had played in two Champions League finals for Valencia.

When we arrived, we were met by two three-storey blocks. The beds were really small. There was a small bedside table and a minuscule wardrobe. Obviously, there was no television or air conditioning and we had to make our own beds. At six in the morning we would be queuing for the bathroom to brush our teeth and then we would meet in the communal living room to drink *mate*. There was no radio, no laptops, nothing. Half-asleep, we went on a bus to breakfast taking with us everything we needed for training. I came from a humble area – as a lot of us did – and I was used to this kind of thing. It was good.

'Meeting genuine amateur sportsmen was lovely,' said Nicolás Burdisso, who at the age of twenty-three had won the Copa Libertadores three times with Boca Juniors. 'It was something we had never experienced and it motivated us throughout the tournament. Living in the Olympic Village showed us an amateur world that had nothing to do with football. You found yourself queuing for food and when an athlete who had won an Olympic medal entered the room, everybody began applauding.' Burdisso remembers it as a very close-knit group and recalls Kily González keeping the younger players entertained with stories about playing alongside Diego Maradona at Boca Juniors.

It was, however, another child of the streets who dazzled in the heat and smog of the Olympic city. These were Tévez's Games. Argentina's games were split between Patras, Greece's great port on the Adriatic, and the Karaiskakis Stadium, home of Olympiakos. They began spectacularly against Serbia, 4–0 up by half-time, 6–0 at full-time. Tévez scored twice. Tunisia and Australia were beaten 2–0 and 1–0. In the quarter-finals, Tévez scored a hat-trick in a 4–0 rout of Costa Rica, which brought Argentina up against Italy in the semi-finals.

The Karaiskakis was full. Italy, managed by Claudio Gentile, fielded Daniele De Rossi, Alberto Gilardino and Andrea Pirlo in midfield. Giorgio Chiellini, who was to underpin the Juventus defence for a decade and a half and play more than a hundred full internationals for his country, was confined to the bench.

Bielsa employed Javier Mascherano to shackle Pirlo. If the surroundings were different from what his team was used to, then Bielsa's methods were as thorough as ever. Mascherano recalls the players being asked to mark themselves out of ten after each match. 'You would come off thinking you'd had a really good game and then he would go through the mistakes you'd made.'

It was scarcely a contest. The midfield trio of De Rossi, Gilardino and Pirlo were totally eclipsed by Tévez. Seizing on a weak clearance from Matteo Ferrari, Tévez unleashed a fierce right-foot volley to open the scoring. Midway through the second half, his through ball set Luis González free in a perfectly weighted counter-attack. Then, with four minutes remaining and the path to the final open, he held off Ferrari to square the ball for Mariano González, a winger whom Bielsa had blooded in the Copa América, to slide home. If Bielsa had long looked for the perfect expression of his principles, this was it.

If Argentina had been one story of the Olympics, Iraq had been the other. The year before they had been expelled from the International Olympic Committee after stories emerged that Saddam Hussein's son, Uday, had personally tortured athletes who had not met his exacting standards. They had been beaten with iron bars or urinated upon. However, by August 2004, Uday was dead; Iraq had been subjugated and was beginning its disintegration into anarchy. Its football team was in Greece, after Iraq's expulsion had been rescinded. Iraq's German manager was, however, not with them. Bernd Stange's driver had been assassinated and he had been warned he would be next. Stange gave instructions to his players by phone. In Patras they had beaten a Portugal side featuring Cristiano Ronaldo 4–2, before overcoming Australia in the quarter-finals. Paraguay in the semi-finals proved too much and the 2004 Olympic final was an all-South American affair.

Because the final would be staged in the Olympic Stadium,

it would kick off at ten in the morning. Although his footballers would be spared the shattering heat that hung over Athens during the Games – the women's marathon began in temperatures of 35 degrees – Bielsa took no chances. The day before the final, he went to the Olympic Stadium to observe the position of the sun at ten in the morning and whether it would have implications for the game.

A goal from Carlos Tévez was enough for Argentina to win gold. It was the kind of goal of which Maradona would have been proud. He anticipated a cross fractionally before Paraguay's keeper, Diego Barreto. It was his boot rather than Barreto's gloves that made contact. It was a street footballer's goal that displayed the quality the Argentines call *viveza* or 'craftiness'. The win was not painless. In the first half Roberto Ayala injured his knee. Even though he was treated during the interval, the pain became unbearable, although Bielsa would not substitute him but encouraged the midfielder to keep going. Ayala sustained himself by thinking of the hurt of the Copa América final and how this would wash it away. Appropriately, the ball was at Carlos Tévez's feet when the final whistle blew. He picked it up with one hand and punched the air with the other. Nobody had deserved it more. 'I am happy for Bielsa,' Tévez remarked afterwards. 'He has had so much criticism and he deserves this. He is a great worker and a great person.'

In the guts of the Olympic Stadium, in the dressing room and at the press conference, emotion was spilling over, especially for those like Kily González who had experienced all the suffering of Japan. 'I want to remember the players of the 2002 World Cup,' Bielsa said in his press conference. 'I feel a great sense of injustice at the treatment that team received. It was a great team that received far less than it deserved. I know it is difficult but I hope that they can also share in this moment.' For Bielsa and for those he took to the World Cup, the Olympic Games were an exorcism of sorts.

The triumph wore better than the stadium. Fifteen years after the Games that Athens could not afford, the Olympic complex stands like the skeleton of some great beast that died on a vast concrete plain. It is as much a ruin as the Parthenon or the Temple of Olympian Zeus. The girders and every other metal surface are encrusted with rust; the signs that once directed spectators to the Velodrome or the Tennis Centre are unreadable. The Olympic pool is still used by swimmers but the press benches from where the teenaged Michael Phelps' six gold medals were acclaimed lie broken and twisted. Occasionally, the odd jogger pads by the graffiti-smeared walls, past a message written in red spray paint that declares to the arena that once hosted such vivid dreams: 'It's immortality, darling.'

The Director's Cut

There was no reason to go. The damage done in Japan was receding into the past. A younger, remodelled Argentina had reached the final of the Copa América and taken gold at the Athens Olympics. There would be another World Cup in which that young team would be harder, more mature, more dangerous. A fabulously talented seventeen-year-old from Rosario called Lionel Messi was about to break into Barcelona's first team.

There was every reason to go. There were some who would never forgive him for the failures in Japan; a first Olympic gold medal was no kind of compensation for a third World Cup. He was still jeered at home games; there was still a section of the press who wanted someone more amenable, someone who would talk a better game and give them exclusives. Someone like Carlos Bianchi, perhaps.

He was exhausted, as empty as he had been when he left Newell's Old Boys.

The qualifying competition for the 2006 World Cup in Germany was well underway when Bielsa and his team returned from the Olympics. They had begun in September 2003 with a 2–2 draw with Chile at the Monumental. Although results had not been as spectacular as last time – there had been a 3–1 defeat by Brazil in Belo Horizonte – there was little doubt they would get there. They would finish second, level on points with Brazil. In September 2004, Bielsa oversaw a 3–1 victory over Peru in Lima. In the dressing room he appeared more agitated than usual. 'It's true it was different,' said Javier Mascherano.

> But at the time nobody considered it anything special. I thought it was because we had played very well, beaten Peru and were getting closer to the World Cup. But he was more emotional that day than when we had won the Olympics. He was shouting and screaming but I thought it would be the beginning of something rather than the end.

Ten days later, Bielsa went to Ezeiza. There was nothing in his demeanour to suggest he was resigning. He had a brief meeting with the head of the AFA, Julio Grondona, went for a jog and at 8pm on 14 September, six years after taking the job, he walked into a press conference to announce he was leaving it. He had won fifty-four of his eighty-three games and lost eleven, although it was the defeats, to England in Sapporo and to Brazil in two Copas América, that were slowest to heal. His win rate was 65 per cent and under him Argentina had averaged almost two goals in every game they had played. These were not remotely the statistics of failure. 'I am resigning from the Argentina team,' he said.

My motives are simple and straightforward. The decision started to take shape on the return from the game in Peru. I feel that I no longer have the energy to take on the tasks demanded by *la selección*. I didn't feel I had that drive any more. I went back over the decision, slept on it and found that I felt the same. I am 100 per cent convinced that I am doing the right thing. I will not regret it.

Interviewed immediately afterwards, Grondona suggested Bielsa had been forced out by his critics: 'The decision is possibly the result of so many years of hassle which can make it difficult to find the energy to continue.' His replacement was José Pékerman, who had recommended Bielsa for the job six years before. Pékerman would build his team around Juan Román Riquelme, a playmaker full of art and grace whose lack of pace had often seen him sidelined under Bielsa.

In Germany, Argentina once more found themselves in a deadly-looking group. However, Ivory Coast were beaten and Serbia were thrashed 6–0 before a goalless draw with Holland allowed Argentina to qualify in first place. The quarter-finals pitched them against the hosts in Berlin, where Pékerman appeared to lose his nerve. Riquelme was substituted along with Hernán Crespo. Stranger still, neither of their obvious replacements, Pablo Aimar and Messi, was brought on. Germany won the match on penalties, which sparked a brawl, with Per Mertesacker on the receiving end. Pékerman resigned immediately afterwards.

By then, Marcelo Bielsa had not managed a team in nearly two years. The first three months after his resignation he spent in a convent in an attempt to detoxify himself from football. 'I took the books I wanted to read. I did not have a phone nor did I have a television. I read a lot and I don't think anyone reads as much about football as I do. I lasted three months before I started talking to myself and answering back and then it was time to go.'

Between 2005 and 2007, he changed addresses three times in Rosario but he could always find refuge at his home in Máximo Paz, a small town about 50 miles from Rosario, swallowed in the vastness of the pampas. Although, strictly speaking, it is named after a man who was once governor of Buenos Aires, it means 'Maximum Peace' in Spanish. This seemed appropriate. Bielsa had a ranch here, set in 200 hectares of land, a place where he could talk to friends, store his enormous collection of football videos and books and be himself. He would go out for a bicycle ride, read the papers.

If there was talk, it was not often about football. There was plenty of time for the famous Argentine barbecues, called *asados*, where haunches of meat are roasted over an open fire. Bielsa's *asados* were often organised by Victor di Lucia, described as 'one of the town's characters' who liked to wear a flower in his ear. Those who were invited knew better than to pump the host for information about football. In June 2017, a few years after Di Lucia's death, Bielsa unveiled a bust of Victor to be placed in his favourite bar, called Kiku.

In October 2006 a visitor came to Máximo Paz searching for Bielsa: Pep Guardiola. He, too, was in a lull in his career. He had finished playing for Barcelona in 2001 at the age of thirty. There had been two frustrating seasons in Italy, at Brescia and Roma, and a lucrative one in Qatar. Now he found himself in the north-west of Mexico, playing for a newly promoted club, Dorados de Sinaloa, in a city on the Pan-American Highway called Culiacán. Guardiola did not play much for Dorados but he had not really come to Mexico to play. He had come to learn from the man managing Dorados de Sinaloa, the man whom Pep Guardiola considered probably the best coach he had worked with, better perhaps than Johan Cruyff.

Juanma Lillo was more Bielsa than Cruyff. He had no playing career to speak of and was wrapped up in the theory and romance of the game. He owned a library that contained 10,000 newspapers and magazines about football. Like Bielsa, Lillo had been championed by Luis César Menotti. In 1995 he had guided Salamanca to promotion to become, at twenty-nine, the youngest manager in the history of La Liga. However, Lillo never remained at any club for very long and there were some in Spanish football who considered him a fraud, a theory that gained credence with every sacking. To Guardiola he was the real thing. He had been fascinated by Lillo ever since the day in September 1996 when Barcelona, managed by Bobby Robson, had encountered Real Oviedo, managed by Lillo. The Catalans had won, 4–2, but there were times when Oviedo had made Barcelona seem ordinary, even amateurish. In Mexico, the two men talked every day about coaching.

It was obvious Guardiola would want to talk to Bielsa. When he and Gabriel Batistuta were playing together in Rome, Batistuta advised him to look him up: 'If you want to be a coach, you have to get together with this man.' On 10 October 2006, over an *asado*, Guardiola, accompanied by the Spanish film director and novelist David Trueba, got together with Marcelo Bielsa. The first hour was taken up with Bielsa questioning Trueba, who had just finished his second film *Bienvenido a Casa* (*Welcome Home*), about the cinema. He only stopped when Trueba said: 'You haven't come all this way to talk about films, have you?' The talk switched to football. 'They started and they could not stop.' Trueba recalled frantic conversations about teams, tactical planning, anecdotes about the game. Bielsa's computer was used to check facts and settle arguments. Then Bielsa positioned Trueba between two chairs to act out a move in a game.

They turned to the practicalities of management such as dealing with the press. Bielsa explained why he never now gave exclusive interviews. 'Why am I going to give an interview to a journalist at a powerful paper and deny one to a little reporter from the provinces? What's the criterion?' When he became manager of Barcelona two years later, this was a policy Guardiola would follow. It would be the same in Munich and Manchester. He would not grant one-on-one interviews but talk to the media only via press conferences, where anyone could ask a question. Then Bielsa turned to Guardiola: 'Why do you, who knows about all the garbage in football, the dishonesty of people in the game, want to return to that environment and manage? Do you like blood so much?' Guardiola replied: 'I need that blood.'

Guardiola went into management and shed considerable quantities of other people's blood, not least that belonging to his mentor, Juanma Lillo. In November 2010, Lillo was managing Almería against Barcelona. In their own stadium, the Juegos Mediterráneos, they were thrashed 8–0. Lillo was sacked the next day. He would not manage another club for four years.

You wonder why Trueba never turned that evening into a script, just as an encounter between Marilyn Monroe and Albert Einstein in a New York hotel became the basis of a play and later a film, called *Insignificance*. Marcelo Bielsa had a passion for film. When he was not working, he told Trueba, he would get through two a day.

A couple of years later, it was early morning on Chile's Pacific coast when the phone rang in Luis Vera's house in Valparaíso. His wife answered and turned to her husband: 'There's a Marcelo Bielsa for you.' Vera was a film director. In September 1973, as General Augusto Pinochet's tanks rumbled through the streets of Santiago and the air force bombed La Moneda, the presidential palace, he fled the country. He was twenty-one. He ended up in Romania, studying film at Bucharest University, and by 1979 he was living in Sweden. Only when the dictatorship stood down a decade later did Vera return to Chile. In 2008 when Bielsa called, he had just released a film, *Fiestapatria* (*Party Country*). It was about an extended family who, after the fall of the dictatorship, meet up on Chile's Independence Day. Bielsa had watched it three times.

They had met briefly before, at Valparaíso's football stadium. Bielsa had been appointed manager of Chile and was watching a game. During the interval, Bielsa was standing by himself with nobody quite having the courage to go over and talk to him. Vera approached him, introduced himself as a director, told Bielsa he had a new film out and gave him his card. Now, on the phone, Bielsa asked, very politely, if they could meet up. By six o'clock that evening Bielsa had driven to Valparaíso in what Vera thought was a well-worn and modest Nissan Tiida. Then they decamped to a fish restaurant by the ocean. By one in the morning they were still talking. 'We spoke a lot about love, about politics – very little about football – and a lot about the cinema,' Vera recalled.

He told me that if he hadn't become a football coach, he would have liked to have become a film director but he doubted whether he had the talent. In a world of football that is manipulated by commercial interests, Marcelo represents a romantic ethic. He is more than a football manager because his outlook on the game is the same as his outlook on life. He sees the world just like a film director.

Vera would help Bielsa keep in touch with the new talent in the industry, introducing him to the work of the Serbian director Emir Kusturica, whose intimate documentary on Diego Maradona was shown at the Cannes Film Festival in 2008. Bielsa's first close encounter with the cinema world resulted from his constant need for a video recorder. Francisco Lombardi was Peru's leading film-maker and was also a director of Sporting Cristal, one of the country's biggest clubs. He was a fan of Bielsa's work at Newell's and in 1992 invited the team to Lima to play a friendly. Bielsa had brought his usual cache of videos to watch before the game but discovered that the kind of recorders he needed to view them was not available in Peru. Lombardi lent him his. It began a friendship. Lombardi would send Bielsa DVDs of his work 'because I knew he would watch them' and one day Bielsa sent him a document which contained a detailed analysis and critique of every one of Lombardi's films. When Bielsa accepted the offer to manage Athletic Bilbao, one of its attractions was its proximity to San Sebastián, which stages Spain's biggest film festival. Lombardi had won its best director's prize twice.

While at Bilbao, Bielsa championed the work of a young Chilean director, Fernando Guzzoni, turning up in his trademark grey tracksuit to help promote *Carne de Perro* (*Dog Flesh*) at San Sebastián. It won the prize for the best new director, earning Guzzoni €90,000. 'He talked to us at length about the film,' Guzzoni said. 'He liked the way the camera got really close to the hero; he appreciated the absence of music. You could tell he knew what he was talking about. He was really warm and friendly, nothing like the cold, monastic image that many people have of him.' Bielsa preferred films that stretched the audience. He was not one for popcorn and special effects. Lombardi's awards were for serious pieces of work. There was an adaptation of *The City and the Dogs* by Peru's most famous author, Mario Vargas Llosa, another by Jim Thompson, the alcoholic American crime writer who wrote *The Grifters* and *The Getaway*.

Carne de Perro also deals with the aftermath of the Pinochet dictatorship, focusing not on a family but an individual – a former torturer trying to escape his past. It was praised by the *Hollywood Reporter* in a review that acknowledged that it could be 'unwatchably unpleasant'.

Lombardi argued that what attracted Bielsa to seek out the company of film directors was that their task – to bring the best out of a cast – was similar to his own job. The training ground is the rehearsal room, the tactical analysis, the script. 'I think Marcelo could have become a film maker,' he said. 'It's something he would have excelled at.'

Mountain Men

There was not much to say on the flight back from Venezuela except an acknowledgement that things had to change.

In the Copa América, Chile had just been humiliated 6–1 by Brazil. It was not the result that grated on Harold Mayne-Nicholls, the head of the Chilean FA. His country had a long history of losing to Brazil, if not quite by this kind of margin. It was the sheer indiscipline of the team on and off the pitch that persuaded Mayne-Nicholls that he needed to change manager. The current incumbent, Nelson Acosta, had little desire to remain. Chile had qualified for the knockout phases of the Copa América with a goalless draw against Mexico in the oil refinery town of Puerto La Cruz. Acosta had given his players permission to go out and enjoy themselves. They had enjoyed themselves rather too much and the next day they were still enjoying themselves.

Some players went into breakfast drunk. Food was thrown; there were fights. Hotel property was damaged. Two days later came Brazil. In the aftermath, Acosta told Mayne-Nicholls he could no longer work with these footballers.

By then, Bielsa's exile from football had stretched to nearly three years. He had already turned down an offer to manage Colombia but Mayne-Nicholls wondered if he might be persuaded to take over Chile. Mayne-Nicholls was of Cornish and Croatian descent. One grandfather had come from Falmouth, another was from the island of Brač in the Adriatic. He became a journalist and then head of media when Chile staged the Copa América in 1991, which Argentina, spearheaded by Gabriel Batistuta, had won. Now he was president of the Chilean FA. His first encounter with Bielsa had come in March 1992. He was now a director of Universidad Católica, one of Chile's biggest clubs, when they drew Newell's Old Boys in the Copa Libertadores. Mayne-Nicholls had been asked to arrange some practice facilities in Santiago for the visitors and he was intrigued enough by Bielsa to watch Newell's train. He watched Bielsa put his team through a single, forty-minute exercise to repeat one routine. The next day from his seat in the stadium, Mayne-Nicholls saw Newell's score from precisely the routine he had watched them practise over and over again.

Soon Mayne-Nicholls found himself in Rosario, talking to Bielsa. The problem was not the state of a team that had failed to qualify for the last two World Cups but money.

The CFA had $12 million to cover the next three years. The cost of Bielsa and his team would be $1.5 million, or more than a third of their annual budget. Acosta had been paid $300,000. 'It was easy to talk to Marcelo but not so easy to close the deal,' he recalled.

The money meant I had to answer a lot of questions about the wisdom of appointing him. In the first year he didn't ask for his money and we had to ask him to go to the Federation and collect his cheque. I told him that if he didn't ask for his money, it would cause a lot of problems. I said: 'If I see there is money in the account, I will use it, and if you come to pick up your money the next day, you are going to be disappointed.' When we made the final agreement, I told him I wanted him to move with his wife and two daughters to Chile. I told him that if he were just coming over for games, it would not look good and I wanted Marcelo to get a touch of our culture and really know the way we live. He came over in August 2007 and started looking for a house and then he called me and said: 'We need to talk.' He said his family would be moving back to Argentina. I was quite angry because it had been part of the agreement. He told me his daughter, Inés, had been called up for pre-selection to the Argentina field hockey team. He said: 'I cannot tell my daughter she has to go to Chile rather than play for Argentina.' I could not argue with that. Ten or so days later, I got a call from him at seven in the morning. It had been raining for two or three days and in winter here in Chile, it's not like London rain, it's very cold and up there in the mountains everywhere would be covered by snow, completely white. Marcelo said we needed to talk urgently. I told him I would take the kids to school and meet him at the technical centre. I arrived at 8.00 or 8.15. He said, 'Can we take a walk?' I was wearing a jacket and tie with some proper shoes and as we were walking along the side of the pitch, I could feel water in my shoes and my socks were wet and cold. He said, 'I need you to authorise one more thing.'

'What is it?'

'I want to live here in the technical centre.'

'Marcelo, look around you. In winter it is dark at six. Look at the neighbourhood. There are no restaurants, no cinema, no life.' By now we had turned a corner to face the mountains. The sky was blue, the mountains were completely white. 'Look at those mountains,' he said. 'I would never forgive myself if I lived somewhere I couldn't see these mountains every day.' He moved into room number one and took over an adjoining room. One became his office, the other had room for a bed and a table but not much more. He lived there for three years. He would watch a lot of films and I think it was there that he really learnt to use the internet.

One good thing about it was he could order food from the kitchens. I think he liked that.

Years of under-investment had left the training centre itself in a state of disrepair. The pitches were poor and the Chilean FA had no money available for improving them. It was then that Bielsa went on the road, giving lectures and charging for them. The money would go towards improving the technical centre. 'If it was a school, he would talk for free. If it was a large mining company, he would charge a lot,' said Mayne-Nicholls. 'The money went into a special account. He always knew how much was in that account and I know he gave at least a hundred lectures. The first money we made meant we could install televisions at the technical centre, then we improved the pitches and then the whole infrastructure of the place.' Although Mayne-Nicholls told Bielsa that he did not have to qualify for the World Cup in South Africa – he was more interested in how Chile played – it was a clear goal for the manager.

Chile's record had been indifferent and erratic. Only in their own World Cup, in 1962, played in the aftermath of the biggest earthquake in recorded history that had left two million homeless, had they been a success. Then, the country had been inspired by the words of the head of the Chilean FA, Carlos Dittborn, who declared when they bid for the tournament: 'Chile must have the World Cup because we have nothing.' The most abiding memory was the Battle of Santiago, as Italy and Chile brawled their way through ninety minutes in which the police came onto the pitch four times. The conflict had been sparked by an article in an Italian newspaper that described the organisation of the World Cup in withering terms: 'The phones don't work, taxis are as rare as faithful husbands, a cable to Europe costs an arm and a leg and a letter takes five days to turn up.' The article claimed the Chilean population was prone to 'malnutrition, illiteracy, alcoholism and poverty'. Since then, Chile had played in thirteen matches spread across four World Cups and failed to win a single one. However, Bielsa's appointment coincided with a dramatic upturn in Chilean football. Just before Bielsa's appointment, Chile had finished third in the Under-20 World Cup in Canada. A team with Alexis Sánchez, Arturo Vidal, Carlos Carmona, Gary Medel and Mauricio Isla had reached the semi-finals without conceding a goal in five games. They had gone down 3–0 in Toronto to an Argentina side featuring Sergio Agüero and Ángel di María. Later Chile would win the Copa América in 2015. Bielsa would not be at the helm when a scuffed penalty from Alexis Sánchez in a shoot-out against Argentina gave them the trophy for the first time, but it was Bielsa who laid the foundations for victory.

When he accepted the offer to manage Chile, Bielsa realised he would not be able to put together the backroom staff that he had alongside him with Argentina. Claudio Vivas was in charge of the youth team at Estudiantes while

Javier Torrente was in Paraguay managing Cerro Porteño. In their place came the imposing figure of Eduardo Berizzo. One of the great qualities of an assistant manager is the ability to be approachable, and Chile's players found him easier to have a conversation with than Bielsa. However, Berizzo was also possessed of a fierce temper. As a player he was sent off four times in a single season with Celta Vigo, which made a substantial contribution to their relegation from La Liga in 2004. Another dismissal while working as Bielsa's assistant meant he was unable to sit on the bench for all of Chile's group games during the 2010 World Cup. Berizzo was one of Bielsa's many players who went into management. He possessed something of his old boss's attitude to life. 'Bielsa taught me that you can never think you have learned everything,' he said. 'Everything is still there to be discovered.' If his spells at Estudiantes and Athletic Bilbao were not successful, he would forever be a hero in Rancagua. The city's club was O'Higgins, named after Bernardo O'Higgins, the Chilean from a County Sligo family who had liberated the country from Spanish rule. In 2013, Berizzo took O'Higgins to the first title in their history.

There were other familiar faces, such as Luis Bonini, the physical conditioning coach who had been part of Bielsa's backroom staff since joining him at Atlas Guadalajara in 1992. He had been a student of the University of the South in Bahia Blanca who had switched from economics to physical education. His first gigs had been in swimming and basketball before Bonini turned his attention to football. He was as rigorous in his field as Bielsa was in his.

Pablo Contreras was a centre-half for Celta Vigo who had been one of the ringleaders of the drunken breakfast fracas during the Copa América and, as a result, had earned himself a ten-game ban. Bielsa offered him a way back into the squad.

Marcelo intimidated us with his words and his gestures. Seriously, I swear we were scared of him and I was one of the older ones. One of us said to Bonini: 'Prof, we are tired.' The work was really intense. Our hamstrings were tired, our abductors burned. Bonini said: 'Okay, tell that to Marcelo.' Marcelo came over to us. 'The professor tells me you are tired.' He turned to Gonzalo Jara [who also played in defence]. 'Gonzalo, are you tired?' Gonzalo said he was fine. Then he asked me: 'Pablo, are you tired?' I was the oldest. I was melting away. 'No Marcelo, I am perfectly fine.' Bonini had been listening to all this and afterwards he came over and said, 'You are all chickens, you bastards. When the man comes near you, suddenly you are all paralysed.'

There was another incident that pointed towards Bielsa's perfectionism. He called over Gary Medel and suggested the midfielder, the very heartbeat of this Chile side, was 3 kilos overweight. Medel replied that he was sure he was not, but went to be weighed anyway. He was 3 kilos overweight.

Arturo Vidal, who had just agreed to join Bayer Leverkusen for $11 million, which would make him Chile's most expensive footballer, disliked Bielsa's training sessions until something clicked. 'Before, I was erratic, running around like crazy all over the pitch. I didn't concentrate well in matches or in training. Then he made me realise the importance of the mental side of my game.'

Chile's first qualifying game for the South Africa World Cup would be against Argentina in Buenos Aires. They were now managed by Alfio Basile, who had taken them to the 1994 World Cup, where everything had been thrown into chaos by Diego Maradona's failed drugs test. He was now back at the helm following José Pékerman's resignation. The reception Bielsa received at the Monumental was a good one, especially from the Argentina players. They were, after all, mainly his players. Lionel Messi, now twenty, had never been managed by Marcelo Bielsa but here he led Argentina's attack alongside Carlos Tévez. They were blocked off, frustrated by Chile's defensive midfield centred around Manuel Iturra while up front Eduardo Rubio and Humberto Suazo troubled Gabriel Heinze. Nevertheless, two goals from Juan Román Riquelme, the man who had benefited most from Bielsa's departure, proved enough.

In November came a 2–2 draw in Montevideo against Uruguay. Marcelo Salas, who could claim to be Chile's finest striker but who was now thirty-two, scored his final two goals in a red shirt. They would be enough to earn Chile their first ever point in the vast bowl of the Centenario Stadium but the memories of that Sunday afternoon would not linger. Three days later, Chile lost 3–0 at home to Paraguay, managed by Gerardo Martino, whom Bielsa had coached at Newell's. The reaction in Santiago and beyond was venomous, although in retrospect Martino was leading a fine side that would beat Brazil and Argentina in qualifying and reach the quarter-finals of the World Cup. As Mayne-Nicholls recalled:

The media began saying, 'Why are we paying so much money for a coach who does not let us watch his training sessions and does not pick up the phone when we call him?' There was also a lot of anger towards the players and the board. The problem was that our next competitive game was not until June 2008. We would have seven months without having much to show the press. We played one friendly against Israel and lost, 1–0. There was a draw and a win against Panama and Guatemala but nothing to suggest things might change. The chief sports writer of our leading newspaper, *El Mercurio*, called for Marcelo's resignation.

When the qualifiers resumed, Chile overcame Bolivia at high altitude in La Paz and then returned to Puerto

La Cruz, the scene of their humiliation by Brazil, and beat Venezuela, 3–2. Next up was Brazil at the National Stadium in Santiago. From demanding that Bielsa should go, the Chilean media swung the other way, calling this the 'worst Brazilian side in living memory' and predicting revenge for generations of defeats. History repeated. The worst Brazilian side in living memory did to Chile what every other Brazilian side in living memory had done and won, 3–0. By the time October came around, the group was in the balance. Chile were clinging onto the fourth and final automatic qualifying place, one point above Uruguay in fifth, two ahead of Colombia. Paraguay were the surprise leaders, Brazil and Argentina tucked in behind them. In Santiago, Chile would be playing Argentina, a nation they had never beaten in a competitive international.

What followed was perhaps the most significant result in the modern history of Chilean football. Carlos Carmona found Gary Medel on the overlap and Medel, nicknamed 'Pitbull' for his sheer competitiveness, drove in a low cross that Fabián Orellana, a twenty-two-year-old debutant who played his football in the wealthy Santiago suburb of La Florida, met first time. Fresh-faced and with flowing locks, Orellana looked how the Victorians imagined young Greek gods. He was only playing because Alexis Sánchez was suspended. They would call the boy 'El Histórico' and the goal would help him get a transfer to Udinese in Serie A. The move that produced the goal was pure Bielsa. In

March 2019 Leeds would score an almost identical goal against Millwall, finished off by Pablo Hernández, although nobody in Yorkshire ever referred to him as 'the History Boy'. Orellana never quite stormed the heights of European football and, although he would win the Copa América, he would never have another night quite like this one. 'He was like a father to me,' he said of Bielsa. 'He was the best coach I have ever had or at least it is difficult to think of anyone better. This win was critical for us because we told ourselves we could beat anyone.'

When the final whistle went, the flares burned and the flags waved and the rest of the Chilean bench poured onto the pitch, Bielsa marched off towards the dressing room, head bowed, offering not a smile. The defeat would hit his opposite number harder. For Alfio Basile this was the end and, in a decision which they could justify only on the grounds of gut instinct, the AFA installed Diego Maradona as his successor. Maradona employed management techniques Caligula might have recognised. He got through seventy different players and, when decisions were questioned, he would grab his crotch and yell at journalists that they could 'suck it and keep on sucking'. The wonder was that Argentina made it as far as Cape Town and the quarter-finals before being dismembered by Germany.

On the other side of the Andes, there was a deep feeling of national pride. 'It was not just an unbelievable day for Chilean football, it was an unbelievable day for the country,' said Mayne-Nicholls. 'It changed our way of thinking and that is Marcelo's biggest legacy. His message was that if you work hard and do the right thing, the results will come.' It instilled better memories of the National Stadium which, after General Pinochet's coup in September 1973, had been used as a holding pen and torture centre for up to 20,000 prisoners. The men were in the stands and on the pitch, the women in the dressing rooms, the offices and the empty swimming pool. Forty-one were killed. What stopped its use as a prison camp was the need to stage a World Cup play-off against the Soviet Union two months after the coup. When officials from Fifa came to inspect the stadium, the prisoners had still not been moved: 'We wanted to yell out and say: "Hey, we are here, look at us,"' said one of them, Felipe Agüero. 'But they seemed only interested in the condition of the grass.' When the Soviet Union boycotted the game, Chile qualified for the World Cup in West Germany by default.

Their qualification for South Africa would be an altogether more uplifting affair. After the victory over Argentina, Chile lost one of their final eight games, predictably enough to Brazil, and guaranteed qualification with a 4–2 win over Colombia in Medellín. 'I had a message from the president of Chile, Michelle Bachelet, that she would like to come to the technical centre the next day and congratulate the team,' Harold Mayne-Nicholls recalled.

We were late leaving Medellín and didn't get back until the early hours of the morning. We told the players they should be ready in their kit for 8.30am. The president arrived; the team was ready but Bielsa was nowhere to be seen. I was becoming more nervous. I had no idea where he was. Then, suddenly, he appeared with two guys I had never seen before. I wondered what they were supposed to be doing with the president and then Bielsa spoke to her: 'I would like you to meet two people who have done more than anyone to get us to the World Cup. This man is our baker and every day he delivers fresh bread to us. This man brings us fruit and vegetables. We could not have qualified without them.' That was Bielsa.

Voortrekker

Marcelo Bielsa's second World Cup did not leave the livid scars of the first but there would be regrets. The preparations were far from smooth. His main striker, Humberto Suazo, who had scored more goals than any other South American in qualifying, was injured and once more the draw was unkind. As one of the first nations to qualify, Chile had their pick of South Africa's training centres. Bielsa left the choice largely in the hands of Luis Bonini. It came down to two. The first was the Ingwenyama Conference Centre and Sports Resort near Nelspruit in the north-east of the country. The training pitches were poor but they were in walking distance of the hotel. The other option was in Kimberley, the centre of South Africa's diamond industry. The mayor of Kimberley had contacted Harold Mayne-Nicholls and offered to pay all of Chile's expenses if they based themselves there. The training pitches were better than at Ingwenyama but they were a ten-minute bus ride away. As president of a football association that was perpetually strapped for cash, Mayne-Nicholls naturally favoured Kimberley. Bielsa told him he had no problem with the choice; he would adapt his training. Bonini objected. 'He told me they would be training sometimes three times a day, which meant six bus journeys,' said Mayne-Nicholls.

The players would be annoyed about having to get on the bus all the time and there would always be one player who was late. More importantly, Bonini told me the players would leave themselves open to injury if they were sitting down all the time. He suggested we use the place near Nelspruit. They would pay some of our expenses but not all. Uruguay were the last country to qualify for the World Cup. I knew their coach, Óscar Tabárez, and the president of the Uruguay federation. They told me they could not find anywhere in South Africa. I put them in touch with the mayor of Kimberley and they stayed for free.

They stayed rather a long time at the Protea Hotel. Uruguay would reach the semi-finals of the World Cup, their best performance since they won the trophy in 1950.

In December 2009 the draw for the World Cup was made in Cape Town. One of those charged with pulling out the balls was David Beckham, the man who had caused Bielsa such pain in Sapporo. It was not as bad as 2002 but Chile would be in with the European champions, Spain. There was Switzerland, who had lost only once in qualification and were managed by Ottmar Hitzfeld, who had won the Champions League with both Borussia Dortmund and Bayern Munich. Honduras might seem makeweights but in Carlos Pavón and Carlo Costly they possessed the two highest scorers in North and Central American qualifying. In the event, Honduras would not score a single goal in the tournament. Like the *voortrekkers*, who abandoned the relative comforts of the Cape to found the ideologically pure Boer republics in South Africa's unforgiving heart, once out of the group there was no easy way through for Chile. Waiting for them in the knockout phases would be Brazil or Portugal. In the quarter-finals, maybe Italy, the world champions, or perhaps Holland.

To make his final squad selection, Bielsa arranged two friendlies on the same day in March. They would face Costa Rica and North Korea four hours apart. Three days before, Chile was struck by an earthquake. It was not quite on the scale of the one in 1960 that had wrecked the country but it still measured 8.8 on the Richter scale and could be felt 1,500 miles away. The matches were cancelled. The south of the country, particularly Concepción and Coronel, was hit hardest. There was looting, rioting and curfews.

The decision to play two friendlies on a single day was

kept to but the games – this time against Northern Ireland and Israel – were not staged until 30 May, close to midwinter in the southern hemisphere. There was rain and mist in Santiago and Humberto Suazo, who had scored ten times in qualification, was injured. He would go to South Africa but his performances were a shadow of what they had been.

Meanwhile, Mayne-Nicholls was in Rome attempting to persuade Chile's finest player, David Pizarro, to make himself available for the World Cup. Pizarro had been a key part of the Roma midfield that had finished second in Serie A, two points behind Inter Milan, who had just won a treble under José Mourinho. Pizarro was thirty and probably at the peak of his powers but had not played for the national team for five years, having announced his retirement in the wake of Chile's failure to qualify for the 2006 World Cup. 'Marcelo had told me that, if Pizarro didn't announce he wanted to play for the national team, he would not call him because it would be unfair to the other players,' said Mayne-Nicholls.

Why would he call a footballer who didn't want to play? But I had known David since he was a kid and I was determined to try. I was in Europe and met David in Rome for a coffee. We talked for two hours but he didn't commit and I always wonder what we might have done had he said yes.

When Chile arrived at the Ingwenyama complex there were problems that extended further than the fact that the supposedly heated swimming pool was freezing. The team and its support staff could fill forty-five rooms. There were thirty-five still unused which the hotel wanted to sell to whoever wanted to stay there. Bonini went to Mayne-Nicholls and asked if the Chilean FA could buy up the remaining rooms. He was told they did not have the funds but a solution was reached which saw Chile's sponsors move in with the team. Bonini gathered everyone together and told them that nobody would be permitted to watch training under any circumstances.

In one sense, the Ingwenyama was a good choice. It was near the Mbombela Stadium in Nelspruit, where Chile would play their opening game against Honduras. With Alexis Sánchez dominant, they ought to have won by more than a single goal but the real surprise came on the final whistle. In Durban, Spain had lost to Switzerland. The group was wide open. Chile met Switzerland in Port Elizabeth and from the moment Valon Behrami earned a red card by thrusting his hand into Arturo Vidal's face after half an hour, the pattern of the game was settled. Fifteen minutes from the finish, Mark González headed into a virtually empty net to give Bielsa a second straight win.

On the training pitches at Ingwenyama, Bielsa and Bonini were in a rhythm. 'I have never come across a coach who is such a perfectionist,' said the midfielder, Rodrigo Millar.

'When he wants to get the most out of a footballer, he squeezes you like a lemon.' Chile were facing Spain in one of South Africa's great rugby stadiums, the Loftus Versfeld in Pretoria. He needed just one more squeeze.

Spain would end the tournament as world champions but this was the night they might have been eliminated. If they failed to beat Chile and Switzerland overcame Honduras in Bloemfontein, then Andrés Iniesta, Xavi Hernández, Iker Casillas, David Villa and Fernando Torres would all be going home. In Santiago, it seemed perfectly possible. In Chile, it was early afternoon. The city was in a party mood. There were street barbecues, restaurants were serving the national dish of beef in red wine and everywhere there were flags and painted faces. This was the equivalent of being in Sydney when Australia were playing England in a Test match: the same sense of wanting to put one over on the old colonial power. In 2014, Chile would beat Spain in the Maracanã and send them out in the group stage, but this time little went right. Gary Medel was booked early on, which meant he would miss the next game if Chile qualified. Then, as Torres chased down a long ball, Claudio Bravo came far out of his area to clear with a sliding kick that went straight to David Villa who, from 30 yards, clipped it expertly into an unguarded net.

A dozen minutes later, Iniesta side-footed home Spain's second but in the build-up, Torres appeared to have been tripped – accidentally to most observers – by Marco Estrada.

The defender was dismissed and many on the Chile bench thought Torres had made far more of it than he might. Two goals and a man down, Chile were almost done, though during the interval Bielsa brought on Millar and a minute after the restart the midfielder scored. Spain's manager, Vicente del Bosque, realising that another Chile goal would put them in danger of elimination, became more defensive. They hung on and in Bloemfontein so did Honduras.

Spain went through as group winners; Chile were sentenced to play in the very epicentre of South African rugby, Ellis Park in Johannesburg. They would play Brazil, the nation that had knocked them out in the World Cups of 1962 and 1998 and would eliminate them in 2014. They would knock them out of this one, too. Without Medel, their 'Pitbull', and with Suazo still not back to full fitness, Chile looked toothless. It was not much of a contest and Brazil might have won by more than three goals. In the aftermath, Bielsa admitted his team had been unable to slow the Brazilians down. Chile had won friends with their style of play but they were still the first South American team to be eliminated. They had progressed as far as Portugal, England or Mexico, further than France, Italy or Ivory Coast.

Once back from South Africa, Bielsa returned home to celebrate his fifty-fifth birthday and took up Harold Mayne-Nicholls' offer of a new five-year contract. It would encompass two very attractive Copas América, one in Argentina, the other in Chile itself. In between would come the World Cup in Brazil. However, Mayne-Nicholls' triumph was short lived. Santiago's big clubs, Colo-Colo, Universidad Católica and Universidad de Chile, thought his presidency had concentrated too much on the national team. They put up a candidate, Jorge Segovia, the president of Unión Española, against him. Against Mayne-Nicholls' better judgement, Bielsa waded into the debate. He called a press conference in which he promised to resign if Segovia won. 'If I want to preserve my right not to think like other people, I must accept that others will not think like me,' he said.

> The day when Harold has to resign from the presidency is the day when I quit my job. I know perfectly well I cannot work alongside Mr Segovia. I have nothing in common with him. It would be impossible. You cannot work with someone in whom you have no confidence. I want to remain while the current president is in charge and if he extends his term of office, I will come with him.

The intervention did little good, other than to make Marcelo Bielsa's position untenable. On 4 November Segovia won the election by twenty-eight votes to twenty-two. However, the Chilean FA ruled that Segovia could not be its president and also the president of Unión Española. In January a new president, Sergio Jadue, was appointed. Bielsa would not work with him either. Refusing to work with those he did not like or was uncomfortable with was becoming an increasingly striking facet of Marcelo Bielsa's personality. In Mexico he had been uneasy with Club América because he disliked the vast television empire that owned it. His time at Olympique de Marseille came to an abrupt end because he could no longer trust the president, Vincent Labrune. A fear that Lazio would not keep their promises thwarted a potentially fascinating move to Serie A.

Jadue tried to keep Bielsa on board by appointing two people he was close to, Julio Venegas and Juan Carlos Berliner, to lead the delegation and be the head of the selection committee for the upcoming friendly against the United States in Los Angeles. There were meetings between Jadue and Bielsa at the technical centre. Bielsa said he would inform him of his decision in writing. After 10pm on 2 February, the new president of the Chilean FA called a press conference to state that since he had not heard from Bielsa, he assumed he would be carrying on as manager. If Jadue was working on a hunch, it was mistaken.

Two days later, Bielsa called a press conference of his own. The audience was left in no doubt of what was to come: 'Sergio Jadue has acted in a manner which I cannot understand and I can no longer have confidence in him.' For once, Bielsa felt he could not spend the night in the technical centre. He was no longer manager of Chile. He went to a hotel near the airport before flying back to Rosario.

Behind him was a platform upon which Chilean football could stand. Four years later, the streets of Santiago would become rivers of joy when, in the National Stadium, Chile beat Argentina to win the Copa América for the first time. The following year, in a special tournament to celebrate the competition's centenary – staged in the United States – they would beat Argentina once more to retain the title.

By then, Sergio Jadue had begun a life ban from football after pleading guilty to charges of racketeering and fraud that had been brought against him in the United States. Harold Mayne-Nicholls, who had been part of Fifa's evaluation committee for the World Cups in Russia and Qatar, was banned for seven years for asking the Qatari authorities if they could find work placements for family members at their Aspire Academy. The ban was reduced to two years on appeal and Mayne-Nicholls went on to become vice-president of Chile's biggest club, Colo-Colo, and head of the sporting charity Ganamos Todos (Let's Win Everything).

Juan Antonio Pizzi, who managed Chile to victory in the MetLife Stadium in New Jersey, remarked: 'It is unarguable that Marcelo Bielsa changed the mentality of the Chilean footballer. Bielsa was the great revolutionary of the Chilean game.' Manuel Pellegrini, who spent his entire playing career with Universidad de Chile and had managed Manchester City to the Premier League title in 2014, thought Bielsa more important than either Pizzi or Jorge Sampaoli, who had taken Chile to their two Copas América. 'Sampaoli won, Pizzi won but I am not talking about wins,' he said. 'Bielsa was the one who had more influence on Chilean football because he dared to do more.'

This would be Marcelo Bielsa's final stint as a manager in Latin America. Bluntly, there was nowhere else to go. Argentine domestic football weakened with every season and with every exodus across the Atlantic. Brazil, who had sacked Dunga after a wholly uninspiring World Cup in South Africa, were not above making left-field choices. In 1969 they had appointed the Communist journalist João Saldanha, an experiment that ended when Saldanha went looking for one of his critics with a loaded revolver. It was, however, necessary to be Brazilian to manage Brazil. Uruguay, just across the River Plate from Buenos Aires, might have appealed but it was the preserve of the great Óscar Tabárez, a man who was at least Bielsa's intellectual equal and who would take Uruguay to four World Cups. There was nowhere else to go but Europe.

PART TWO:
EUROPE

Atlantic Crossing

He could be seen early in the morning walking on the beach at Getxo, head stretched forward, lost in thought, dressed in his tracksuit uniform. Above him on the cliffs would be the old windmill, to one side would be the mouth of the River Nervión emptying into the Bay of Biscay. You wonder if he noticed. Sometimes he would climb the steps to the little harbour at Algorta where he might have breakfast. Javier Irureta watched Marcelo Bielsa and wondered if he should approach him. Someone else went over to greet Athletic Bilbao's new manager. Bielsa grunted and kept on walking.

Irureta had played for and managed Athletic. In 1977 he had been part of a side that had reached the Uefa Cup final and finished third in La Liga. Under Bielsa, Athletic Bilbao would do something similar. The San Mamés, the great cathedral of Basque football, would be a stage on which Marcelo Bielsa would do some of his finest work.

He had long wanted to manage in Europe. In April 1997, he had given an interview on Mexican television. It was a bizarre format in which he was asked a question about a subject relating to each letter of his name. E was for 'Europe'. His preference would be to manage and coach in Argentina, something he would do a few months later with Vélez Sarsfield. However, he admitted his frustration with the state of Argentine football because the best players were no longer in Argentina. Some fourteen years later, this would be even more true.

There were plenty of choices. Inter Milan were seriously interested. Having won the European Cup for the first time since 1965, Inter had endured a chaotic season. José Mourinho, the man who had delivered the triumph against Bayern Munich – part of a Treble that included the Scudetto and the Coppa Italia – had decamped to Real Madrid. His replacement, Rafa Benítez, a man Mourinho loathed, was never comfortable at San Siro. Shortly after taking them to the World Club Cup in December 2010, he publicly urged the Inter president, Massimo Moratti, to either back him in the transfer market or sack him. Moratti sacked him. Benítez was replaced by Leonardo, the urbane, elegant Brazilian who had managed AC Milan the season before. He took them to second in the championship before leaving to become the sporting director of Paris St Germain.

There was strong dressing-room pressure for Bielsa, led by Inter's captain, Javier Zanetti, and Esteban Cambiasso, who had played under him for Argentina. 'Bielsa was very important to me,' Zanetti said. 'I have learned something from everyone but Bielsa taught me the best way to live and interpret football.' By turning Inter down, Bielsa lost not just his best shot at managing one of the giants of European football but also of participating in the Champions League, a competition he was never to be part of. Moratti made another disastrous choice. Gian Piero Gasperini, who had taken Genoa to promotion and fifth place in Serie A while winning Mourinho's admiration, lasted five games, four of which he lost, none of which he won. Inter's time as a dominant force in Italian football was coming to a close.

For Bielsa there were also offers from Sevilla and Real Sociedad. He could not come to an agreement with Sevilla but was seriously interested by Real Sociedad. He had gone to San Sebastián to watch Real at the Anoeta and was impressed by the club and the quality of their players. Bilbao seemed less of an option. Under Joaquín Caparrós, Athletic had finished sixth in La Liga and qualified for the Europa League. Caparrós had been at the San Mamés for four years but his contract was up and there were presidential elections. The incumbent, Fernando Macua, was a Bilbao lawyer who had been in his post as long as Caparrós, who had been appointed in 2007, the year Athletic escaped relegation by a point. Caparrós's football was dull and defensive but he was popular with the players. Macua was expected to win but was up against a former player. Josu Urrutia had been with the club since he was nine, had spent fifteen years in the first team and been part of the side that finished runners-up to Barcelona in 1998, their best performance since winning the title in 1984. It was the kind of charisma that Macua could only dream of but it would be up an uphill struggle for Urrutia. Athletic Bilbao had been performing well: there was no crisis for him to exploit. His main policy was to bring in Marcelo Bielsa as manager. After a month's worth of phone calls from Bilbao to Rosario, he had agreed a one-year contract, although Urrutia was forced to admit that nothing had been signed.

Macua argued that Bielsa was a risk, pointing out he did not know the squad and that, a few weeks at Espanyol apart, he had never managed in Europe. It was something Urrutia leapt upon. 'If someone thinks that, then they have no football culture,' he said. 'If someone doubts the ability and prestige of this man, I recommend getting some information on him. Athletic should take a risk.' Then, quoting Piru Gaínza, Bilbao's greatest forward, who won two league titles and seven domestic cups with Athletic between 1943 and 1958, he said: 'To improve, you have to take a risk.' He added. 'We have the guarantee of a proven, committed person.' Against the odds, Urrutia won the election. Bielsa came to Bilbao.

One of the first people he spoke to was Santiago Segurola,

one of Spain's most celebrated journalists, whose writing contained a passion for the city of Bilbao and its football club. He was born in Barakaldo on the left bank of the Nervión, alive with the cranes of the shipyards and the smoke of the factory chimneys. His father had played football in Cádiz and Granada but in December 1936 he had been badly wounded during the Civil War, fighting in a Basque battalion against Franco. He no longer played professional football but he instilled in his son a love of Athletic Bilbao.

Athletic Bilbao is unique in that it selects only footballers from the Basque Country, an area of north-eastern Spain that spills over the Pyrenees into south-west France. It is roughly the same size as Yorkshire but with a smaller population. In 1991, after twenty-three years without a championship, Yorkshire cricket abandoned its policy of selecting only those born in the Broad Acres. Despite the pressure of being a club whose proudest boast is that it has never been relegated, Athletic has stuck with its Basque-only policy. To Segurola, in an age of impersonal supermarkets, Athletic chose to remain something unique. 'It is not just about the market. For me, it is something wonderful. It is a close link, a human link, it's earthy. It's not based on money or success or globalisation or China and Japan. It says: "This is who we are. We live with our problems and we do it with honour."'

Franco may have repressed Basque, an ancient language

unrelated to any other in Europe, but Bilbao did well under the dictatorship. Between 1940 and 1980 its population doubled, symbolised by the vast blast furnaces of the Altos Hornos steelworks on the banks of the Nervión, fed by coal shipped in from nearby Asturias. By the steelworks people lived in self-built shacks called *chabolas,* which resembled Brazilian *favelas.* Franco's death in 1975 may have allowed the captains of Athletic Bilbao and Real Sociedad to parade the banned Basque flag before the derby at the Anoeta but it opened up Spain to the chill winds of foreign competition. Within ten years, unemployment had risen from 3 per cent to 25 per cent. One in every two young men in Bilbao had no job. In the industrial heart at Barakaldo, Segurola estimated nearly seven out of ten were without work. Decades of pollution from Altos Hornos and all the other waterfront factories had led to the Nervión being declared ecologically dead. In August 1983 the poisoned river burst its banks and flooded the old town to a depth of up to 10 feet.

In the middle of all this, Athletic Bilbao became champions of Spain. They had not expected to. On the final day of the 1982–83 season, Athletic and Real Madrid were a point in front of the rest. Real, with the better goal difference, were at Valencia, who were in the relegation zone; Athletic were in the Canary Islands, facing Las Palmas. At the Mestalla, Valencia won to save themselves. Athletic Bilbao, after going behind, thrashed Las Palmas 5–1, to relegate them and seize the title for the first time since 1956.

Segurola said that to understand Athletic Bilbao you have to understand how much this title meant. 'There were nationalist resurgences, unemployment, drugs in the ports and a huge problem with addiction. The arrival of Aids. It was a very dark period and there was a need to cling on to something. Athletic was something sacred.' From the airport, Javier Clemente's squad was taken to the Nervión estuary and put on a barge with the trophy. They sailed downriver for twelve hours. A million people lined the banks to see a team of local heroes go past. The following season they won the Double.

Bielsa was probably the biggest name to come to Bilbao since Howard Kendall left the league champions Everton to work in the Basque Country in the summer of 1987. When Kendall recounted his arrival in Bilbao in his memoirs *Love Affairs and Marriage* it is striking how similar his brief was to the one Bielsa was to encounter nearly a quarter of a century later.

I was not expected to win the league because Real Madrid and Barcelona were expected to sweep up everything. Cup success would be a bonus. I was expected to go and prove that Basque football could compete and to qualify for Europe. I thought it was a great challenge ... I never found the Basque-only transfer policy limiting or frustrating. I knew what I had to work with and enjoyed working with what I had.

Kendall would live at the training ground at Lezama, rather than a hotel or a rented house. He made use of a single bedroom with an en-suite bathroom and went downstairs to his office. Training was conducted in public, something Kendall at first vehemently opposed but then came to love. When Bielsa took training at Lezama he would sometimes pick out a child and ask them to give his instructions to the team. Like Kendall, Bielsa would encounter the presence of Javier Clemente around the place. Clemente was a combative figure who during Athletic Bilbao's golden years had clashed frequently with César Luis Menotti, who was then in charge of Barcelona. Menotti had thought Clemente's tactics destructive and defensive. Clemente responded by calling the Argentine a womaniser and a 'pretentious hippy'. After the final of the Copa del Rey against Barcelona which sealed the Double for Bilbao, the two teams engaged in a vast rolling brawl. Like Kendall at Everton, Clemente would manage the club on three separate occasions, each less successful than the last, but he was always around, always had access to powerful ears and was a constant critic of Bielsa's methods.

The early matches provided him with ammunition. Preseason had climaxed with a game against Tottenham at White Hart Lane that was caught up in the riots that turned this area of north London into a furnace. After five matches it seemed like a metaphor. Athletic Bilbao had won none of them and were second bottom with two points. Their next game was the Basque derby against Real Sociedad at the Anoeta. All of Fernando Macua's warnings – that Bielsa was a risk, that he did not know La Liga and he did not know the squad – seemed true.

Two goals from Fernando Llorente proved enough to beat Real Sociedad and inside the squad something clicked. They would lose only one of the next thirteen matches and by mid-January they had risen fourteen places to fifth. 'Nobody knew Bielsa well,' said Segurola – not Urrutia, not the players, not the public nor the press. There were people who were suspicious of him. They didn't know Bielsa's style, which in many respects was the closest you could get to the essence of Athletic. Segurola explained:

They were dynamic, aggressive, honest, attacking. The reality was that for years Athletic had been a defensive, conservative team. Bielsa took Athletic out of mediocrity. He showed the players that they could play in another way. He made a team that was optimistic, hard-working, intrepid; a team that didn't look for excuses. If they won, they won. If they lost, they lost. If they won playing badly, they said it. If they lost playing well, they also said it. Bielsa's demands were a shock to the players. They were used to this paternalistic regime saying: 'Our lads are in a more difficult situation than the rest [because of the Basque-only policy]. It was something that gave the players an excuse. When a player has an excuse, he will lose. Bielsa gave no excuses at all. The impact was savage.

He was making an impact beyond the dressing room. One morning a group of boys asked Bielsa if he could sign their sticker album. Bielsa asked them to hand the album over and told the boys to meet him the next day. He returned and presented them with an album signed by every member of the Athletic Bilbao squad.

One of the last acts of Macua's presidency had been to sign Ander Herrera. He had been born in Bilbao – and was thus eligible to play for Athletic. It was to prove an inspired decision. Herrera's first love had been Zaragoza. His father, Pedro, had played at La Romareda and was general manager in 2004 when they reached the final of the Copa del Rey. Zaragoza faced Real Madrid in their swaggering, *galáctico* pomp. It was the team of Zidane, Beckham, Ronaldo, Figo.

Ander was thirteen when he travelled to Barcelona to watch what was anticipated to be an easy, low-gear victory for a club that expected a Treble. What followed had the young Ander in tears. David Beckham scored from a fabulous free kick; so too did Roberto Carlos. Zaragoza hit two, both teams were reduced to ten men and, in extra time, Luciano Galletti snatched victory for little Zaragoza.

Like his father, Ander played midfield at La Romareda before the transfer to the San Mamés.

I was going from a team like Real Zaragoza that was fighting just to keep alive, to the romantic football of Marcelo Bielsa. It was a big change for me. We played amazing football. Marcelo Bielsa should always be in football. He would tell us: 'Don't waste time arguing with the referee, keep running, keep fighting. If you score a goal, the best way to defend the lead is to score another one.' For three to four months we were almost unbeatable. I talked to Alexis Sánchez when he was at Barcelona and he said: 'Oh my God how much do you run?' Nobody ran harder than us.

The peak came on a November night when Barcelona came to the San Mamés. Five years after they had talked into the small hours in Máximo Paz, Bielsa and Guardiola were facing one another as the rain sluiced down. Pinned to one of the stands was a banner that displayed a portrait of Bielsa and the words: 'Athletic, Carajo!' Guardiola had selected nine of the Barcelona side that had sliced Manchester United apart at Wembley to win the European Cup six months before. What followed was extraordinary, relentless and uncompromising. If Muhammad Ali versus Joe Frazier at Madison Square Garden had been recast as a football match, this would have been it.

The pace was exhausting: at times you thought the game had to slow, had to pause, had to take a breath. However, even in the second half when there were pools of water glistening beneath the floodlights on the pitch, spraying up over every boot that landed on it, and the ball would stop alarmingly, the driving beat of the game never stopped. Mostly, it was Barcelona pushing forward, Athletic Bilbao responding with punishing counter-attacks. 'You came at us like beasts,' Guardiola, whose voice was thin, cracked and hoarse by the end, told Bielsa at the final whistle. 'A song to football,' Guardiola called it in the post-match press conference. He had never before encountered a team that played with this kind of intensity.

The rain triggered the opening goal. Javier Mascherano slips, Markel Susaeta drives down the left flank and pulls the ball back to Herrera, whose shot from the edge of the area just skims Victor Valdés's gloves before striking the back of the net. Three minutes later, Barcelona equalise. Eric Abidal, a man who had undergone surgery for liver cancer eight months before, pounds down the flank from left back and delivers a cross into a box where there is just Cesc Fàbregas and a defender. Fàbregas stretches every sinew to make the header.

The game remained locked at 1–1 for a further fifty-five improbable minutes and the goal, when it came, was almost unworthy of the night. Iker Muniain, aged just nineteen, had just turned and played the ball beautifully between Sergio Busquets and Andrés Iniesta. A few minutes later, rather more mundanely, he delivered a corner. Abidal cleared it against Fernando Llorente's shins; the ball struck

Gerard Pique's knee and slid past Valdés into the net. There were ten minutes remaining, ten minutes that were played almost entirely in Athletic's half. They clung on. Fernando Amorebieta was dismissed, Llorente, his sodden shirt ripped in a confrontation with Mascherano, was withdrawn and thirty seconds into stoppage time, Barcelona broke through. Gorka Iraizoz could not hold Iniesta's back-flick and as the ball spun clear, Lionel Messi pounced. It was his fourteenth goal of the season. It was early November. Bielsa was giving Athletic the kind of football they had not experienced for a decade, perhaps not since the last title win in 1984. He was becoming a hero.

Athletic Bilbao had never won a European trophy. In 1977, they had reached the Uefa Cup final, overcoming AC Milan and Barcelona, but had lost to Juventus on the away-goals rule. Bielsa had inherited a place in the Uefa Cup's long-winded successor, the Europa League. Bielsa was never to manage in the Champions League, would never have a platform on which he could take on the big beasts of the European jungle, the Bayern Munichs and the Juventuses, but this campaign would show what he was capable of.

Athletic very nearly fell at the first. They had to play a qualifier against Trabzonspor and drew the first leg goallessly. The return might have been awkward but the Turkish champions, Fenerbahçe, were being investigated for match fixing, which would see their president, Aziz Yıldırım, jailed. They were thrown out of the Champions League and

Trabzonspor were invited to take their place. Athletic were given a bye into the group stage. Pitted against Paris St Germain, which had just been taken over by the government of Qatar, and Austria's wealthiest club, Red Bull Salzburg, their path was by no means straightforward.

Athletic began with a 2–1 win in Slovakia against Slovan Bratislava and beat Paris St Germain 2–0 at the San Mamés. Only one game, the last, was lost against PSG at the Parc des Princes. Athletic had already qualified for the knockout stages and Bielsa had chosen to rest players. Even so, with five minutes remaining, the score was 2–2 until an own goal and a penalty settled the evening. The reward was February in Moscow. On a frozen pitch in a largely deserted stadium, Lokomotiv won 2–1. In the return in Bilbao, Athletic were reduced to ten men just before the hour when Amorebieta was dismissed once more. Three minutes later, Iker Muniain slid in to meet a flick on from Fernando Llorente and they clung on to reach the last sixteen.

Muniain was a jewel. He was from Pamplona and had broken through astonishingly young. He was sixteen years and seven months old when he made his debut for Athletic in a Europa League game against Young Boys Bern at the San Mamés and he scored in the second leg in Switzerland. He was Athletic Bilbao's youngest debutant since 1914. Sometimes his age would count against him. He once tried to gain entry into a nightclub in Pamplona and, when he was refused, he retorted: 'Don't you know who I am?'

'Yes,' replied the bouncer. 'You're Iker Muniain and you're seventeen years old. Now fuck off home.'

His career never quite fulfilled its promise, perhaps because his small size, his speed and his youth made him a target for every scything challenge in La Liga, perhaps because he suffered from a lack of confidence. He played his first international for Spain in a 5–0 thrashing of Venezuela in February 2012 and was selected for the London Olympics. He would not be selected again for another seven years. In a study of the player published in November 2013, a few months after Bielsa had left the San Mamés, the journalist David Cartlidge wrote: 'Those close to the dressing room at Athletic see Muniain as a fragile character, overly self-critical and someone who takes losses personally.' Muniain dazzled in Bielsa's first season in Bilbao, especially in the two matches against Manchester United in the last sixteen of the Europa League. It was the first time since David Beckham's penalty in Sapporo that Bielsa attracted the attention of a substantial English audience.

The previous season Manchester United had reached the Champions League final, facing Barcelona at Wembley. There, they had been dismantled by the brilliance of Messi. At Old Trafford, another citizen of Rosario would deepen the feeling that the club was starting to fade as a European force. 8 March 2012 counted as one of the great displays of the kind of football Marcelo Bielsa demanded and loved. Wayne Rooney scored the first and the last goal but in between Athletic scored three times and even Sir Alex Ferguson confessed that, but for the brilliance of David de Gea, they ought to have scored several more. It was a night of running and passing and pressing, of green-shirted players swarming forward while above them thousands of Basques, wearing their home colours, rhythmically waved red and white scarves above their heads. Bielsa paced his technical area like an expectant father in a 1950s hospital corridor.

His children did not let him down. One Manchester United full-back, Rafael da Silva, was tormented by Muniain while on the other flank, Patrice Evra was pushed to the very limits by Markel Susaeta and Andoni Iraola. Fernando Llorente, who should have had a penalty after being dragged down by Chris Smalling, headed home a low cross, driving his way through Da Silva and Smalling to do so. Óscar de Marcos ran on to meet Ander Herrera's delightful chip over a line of United defenders, though Ferguson rightly thought he was offside. What struck you about the third goal was how fast Muniain ran to drive in a shot that De Gea had parried. He ran twenty yards like an Olympian and this was the last minute of the game.

Ferguson expressed his astonishment that Bielsa had put his team through a two-hour training session at Manchester United's old training ground, the Cliff, and then trained them for another hour on the pitch at Old Trafford. He thought Bielsa was able to do it because they could relax in some league games, whereas Manchester United were always pressed hard. It suggested Ferguson did not understand how Bielsa worked.

However, on their return to Spain, they lost at Osasuna. They beat Manchester United in the second leg at the San Mamés but in La Liga, Athletic Bilbao lost four and drew one, at home to Sporting Gijón. At Old Trafford, Marcelo Bielsa had unveiled a masterpiece, something that resonated throughout Bilbao and beyond, but there were some who thought they saw cracks starting to appear on the canvas.

Grand Designs

I cannot lie to you; in the final months we couldn't even move. Our legs said 'stop'. We always used to play with the same players and we were not at our best in the finals. We were a completely different team to the one that we had been before because, to be honest, we were physically fucked. We couldn't run any more. We played, I think, sixty-five games that season – thirty-eight in the league, a cup final in Spain and the Europa League final. If you see the stats, Marcelo Bielsa used to play the same team so you can imagine how we finished that season. I am not blaming the manager because he did amazingly for us and we should be very thankful because of the beautiful football but in the last month we couldn't even move and that is the reality.

The words are Ander Herrera's, spoken in an interview with the journalist Graham Hunter. They appear a damning testimony of how Athletic Bilbao collapsed as the season reached its climax. They had burned brilliantly and brightly but, at the end, they burned out. In the Europa League the flames flickered almost until the end. In the quarter-finals against Schalke they produced a performance that was the equal of the 3–2 victory at Old Trafford. Schalke had reached the semi-finals of the Champions League the season before and with an attack led by Raúl and Klaas-Jan Huntelaar they went on to finish third in the Bundesliga this season.

The first leg was in Gelsenkirchen and was a better match than the one at Old Trafford because Schalke, unlike Manchester United, matched Athletic Bilbao blow for blow.

Raúl scored twice, the first a pure striker's goal, stolen at the near post, then a superlative volley delivered from the edge of the area. In the return fixture at the San Mamés, Raúl scored his seventy-seventh and final European goal. The climax of the first leg was astonishing. Athletic scored three in the final twenty minutes. Huntelaar struck the post and Raúl might have had a hat-trick but it was the sight of Athletic breaking away in the ninety-third minute, still running, still pressing, with Iker Muniain driving in the fourth, that decided everything. It was the only goal Bielsa celebrated, punching the air as ball hit net. It was 4–2 and Schalke would have to win by three clear goals in Bilbao.

They scored twice but so, too, did Athletic. They would play Sporting Lisbon in the semi-finals.

The first leg at the José Alvalade was lost 2–1. In the dressing room there was a confrontation between Bielsa and his captain, Andoni Iraola, who reacted badly to his manager's criticism of his performance. Iraola had been driving up and down Athletic's right flank from his position at full-back all season. He was carrying an injury and he was taking injections to dull the pain. Spain would be defending their European Championship title in the summer and he must have had a chance of making Vicente del Bosque's squad. In the end, he was not fit enough. Ander Herrera was suffering from a groin injury and asked for time off to recuperate so he would be available for the key matches. Bielsa told him it was impossible. Fernando Llorente was carrying a knee injury.

Then, Athletic Bilbao roused themselves one more time for a last extraordinary performance. The semi-finalists were all from the Iberian peninsula – Atlético Madrid were playing Valencia in the other semi-final. The San Mamés, the old cathedral of Basque football, was a place of scarves, banners and hope. The television commentator now referred to the team as: 'Athletic Club de Bilbao de Marcelo Bielsa'. The identification between the club and its manager was complete.

The second leg against Sporting Lisbon was probably Llorente's finest game for Bilbao. He was involved in all three goals, chesting Muniain's cross into Susaeta's path and delivering a beautiful, delicate pass for Ibai Gómez to score the second. There were two minutes left, the scores were level on aggregate and both teams had struck the frame of the goal. Gómez delivered a low cross that Llorente's long leg met fractionally before his marker. The ball skidded off the post and into Rui Patrício's net. Perfectly properly, the ball was at Fernando Llorente's feet when the referee, Martin Atkinson, signalled the tie was over. He lay on his back staring up at the sky, listening to the noise from the stands, and wept. Athletic Bilbao would win no more matches that season. Five of the last six were lost and they included the finals of the Europa League and the Copa del Rey.

The final of the Europa League, in Bucharest's National Stadium, would see them face Atlético Madrid managed by Bielsa's protégé, Diego Simeone. It was Spanish club against Spanish club, Argentine manager against Argentine manager, Atlético against Athletic, two teams who played in red and white stripes – although Athletic wore the green away shirts they had donned at Old Trafford. If there were similarities off the pitch, there were none on it. Athletic Bilbao were brutally shunted aside by Atlético Madrid.

In the 2011 final in Dublin, Radamel Falcao had been the difference as Porto overcame Braga. Now, in another final between two clubs from the same country, he scored twice and struck the post. The first was a fabulous drive from the edge of the area, the second a turn through 360

English football's first real sight of Marcelo Bielsa was when Argentina came to Wembley in February 2000. Here, he briefs his players before what turned out to be a goalless draw.

With a portrait of Muammar Gaddafi looking on, Bielsa briefs the press alongside Juan Pablo Sorin as Argentina prepare to face Libya in April 2003.

Above. Luck was rarely on Marcelo Bielsa's side during his time with Argentina. Having dominated the final of the 2004 Copa América, Bielsa contemplates defeat to Brazil in a penalty shoot-out in Lima.

Left. The timing of Bielsa's departures are seldom expected. Here, a month after leading Argentina to Olympic gold in Athens, he says farewell to *la selección*.

The brother of two politicians, Marcelo Bielsa has always possessed the common touch. Here, in El Salvador, he is speaking to children in the El Rosario district as part of the Futbol Forever programme, which uses the sport to campaign against gangs and gang violence.

In Bilbao, Bielsa inspired the kind of football Athletic's fans had not seen for a generation. In Madrid in May 2012, they gathered for the last match of a remarkable season, facing Pep Guardiola's Barcelona in the final of the Copa del Rey.

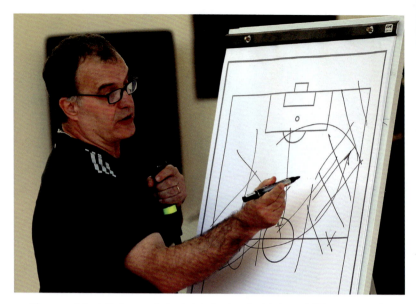

'There are defeats that are useful and victories that don't help at all.' This was one of the lessons delivered in a ninety-minute lecture to the Italian Football Federation in March 2015. Among the audience in Coverciano were Antonio Conte and Rafa Benítez.

'El Loco: Make Us Dream!' reads the banner held aloft by Olympique de Marseille's most passionate fans, the South Winners, at the Vélodrome. For a time, it seemed the dreams would extend to winning the Ligue 1 title.

Marcelo Bielsa's bench may be pointing the same way in Marseille's encounter with Paris St Germain but, ultimately, PSG's sheer financial muscle proved too much.

Marseille, like Bilbao, was a city that considered itself apart from the rest of its country. Bielsa was the perfect fit. Here, fans pay homage before a friendly with Livorno in July 2015.

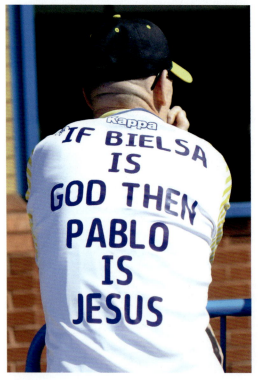

Above. Leeds United was a comatose rather than sleeping giant when Bielsa arrived in Yorkshire in the summer of 2018. It was the greatest coup by a club outside the top flight since Kevin Keegan came to Newcastle in 1982. Elland Road became a furnace of passion.

Left. Support for Marcelo Bielsa was unwavering at Leeds United and Pablo Hernández, 33 when the season began, enjoyed a renaissance.

In the long years since Leeds' relegation in 2004, they had been a club ignored.
Now they were headlines. Bielsa gets ready for his close-up before the 2-0 defeat
at Brentford in April 2019.

One of the rituals of matchday at Elland Road is Bielsa greeting young fans,
sometimes offering them a lollipop and sometimes an autograph.

'Give a goal, give a goal.' Pontus Jansson cannot quite believe he is being asked to allow Aston Villa to score. Marcelo Bielsa's gesture to right a wrong made headlines around the world and won Leeds the Fifa Fair Play Award.

A man and his nemesis. Marcelo Bielsa crouches, while Frank Lampard and Derby County exact their revenge for Spygate in May 2019.

degrees that put Athletic's left-back, Jon Auternetxe, on his back. Simeone's use of two holding midfielders in front of the back four neutralised the threat of Susaeta, Llorente and Muniain. It finished 3–0. 'What we did against Atlético Madrid is one thing I will have in my heart forever,' said Herrera. 'We were favourites and everyone expected us to win. I find some similar things with the final Manchester United played against Ajax in the 2017 Europa League final. It was kids against men. I don't blame ourselves for the final against Barcelona because that was one of the best Barcelonas in history.'

The final of the Copa del Rey was staged in Madrid, at Atlético's ground, the Vicente Calderón. It would be Pep Guardiola's final game in charge of Barcelona, the end of an affair that had begun as a thirteen-year-old on the training pitches of La Masia. Lionel Messi's first shot at goal came after twenty-five seconds. As a contest it lasted twenty-five minutes, time for Pedro Rodríguez to score twice and Messi to drive right-footed into the roof of the net. Athletic Bilbao looked exhausted, broken, but it would be hard for any team on the planet to cope with the farewell Barcelona laid on for their manager.

'Perhaps they were tired but they were much more than tired,' Santi Segurola reflected.

It was a team with a small squad, a team with two problems. First, there was a fatigue, a mental fatigue and second, they played the two best teams of their respective eras. We are not just talking of Barça but the Barça of Guardiola, of Messi, of Xavi, of Iniesta . . . who else do you want me to mention? They were all there. They had lost to Barcelona in the final of the Copa del Rey two years before, in Valencia, under Caparrós. For the final in Madrid, 75 per cent of the stadium was Athletic. They bought tickets from the Barcelona fans. They paid a fortune for them. The other final was against Atlético Madrid. Then, we didn't know it but the team that started out that final was the best Atlético Madrid of all time – the Atlético of Simeone. He had arrived in January of that year. He began building a team with Juanfran, Godín, Miranda, Filipe Luís, Falcao. It was the base of a team which won the league, which made European finals, which won two Super Cups. This was the team.

At the Copa del Rey most of the drama took place after the match: in a hospitality box at the Calderón and the following day in the dressing rooms at Lezama. In the executive boxes some Athletic Bilbao officials attempted to persuade Josu Urrutia that Bielsa's contract should not be renewed. They told the president the players had wearied of their manager. The training sessions had become exhausting, the talks repetitive. However many plaudits he had won, it was time to go. The anti-Bielsa directors had the support of Javier Clemente, who thought the team was 'physically dead by January' and went straight to the microphones of Radio Marca to say so. 'Marcelo Bielsa needs to learn what Athletic Bilbao means,' he said.

If he stays next season, he needs to do better in the finals and match his play to the style of the club. In the end, all we have been left with is a series of phrases. Bielsa is a manager who is frugal with his words. He doesn't say anything. It's a mystery and we don't know what's going through his mind. That's why they call him El Loco – because of his character and his temperament.

The day after the Barcelona defeat, Bielsa addressed his players at the training ground. The conversation was recorded and five months later was leaked to the press.

In the next few days the club and I are going to decide whether I stay here at Athletic next season. If I don't see you again, I want to wish you well. I want to say to you briefly that the season ended very badly, really badly. I am responsible for the way it finished and I want to tell you very clearly why. You played a great game against Sporting Lisbon and, after that, everything went wrong. Yesterday's game confirmed my point of view because the players who respond to my way of thinking, to my way of looking at football, people like De Marcos, Amorebieta, Susaeta, Muniain were not at the right level for the match. It's a scar, a wound. Yesterday, I heard some of you chatting and joking. That seems to me to be unacceptable, unacceptable lads – to mobilise an entire people and then to let down an entire people by not reaching the level of the hopes you generated. I am truly ashamed to have let down the fans of Athletic Bilbao because we have let them down, lads. How can you not feel responsible when the players who are supposed to best represent my ideas of football are those who have shown the least involvement in these matches? I don't know if you see what I am trying to say. Outside of that I want you to recognise that you are very young, you are immature millionaires, that you don't have to worry about the future because everything is done for you and you are allowed to laugh when certain people have had to come back from Madrid on foot. And when you've just lost a final.

Bielsa was offered another one-year contract that would see out Athletic Bilbao's final season in the San Mamés. Athletic would not just be getting a new stadium, a 53,000-seater venue that from the outside looked not unlike Munich's Allianz Arena and which cost €211 million. The training ground at Lezama would also be completely overhauled for €1.2 million. There would be new dressing rooms for the players and the coaches, a new canteen, a lounge and new press room. The offices would have to be moved temporarily to the car park but they too would be rebuilt. There would be a new running track. As he would show at Leeds, Marcelo Bielsa was perfectly happy working in an old, atmospheric ground but he set great store by training grounds and the redevelopment of Lezama was important to him. Bielsa, the brother of an architect, had provided what he called 'an austere plan to remodel Lezama'. In Argentina he had been in almost daily touch with the contractors, sometimes spending four hours a day on the phone. He assumed half the work would be finished by the time the squad assembled for pre-season training on 2 July.

When he returned to Spain, the training ground looked like an episode of *Grand Designs* gone horribly wrong. There were cement mixers rolling, pipes still to be fitted, construction lorries and protective helmets everywhere. The building would continue until December. Bielsa walked round the site in a fury. He estimated that only 15 per cent of the work had been done and took photographs of what he thought was shoddy workmanship. There was a confrontation with the project manager. 'The problem is not that the work isn't finished, it was that it was done so badly,' he said.

When I saw how bad it was, I was outraged. I went to see the person in charge of the works. I offended him with what I said and he also spoke badly to me. I believe that what has been done is a scam, a robbery and a deception. Having to take pre-season in these conditions discredits me as a coach.

He added he would not be living at the training ground because the rooms had been too expensively refurnished. The state of the training ground wrecked Bielsa's relationship with Josu Urrutia. The work had been carried out by Bilbao's most prestigious building firm, Construcciones Balzola. They had built the spectacular curved titanium frontage of the Guggenheim Museum, whose design by Frank Gehry symbolised the rebirth of the Nervión waterfront from the rusted, rotting docks. They had also built the Bilbao Museum of Fine Arts. The club issued a statement on its website, distancing itself from its manager. 'The club disagrees with its manager in his negative assessment of the works, the degree of compliance with the contract to carry it out and the professionalism of the people involved in the construction project. Athletic apologises for the damage the declarations of a club employee may have caused to the construction company and its workers.'

If Bielsa was unhappy with the state of the training ground he was dismayed by the club's transfer policy. In August, Javi Martínez was sold to Bayern Munich for €40 million. As Arsenal discovered when they abandoned Highbury for the Emirates, new stadiums have to be paid for. Nor was Bielsa enamoured with the men who had been brought in as replacements, the striker Artiz Aduriz and the left-back Isma López. He told a press conference that he had 'not requested these players and I pointed out other positions that should be reinforced. They are not those of Aduriz and Isma.'

Isma López, who was signed from Lugo, a little club in north-west Spain that had just won promotion to the Second Division, would play only eight matches for Athletic Bilbao before being sold on. However, Bielsa was mistaken about Aduriz, who was from San Sebastián and had learned to play football on the sands of the city's famed Playa de la Concha. Perhaps Bielsa was suspicious of the fact that this was the third time Aduriz had signed for Athletic and he was now thirty-one. This was hardly his kind of transfer. However, Aduriz, who growing up would swap summers on the Playa de la Concha for winters climbing and skiing in the Pyrenees, would have a golden Indian summer back in Bilbao. He scored fourteen goals in his first season, a total he would better in each of the next four. At the age of thirty-five Aduriz would be part of the Spain squad for Euro 2016.

In part Aduriz was given the games he needed to succeed because Fernando Llorente's head was elsewhere. His contract was up in the summer of 2013 and Llorente was looking for other clubs, especially Juventus. He was twenty-seven, he had been at Athletic Bilbao all his career and time was running out if he were to be the subject of a major transfer.

He had suffered from a knee injury as the season reached its dramatic climax and he agreed with Clemente that the squad had been exhausted by Bielsa's regime. Footballers who plan to leave can be poisonous commodities. At Liverpool, Steve McManaman ran down his contract with a series of desultory performances as he waited to join Real Madrid. Liverpool finished seventh in 1999. Twenty years later, the failure to remove four players who were out of contract from Tottenham's first team poisoned the atmosphere and directly contributed to the downfall of Mauricio Pochettino.

It would have been better had Urrutia simply sold Llorente to Juventus for whatever price he could get – not even the Old Lady of Turin was going to pay the €35 million buy-out clause of a contract that had ten months to run. However, Llorente remained at the San Mamés, although Bielsa perfectly sensibly kept him on the bench. The crowd took the manager's side. Llorente was whistled at Athletic's opening fixture of the season and the whistling never ceased.

Bielsa's second season in Bilbao, like his first, started badly. Only one of the opening six fixtures in La Liga produced a win. Athletic conceded fourteen goals and lost the derby, 2–0, to Real Sociedad. Spectators watching training at Lezama saw Bielsa send Llorente to the newly refurbished dressing rooms. 'I decided that his contribution was not required,' Bielsa said afterwards. 'If that indicates conflict, then it is indeed a conflict.' Llorente did not start the next game, a 3–1 win over Sparta Prague.

Unlike in his first season at the San Mamés, there would be no upswing. The two competitions in which Athletic had dazzled, the Europa League and the Copa del Rey, fizzled out. Athletic failed to win a single group game at home and in the Copa del Rey they were drawn against Eibar. It was a Basque derby. Eibar was a town of some 27,000 that had been devastatingly bombed at the same time as Guernica during the Spanish Civil War. Wolfram von Richthofen, the commander of the Condor Legion – the Luftwaffe squadron sent to aid Franco's advance – noted in his diary for 26 April 1937 that Eibar's destruction had been 'an interesting phenomenon.' In November 2012, Eibar's football team was in the third division although within eighteen months two promotions would see them in La Liga for the first time in their history. The first leg, in Eibar's little municipal stadium which held 5,000 spectators, was drawn goallessly. In the return at San Mamés, Mikel Arruabarrena, who had been part of Athletic Bilbao's youth teams but who had never started a senior game for the club, put Eibar ahead. With two minutes remaining, Aduriz levelled but it was too late. Athletic were out on the away-goals rule. Bielsa described the result as 'inexplicable'.

There was little left to play for. The season dissolved into a series of results that did little to lift the mood in Bilbao or Athletic much up the table. This was the last season they would play in the old San Mamés, which had been Athletic's home since 1913. It was the oldest stadium

THE QUALITY OF MADNESS

in Spain. They called it 'the Cathedral' and there should have been some kind of high mass to see it off. There were some high points in the season: a 3–0 victory over Atlético Madrid, a win over Valencia and another 2–2 draw with Barcelona. However, the last derby with Real Sociedad was lost and the final league game in the San Mamés was a 1–0 defeat to Levante. It deserved a better goodbye. So, too, did Marcelo Bielsa. This time Josu Urrutia did not renew his contract. 'The second season affected Bielsa, he suffered a lot,' said Santi Segurola.

The relationship with the directors, or some of the directors, was broken or at least strained. In general, however, he had tremendous support from the public. I don't just mean at the San Mamés but people who didn't go to the ground, perhaps people who didn't have the money to be members of Athletic but who are still unconditionally Athletic, who have not a single grain of cynicism but just an emotional, honest connection. This was never lost. He was sacked in mid-June, late on a Friday when people were setting off to their summer houses or to the beaches. Athletic dismissed him with a statement that lacked a bit of style. Bielsa had a tight relationship with ordinary people there. He liked to explore the villages around Bilbao to get to know the coastline. He has a close relationship with normal people, working people. There are still those who go and visit him in England. Bielsa is a mythical figure at Athletic and the more time goes by, the bigger the myth becomes. He left an eternal imprint, not only in the team and at the club but especially with the people. It's a team that's rooted in the earth. Bielsa is charismatic, hard-working, peculiar. I miss him in that way. People say Bielsa is crazy. I have never seen him as crazy. He is singular, smart, very intelligent, very demanding, but he's not crazy.

Bielsa had spent his time in Bilbao in a hotel called the Embarcadero, a modest, stylish place overlooking the harbour at Getxo from where the boys of 1983 began their journey down the dead, polluted river with the La Liga trophy. The Nervión was clean now. In the bay the water sparkled and Bielsa decided to spend two more weeks there. In the course of that fortnight people would go to the garden in front of the Embarcadero's reception and leave little gifts or cards with messages inside. If they had left an address, Bielsa wrote a note of thanks. As the days went by, more presents arrived. As Santi Segurola remarked, 'It was a kind of Christmas.'

Master and Commander

He arrived like a rock star. There were crowds, there were banners, there were cameras and microphones pushed towards him. Smoke canisters were released. Everywhere Marcelo Bielsa went, there was expectation.

Olympique de Marseille's head of security, Guy Cazadamont, picked up Bielsa and his translator, Fabrice Olszewski, from Marseille's airport, Marignane, on 24 June 2014 and drove them in a people carrier to the club's training ground, the Commanderie. There were about a hundred fans waiting at the entrance. As they got out of the car, Bielsa made a gesture to Cazadamont that he wanted to go to the supporters. He would have been particularly intrigued by one banner written in Spanish. *Haznos Soñar* – 'Make us Dream.' Some of the supporters gathered at the gates of the Commanderie were from Olympique de Marseille's most passionate fan base, the South Winners – so called because of the first banner they raised in the Vélodrome, which said 'Win for Us'. They set themselves apart with orange bomber jackets and a passionate dislike for the ultras of Paris St Germain. They would be inspired by Bielsa's brand of football.

Salim Lamrani, who would become Bielsa's translator at Lille and Leeds and had been brought up as a fan of Olympique de Marseille, wrote: 'News of his signing triggered the kind of delight among supporters usually reserved for the greatest players. In the history of Marseille, no coach had ever fired such passion among the fans.' Samir Nasri, who had been born in Marseille's northern suburbs, played at the Vélodrome and continued to support the club long after leaving for the Premier League, remarked: 'It felt like we had signed Cristiano Ronaldo.' If Bielsa was treated like a rock star, albeit a diffident, intellectual Leonard Cohen type of rock star, then Olszewski, with his long hair and goatee beard, would have been a decent fit for a lead guitarist. At the beginning he behaved like one. Early on during a game, he went to the players' lounge and ordered a whisky and Coke. The waitress kept refilling it. 'I went down to the dressing room and the press officer put her hand on my shoulder and said: "Fabrice, you are doing the press conference." I was completely drunk, shit scared. If you go back through my first press conference, you will find that what I said is not really what the coach said.'

He had grown up in Chile and in the Champagne region of France and had met Bielsa during the Toulon Under-21 tournament six years before. His style of translation was individualistic and once, when the manager was asked a question in Spanish, Olszewski 'translated' it into Spanish, causing Bielsa to ask the assembled journalists for a round of applause. Their relationship was sometimes intense. Olszewski was confident enough to tell Bielsa to his face: 'You're like Van Gogh. You are a genius but in terms of human relationships it's a bit complicated.' Bielsa was flattered by the comparison but would challenge him to a fist fight when Olszewski refused to translate what he considered a domineering and insulting series of instructions to the club's twenty-year-old midfielder, Momar Bangoura. 'This is the only way to resolve this,' Bielsa told Olszewski. The fight was declined.

Immediately after his arrival at La Commanderie, Bielsa wanted to take a training session. In Brazil, it was the middle of the World Cup – Argentina were due to play Nigeria in Porto Alegre the next day. There were not many players available but Bielsa made do with some from the youth team and those who had not been required for the greatest show on football's earth.

In public, Bielsa seemed enthused by the city and its football club. 'One of the reasons I came here was to see the Stade Vélodrome full; it is one of the most beautiful sights sport has to offer,' he said. The Vélodrome, with its curved, continuous roof and its views onto the lavender-covered hills of Provence, was the great stadium of French football. It had staged two of the finest matches of the 1998 World Cup: the Dutch victory over Argentina, inspired by Dennis Bergkamp's fabulous winner, and the titanic struggle in the semi-final between Brazil and Holland that followed. He had signed only for a year, albeit at a salary of €300,000 a month, but the Vélodrome was as fitting a stage for Bielsa's talents as the cathedral of San Mamés or the Coloso del Parque.

However, it was the training ground, the Commanderie, that was the centre of Bielsa's world. It was a modern, sleek, white building, constructed in 1991 when Olympique de Marseille looked as if it might succeed AC Milan as Europe's dominant force. The club had booked him a suite at the Intercontinental on the Old Port, which had been the very heart of Marseille since the Greeks set up a trading post here six centuries before the birth of Christ. Bielsa, as always, disliked hotels and asked for a room at the Commanderie to be made up for him. He wanted beds for the players to rest between training sessions.

Like the city that spawned it, Olympique de Marseille's history was drowned in drama, heroism and scandal. There was no club in France remotely like it. For Marcelo Bielsa it was the perfect platform. The modern club had been created in 1986 with the arrival of a Parisian-born businessman named Bernard Tapie, who looked like the square-jawed star of an American TV series. Tapie had made his money with a chain of health-food stores called La Vie Claire. His cycling team had won the Tour de France in successive years. One of Tapie's first acts would be to remove the cycling track that had given the Vélodrome its name. Marseille were mouldering, twelfth in Ligue 1. Within three years, Marseille would win the title for the first time since 1972, when the city had been known for drugs and violence, the backdrop to *The French Connection*. Tapie would give the Stade Vélodrome players of the quality of Jean-Pierre Papin, Didier Deschamps, Chris Waddle, Eric Cantona, Fabien Barthez and Rudi Völler. He became a socialist politician, a minister under François Mitterrand.

In 1991 Marseille reached the European Cup final, losing agonisingly to Red Star Belgrade on penalties. By then, Tapie had the consolation of owning Adidas. Two years later came the ultimate consolation. Marseille beat AC Milan to become champions of Europe. Then came the match-fixing scandal. Just before travelling to Munich for the final with Milan, Marseille had wrapped up the title with a 1–0 win over Valenciennes. No Marseille player had been injured, so they were all available for the final, which was just as well because Valenciennes had been bribed to ensure there would be no rash tackles. The story broke.

There had long been tales of Marseille bending rules, buying referees. When he was in charge of Monaco, thoughts of Bernard Tapie turned Arsène Wenger's stomach. The pair had to be separated in the tunnel at the Vélodrome. Compared to Tapie, Wenger would count José Mourinho as a friend. Now there were arrests, prison sentences. Financial irregularities were uncovered which resulted in Marseille's automatic relegation to the Second Division. In 1995, Tapie was jailed for two years.

Bielsa's predecessor had been José Anigo, who had played for the club, managed them to the 2004 Uefa Cup final and was now Marseille's sporting director and temporary manager. Marseille finished twenty-nine points behind the champions, Paris St Germain. They were twenty points adrift of Monaco. Not only had they failed to qualify for the Champions League, they had not even made the Europa League. That Anigo was able to focus on anything at all was astonishing. Three months before he took over, his son, Adrien, had been driving down the Avenue Jean-Paul Sartre in his Renault. Two motorcyclists pulled up alongside him and shot him dead through the window. Adrien had been a member of a gang called the Massed Raiders and had been jailed for armed robbery. Gangs armed with Kalashnikovs were operating openly in Marseille. The time of *The French Connection* had returned. The fact that Marseille was the current European City of Culture merely added to the embarrassment.

In his office at the Commanderie, Bielsa discovered he was less in control than he had imagined. The president, Vincent Labrune, had a background in television and film.

He enjoyed the company of football agents and liked to do his own deals, which he would then leak to the media. None of this was likely to ease his relationship with his new manager. Bielsa would have been even less confident had he heard a remark Labrune had made to an agent, reported by *Libération*. 'He's here for a year. He will clean up the club.'

Bielsa had given Labrune a list of a dozen players he wanted to sign. Most were defenders or defensive midfielders. Among them were Javier Manquillo and Toby Alderweireld from Atlético Madrid, Martín Montoya, who was playing right-back for Barcelona, and Mauricio Isla at Juventus. These were ambitious names but Bielsa might have expected to have got one or two. He had been promised, or thought he had been promised, a spend of €35 million to give him a squad with two players for every position. The failure to land other players appeared inexplicable. Gary Medel, whom he had managed at the 2010 World Cup, preferred Cardiff. Another target was Benjamin Stambouli from Montpellier. Stambouli had been born in Marseille; his father and grandfather had both managed the club. It should have been a fairly straightforward signing. Instead, Stambouli went to Tottenham for €5 million. He lasted a single season at White Hart Lane; his games were largely confined to the backwaters of the Europa League or the League Cup.

Before accepting Labrune's offer, Bielsa had studied every game Marseille had played over the past two years. He would have done better to have cast his eye over the balance sheets, which were displaying an alarming slide both in real terms and relative to Olympique de Marseille's opponents. When Marseille defended their French championship in 2010, they were the wealthiest club in France. According to the Deloitte Money League, their revenue in 2010–11 was €150.4 million, slightly less than Juventus, slightly more than Roma. Olympique Lyonnais, with €132.8 million, was the country's second-richest club. Three years later, Bielsa inherited a club whose revenues had fallen by €20 million. They now earned slightly less than Aston Villa, slightly more than Sunderland. In those three years, Juventus, a club Marseille could compare themselves to, had increased their revenues by €126 million. However, even the Old Lady of Turin stood in the shadows of Paris St Germain, which was now a wholly owned subsidiary of the government of Qatar. Its income of €474.2 million made it the fifth-richest club in the world, within touching distance of Barcelona and Bayern Munich. It earned more than the rest of the French League put together.

There would be departures from the Vélodrome that would shock Marcelo Bielsa, not just because of the quality of the players but because there had been no serious attempt to keep him informed of them. Labrune would adopt a similar policy when it came to arrivals. The most significant loss was Mathieu Valbuena. He had been plucked from non-league football, replaced Franck Ribéry when he left for Bayern Munich and was affectionately known as 'the

Little Bike' because of his speed, size and endurance. When he had fallen out with Deschamps, the club had declared Valbuena 'untransferable'.

Now Valbuena was transferable and he would be transferred to Dynamo Moscow, who, despite their history, were no longer one of Russian football's great powers – they had not won a title since 1976. Bielsa only found out about the deal the day before Valbuena was due to leave. When they met, he told him he had been France's best player in the World Cup in Brazil. 'I want you to know that those who say you weren't in my plans are liars. I would have been really mad not to have wanted you in my team.' He had also wanted Lucas Mendes to stay, but there was no time for a conversation. Mendes was a twenty-four-year-old Brazilian left-back, who had played two full seasons at the Vélodrome. He was leaving for Qatar to play for El Jaish. Marseille would more than double their money on the €2 million they had paid his hometown club, Coritiba. Given the identity of the club he was joining, Bielsa might have fancied his chances of persuading Mendes to stay. El Jaish had been pilloried for refusing to allow Zahir Belounis, a French footballer, to leave the country after he accused the club of non-payment of wages – Qatar is a country you cannot leave without your employer's permission. In October, Belounis had given an interview to CNN in which he said: 'Life has become a nightmare for me, my wife and my two small daughters. They killed me inside.' After nineteen months Belounis was allowed to leave following intense lobbying from the French government. Mendes set off regardless.

Bielsa discovered he was to be given little choice about incoming players and he particularly objected to Mendes' replacement, Matheus Dória, a nineteen-year-old Brazilian signed for €7 million from Botafogo just before the transfer window closed. In a breathless announcement, Marseille described Dória as 'the future of Brazilian football'. Perhaps significantly, he was photographed not with his manager but with Labrune. The president was not to know it, but even before his twentieth birthday Dória was already part of Brazil's past. His international career, which consisted of three minutes in a friendly against Bolivia – brought on by Phil Scolari when Brazil were 3–0 up – would not be extended. He was not even part of Olympique de Marseille's immediate future. Bielsa publicly condemned his signing: 'To me, you need twenty matches to analyse a player.

'The fact he was due to replace Lucas Mendes would not have advanced the team. Lucas Mendes had been at Marseille for two years and he belonged there because he knew how to adapt to the team. The president promised me he would not sign footballers from abroad because Olympique de Marseille does not have the resources to evaluate footballers who do not play in France.'

Dória did not play a single first-team game for Bielsa, who consigned him to Marseille's B team. He was loaned back to Brazil with São Paulo, played for Granada and then ended up in Malatya in eastern Turkey.

By now, Bielsa realised he would not be in charge of a first-team squad of twenty-two with two players for every position. There was never a chance of a €35 million transfer budget, much less of his being given a say in how it was spent. 'The balance of the transfer market has been negative,' he told reporters. 'The president made me promises he knew he would be unable to keep. If he had told me this sincerely, I would have accepted it but, in these circumstances, I feel like rebelling.' Reports of the press conference were accompanied by a photo showing Bielsa gesticulating, head raised – which it rarely was when talking to journalists. Standing by the podium was Marseille's head of press, Elodie Malatrait, one hand covering her face, the other holding her phone. She seemed the picture of utter despair, although Malatrait has denied the image gave a true picture of how she was feeling. 'He doesn't look at journalists when he talks and that became a hot topic for them,' she said. 'They thought it showed a lack of respect or a lack of courage but that is not Bielsa. He was a mixture of shyness and power. He infuriated us at times with his attitude but, at the same time, you just wanted to give him a hug. He had a likeable side.'

The season began with little optimism. The opening match was in Corsica, against Bastia. It was frantic: three goals in the opening seventeen minutes, six in total, the points shared. Claude Makélélé, Bastia's manager, was generous in his assessment of Marseille, remarking that they had given Bastia plenty of problems and they would do the same to other teams. Perhaps Makélélé was being overly generous. Bielsa's first home game was a Provence derby with Mont-pellier. The Vélodrome had been spectacularly refurbished for Euro 2016, the curved roof pushed even higher, the angles made even more elegant. Marseille delivered a per-formance that in architectural terms was unworthy of a prefab. Montpellier won easily, 2–0. Éric di Meco, who had won the European Cup with Marseille and was now a city councillor, remarked of Bielsa: 'If he succeeds with that team, he's a magician.' Bielsa did succeed. There were eight straight wins and suddenly he was Merlin, he was Gandalf.

Nice were beaten 4–0 in the Vélodrome, Rennes 3–0. In September, Marseille travelled to Reims, the club that had once carried the flag for France in the early years of the European Cup. André-Pierre Gignac missed a penalty in the opening exchanges and scored two before twenty minutes were up. Marseille won by five. Gignac had scored eight times in Marseille's first seven games. A tall, powerful header of the ball, Gignac was one of the nearly men of French football. He grew up in Martigues, along the coast from Marseille, where the beaches and the light had once attracted colonies of artists. Gignac was from Spanish gypsy stock: 'My family live in caravans and work the markets.' In 2008–09 he had been Ligue 1's leading goalscorer, taking

Toulouse from seventeenth to fourth. His goals earned him a transfer to Olympique de Marseille but they would only win him a place on the fringes of the French national team. His most famous goal, the second in a 2–0 win over the world champions, Germany, in November 2015, was drowned out by the explosions around the Stade de France that signalled a night of terror culminating in the massacre at the Bataclan concert hall.

Gignac took immediately to Bielsa and it was a relationship that endured after both men had left the Vélodrome. In April 2019 he gave an interview to *L'Équipe*. Bielsa's first season at Leeds was nearing its climax while Gignac was in his fourth season in Mexico, playing for Tigres in the suburban sprawl of Monterrey. When his contract with Olympique de Marseille expired in June 2015, Bielsa tried to persuade Gignac to join Manchester United, managed by Louis van Gaal, a man Bielsa had long admired. 'He wanted to galvanise me,' Gignac recalled. 'He knew I adored Manchester United because of Ruud van Nistelrooy.' Instead, Gignac made the quixotic decision to sign for Tigres, based in the University of Nuevo León. There were attractions. His debut would be in the semi-final of the Copa Libertadores, in Porto Alegre against the Brazilian side, Internacional. In the second leg, Gignac would score the goal that sent Tigres through to the final, where they would meet River Plate. The first leg in the University Stadium was a goalless draw, the return in Buenos Aires was badly lost. The transfer, however, proved a success. 'We still exchange texts or he sends messages via his assistant, Diego Reyes,' Gignac said four years later.

> Marcelo is a man who doesn't like to talk. He writes me little notes. He sent me a letter when I scored my hundredth goal for Tigres. That bloke changed my career forever. He changed the way I look at football. He invested in me like nobody else had done. He told me in another letter that I was an amateur player in a professional game. Words like that give me goosebumps.

After the demolition in Reims, Gignac scored the last-minute winner in Caen and the second goal against his former club, Toulouse. It was now eight wins in a row. Most of the wins had been observed by Bielsa sitting on a plastic drinks cooler. To Christophe Dugarry, it had been a seriously impressive beginning. Dugarry was speaking as a former Olympique de Marseille player, someone who had won the World Cup with France. 'He has certainly got some good players but how many are of international calibre? Three, perhaps four. I have never seen a manager stamp his mark on a team so quickly.' Raymond Domenech, who had led France to the World Cup final in Berlin eight years before, said: 'I had the chance to look in on one of his training sessions. Bielsa is someone who spends time with his players. He does a lot of work on an individual basis and what he has done with essentially the same team as last year is admirable.'

His training was relentless. There was a practice match between those who would start the next match and those who would not. Dimitri Payet had played appallingly and then, a few minutes before the end, he scored a fabulous goal, something made out of nothing. 'Great, Dimitri, great,' shouted Jan Van Winckel, Marseille's conditioning coach, but the congratulations did not last. Bielsa went marching onto the training pitch, accompanied by Fabrice Olszewski, yelling at Payet: 'No, no this has been a mess, a complete mess. Go to the dressing room. You're not coming with us. Go away, go.' Payet walked away, crestfallen. 'He was right,' Olszewski recalled. 'He later explained to me that if he had congratulated him, then he would allow Dimitri to believe that everything he had done that morning was fine and that was not something he could allow.'

Standing in front of them were the two biggest obstacles to Marseille's remaining top – Olympique Lyonnais and Paris St Germain, who had yet to lose a match. They would face both away from home in the space of three weeks. Lyon were the club that had suffered most from the Qatari-fuelled rise of PSG. In June 1987 they had been bought by Jean-Michel Aulas, a businessman as flamboyant and successful as Bernard Tapie had been at Marseille, although Aulas would last rather longer. Lyon won seven straight championships.

Their business model was to buy young talent cheap and sell them on for the highest possible price. Michael Essien, Mahamadou Diarra, Karim Benzema and Eric Abidal all passed through the Stade de Gerland before being sold on for sizeable transfer fees. In 2008, Lyon had an income of €155 million, making it the richest club in French football, earning nearly €30 million more than Marseille. Two years later, Lyon reached the semi-finals of the Champions League, knocking out Liverpool and Real Madrid before going down to Bayern Munich. It was the best performance by a French team since Marseille had lifted the European Cup seventeen years before. Aulas was praised for his business model but no kind of wheeler-dealing could compete with the pipeline of Qatari money flowing into the Parc des Princes.

Marseille might have beaten both Lyon and Paris St Germain; instead they lost both games, cutting their lead over PSG at the top of Ligue 1 to a single point. Lyon in third were two points behind. They dominated the opening exchanges in each match. At the Stade de Gerland, Anthony Lopes made one excellent and one world-class save from André Ayew. At the Parc des Princes, Gignac's early downward header struck the foot of the post.

Both games saw refereeing decisions that those who travelled from Provence found hard to explain. Against Lyon, Florian Thauvin was denied two penalty claims while in Paris with the home side one up, Bielsa saw his holding midfielder, Giannelli Imbula, dismissed – a red card that would be overturned on appeal. Attacking a depleted team, Edinson Cavani scored the second.

There would be one more defeat, at Monaco, where Marseille were beaten by a Bernardo Silva goal, before Ligue 1 shut down for its winter break. Marseille were top with forty-one points, three clear of Paris St Germain, four of Lyon. They had lost four games but three of those defeats were explicable. Marseille had been unlucky to lose to Lyon – the former French president, Nicolas Sarkozy, remarked that on the balance of play Bielsa had deserved a 2–0 victory. In Paris they had been undone by a poor refereeing decision while the only loss in the Vélodrome had been in the first game, when Bielsa's radical philosophy had not had time to gel. Only the last reverse, along the coast at Monaco, could not be easily explained away, but in Marseille it was Christmas.

In nearby Allauch, shepherds drove their flocks through the streets. At the top of the city's main drag, the Canebière, at the Reformes church, there was a mass for the makers of the *santons* – the figurines that adorn a nativity crib. Around the Old Port there were the lights and sounds of the Christmas market. Beneath the laughter, and the smell of the Provençal soaps and perfumes, was the knowledge that Olympique de Marseille were top of the league. However, by the time the Black Madonna was paraded around the Place Saint-Victor on 2 February for the archbishop to bless the city and the sea, the club was beginning a nervous breakdown.

Avalanche

The avalanche that swept away Olympique de Marseille's dreams of the title and eventually drove Marcelo Bielsa from office began where so many avalanches happen: in the Alps. Grenoble were an example of where ambition can take you in football. They were a small club in a region where skiing was the dominant sport. Youri Djorkaeff played for them; his father, Jean, had once managed the club. The team lived modestly in the French second division until in 2004 they became the first football club in the country to fall under foreign ownership. The owners were a Japanese company called Index Holdings, who made games for mobile phones. Index built Grenoble a new ground with 20,000 seats, grandly named the Stade des Alpes, and shortly after its opening they were promoted to Ligue 1 for the first time since 1963. The club's president, Kazutoshi Wanatabe, gave a speech. The club, he said, 'was at the foot of a great mountain. At the summit is the Champions League.' Grenoble did indeed have a long path in front of it, which led not to nights in the Bernabéu but to bankruptcy and the fifth tier of French football.

In 2009 Grenoble began their second season in the big time by losing their opening twelve matches, something Manchester United had once done in 1930. The result was the same: relegation in last place. By the 2010 winter break, Grenoble were bottom of Ligue 2 and owed €2.9 million. In the middle of all this, they judged that one of their academy products, Olivier Giroud, was not good enough for first-team football.

This was nothing compared to Index Holdings' debts, fuelled by fraud and disastrous foreign acquisitions. They were enough to liquidate the club, which was relegated to the Second Division of the French Amateur Championship. In January 2015, Grenoble were still feeling their way back but being drawn at home to Olympique de Marseille in the Coupe de France was a reminder of the glamour that had once, briefly, been theirs. The game was scheduled for television coverage. To ensure that Grenoble, who were now in the French fourth division, would receive the television revenue and the receipts for a sold-out Stade des Alpes, the pitch, which was marked out for both football and rugby, was covered in tarpaulin and heaters brought in.

Grenoble's Twitter account joked that their best hope was to stop Marseille's bus from getting to the ground.

The bus arrived and within six minutes, André-Pierre Gignac had put Marseille one up with a supreme individual goal that he celebrated with the South Winners. What followed was the kind of tie that would be polished and treasured by those who believe football is nothing without romance. Grenoble equalised and when Gignac scored again, they equalised again. Paul Cattier, a graduate of Grenoble's academy, played the game of his life in goal. Florian Thauvin, who had begun his career at the Stade des Alpes but been sold when Grenoble careered into bankruptcy, had three chances to settle the match and squandered them all. It would be his penalty that Cattier saved in the shoot-out.

It is hard to envisage what more Bielsa might have done. Because he was due to travel to the Africa Cup of Nations, he replaced André Ayew with Dimitri Payet. Ayew was brought on as a substitute and eight minutes into extra time, he scored Marseille's third. Bielsa also employed his twenty-year-old reserve keeper, Brice Samba. Like Paul Cattier, Samba would always remember this night but his memories would be viewed through closed eyes. In the final minute of extra time, Grenoble scored their third. The match went to penalties. Cattier saved, Samba did not. His career as a Marseille player was effectively done.

A cup defeat, however humbling, does not always lead

to a hangover. The week after Hereford's defeat of New-castle in 1972 – the one that is invariably shown whenever the FA Cup is deemed in need of rekindling – Newcastle went to Manchester United and won. (They would not win again at Old Trafford for another forty-one years). Marseille, however, kept losing. The next eight games saw fifteen points dropped against mostly average teams: defeats at Montpellier, Nice and Caen. Draws against Rennes, Reims and Saint-Étienne. The lead lost to Lyon; second place lost to Paris St Germain. Monaco advancing fast. All the old enemies gathering.

Bielsa had lost André Ayew and his centre-back Nicolas Nkoulou to the Africa Cup of Nations, staged in Equatorial Guinea. Nkoulou did not linger in the tournament – Cameroon were knocked out in the group stages. However, when he returned to France, it was for a knee operation that would keep him out of action until April – he had not played since the winter break. Ayew spent rather longer in Equatorial Guinea. Ghana, managed by Avram Grant, reached the final, where after a goalless draw with Ivory Coast, it took twenty-two penalties to decide the result. The sequence ended when Ivory Coast's keeper, Boubacar Barry, saved from his opposite number and then scored. Five days later, Ayew was back at the Vélodrome scoring the second against Reims, whose equaliser in stoppage time summed up the second half of Marseille's season.

Ayew had planned to quit Marseille after the World

Cup in Brazil. His younger brother, Jordan, who had been at the Vélodrome all his career, did leave for Lorient but on the last day of the transfer window, Vincent Labrune persuaded André to stay. He admitted he was unsure about being managed by Marcelo Bielsa:

At the beginning, frankly, I didn't understand very much. I didn't understand the point of this or that exercise but in time and after several conversations with the manager I realised how he wanted us to work. I was pleasantly surprised by him. He's one of the best. For sure, he hasn't won the trophies of a Guardiola or a Mourinho but it is extraordinary how he gets his message across to you.

Olympique de Marseille's television channel gave a glimpse of how Bielsa communicated with his players. In early March, Marseille had travelled to Toulouse and won their first away game in five months. It was no ordinary victory; it was a 6–1 demolition. They were four up before the interval. Michy Batshuayi, who had begun to eclipse André-Pierre Gignac as Marseille's most potent striker, scored twice. It was a Friday night. Marseille were second, above Paris St Germain on goal difference, one point behind Lyon. Over the weekend their rivals produced routs of their own: Lyon were 5–1 winners at Montpellier while Lens were crushed 4–1 at the Parc des Princes. The gap was back to four and three points but the victory in Toulouse, and the manner of it, had proved Marseille were still contenders. Lyon were up next at the Vélodrome. Naturally, it was chosen as Sunday's televised game and when, on the Saturday, Paris St Germain lost at Bordeaux, the stakes were raised. Facing Ligue 1's leading scorers, Bielsa experimented, employing three central defenders and placing his three quickest players, Benjamin Mendy, Giannelli Imbula and Brice Djédjé, across midfield. Ayew, Thauvin and Gignac would lead the attack with Dimitri Payet behind them. Despite his two goals in Toulouse, they were preferred to Batshuayi.

The Vélodrome was fuller and louder than it had been all season. Marseille were the better side. Gignac struck the post and Jérémy Morel was sent off for a reckless tackle, though the defender may have got the ball. Then, in a scramble on the line, Lucas Ocampos appeared to have scored, only for the referee to rule the ball had not crossed the line. The game finished as a goalless draw. Lyon maintained their four-point lead. As they stomped into the home dressing room, Bielsa's players were convinced the gap should be one. It was now that Bielsa began to speak. The players were seated; their manager, wearing a tracksuit, walked up and down the dressing room, talking in Spanish, which was translated into French. He did not look at anyone in particular and the effect was of a teacher, delivering a lecture to a group of intelligent sixth-formers. 'It is very difficult to accept injustice,' Bielsa said.

If you play like you have played today, at the end stands the title. You will get what you deserve. Nothing at the moment will calm you down because you have been killed by this game. Accept the injustice, which balances out at the end. There are nine matches left. If you play like that in those nine matches, be in no doubt, you will get the compensation you deserve – even if it seems impossible to you now. Swallow the venom. It will make you stronger. You will get what you deserve.

Then, raising his voice for the first time, he pointed at his players and said: 'I congratulate you all, every one of you.' The team applauded.

Some of this is fairly standard stuff. 'If you continue play like this, you will get what you deserve' is a phrase uttered by any number of football coaches from the school playing fields to the dressing rooms of the Champions League. However, it is the words Bielsa built around that message that are striking. 'You have been killed by this game . . . Accept the injustice . . . Swallow the venom.' When the speech climaxes with 'I congratulate you all, every one of you,' he almost bows, like an actor. It had the required impact. The following weekend, Marseille found themselves in the coalfields of northern France, playing Lens. They won, 4–0.

Although dressing-room rants make for good anecdotes – there is a film of Neil Warnock turning to one of his defenders who had lost his marker and asking: 'Where were you? In fucking Latvia?' – players generally prefer calm in their managers. Bielsa is not a ranter. The most famous dressing-room scene of all, Liverpool's during the interval of the Champions League final in Istanbul, is generally recalled for its chaos: Rafa Benítez telling Djimi Traoré he was subbed, then telling him he was unsubbed, then sending Liverpool out with twelve players, then telling Didi Hamann to go on. However, what Jamie Carragher remembers is the moment of calm in which Benítez, speaking a language he was not then comfortable with, explained how Liverpool, three down to AC Milan at the break, would go to a 3-5-2 formation with Steven Gerrard and Luis García pushing up against Andrea Pirlo. It changed everything.

For Olympique de Marseille everything now hinged on the game against Paris St Germain at the Vélodrome on Sunday 5 April. Once more they began well – Gignac's powerful, downward header, muscling above Thiago Silva to meet Payet's flamboyant cross, put Marseille one up. They held the lead for five minutes. Blaise Matuidi turned Dja Djédjé on the edge of the Marseille area and shot. The drive faintly brushed Steve Mandanda's gloves before it hit the net. Two minutes before the interval some classic hard, high pressing ripped open a hole in the PSG defence; Gignac ran through and scored. Marseille lost the game because of Zlatan Ibrahimović, whose tally of 156 goals in 180 games made him PSG's record goalscorer. He did not add to those stats in the Vélodrome but he did turn the match.

Four minutes after the interval, he took a frankly dreadful free kick, falling over as he did so. The ball scuttled into the Marseille area, struck a team-mate on the backside and was helped into the net by PSG's Brazilian defender, Marquinhos. The game had barely restarted when Zlatan and Jérémy Morel strove to meet a low cross. In a tangle of legs, the defender got there first and diverted the ball past Mandanda for the fifth and last goal of the match. That Ibrahimović was at Paris St Germain at all was a demonstration of what Marseille and Lyon now had to compete with. In the summer of 2012, he had been water-skiing in the Baltic near his home on the island of Vaxholm. He was playing for AC Milan. He enjoyed it and was very well paid. He returned home to find five missed calls from Mino Raiola. When Ibrahimović got in touch with his agent, he was told Paris St Germain's sporting director, Leonardo, wanted to speak to him. Zlatan had little interest in playing in Ligue 1 and told Raiola to send Leonardo a list of demands so preposterous that no sane football club would accept them. Twenty minutes later, Raiola called back to say Paris St Germain had agreed to everything.

Once more, Marcelo Bielsa's players drank the venom. This time the poison was fatal and Olympique de Marseille were not long a-dying. They lost their next three games, culminating in an extraordinary slugfest at home to Lorient, which finished with the Breton side winning 5–3. *L'Équipe* analysed the defeats that had undone Marseille. Against Caen in February, Marseille were two goals up at home with twenty-seven minutes remaining and somehow contrived to lose, 3–2. Caen's manager, Patrice Garande, pointed out that in the hunt for more goals, too many Marseille players had pushed forward. Bielsa's 4-2-3-1 formation had become a 4-1-4-1 with only one defensive midfielder screening the defence. Suddenly, they were vulnerable.

For the 1–0 defeat at Nantes, *L'Équipe* blamed Bielsa. There had been so many changes at the Stade de la Beaujoire that his tactics had become 'illegible'. At the interval, trailing 1–0, Bielsa had removed a defensive midfielder, Imbula, for an attacking one, Thauvin, who was placed on the left flank. Gignac, who nearly always led the line, was placed behind Batshuayi. Thirteen minutes later, Ocampos was brought on. Thauvin moved to the middle, Romain Alessandrini went to the left wing while Gignac was pushed back into his usual position, ahead of Batshuayi. With eleven minutes remaining, Mario Lemina became the third Marseille footballer to play left wing while Ocampos switched sides. The result was a mess. Marseille controlled the game, had 64 per cent of possession but managed only six shots, of which just two were on target.

They had even more of the ball against Lorient, whose tactics were to defend deep and attempt to hit Marseille on the counter-attack with André Ayew's brother, Jordan, spearheading the thrusts. Jordan scored after nine minutes and before a quarter of an hour was up, they had scored again. By the time, Batshuayi had been brought on, Marseille had no fewer than five forwards on the pitch. Having pulled the game back to 3–3, they conceded twice more in the final six minutes.

There were no more defeats. The last four games were won, three of them easily and all in some style. The fourth was at the Vélodrome against Monaco, who amid the chaos had overtaken Marseille to claim the third and final Champions League place. Bielsa had until now not beaten any of the three clubs that along with Marseille represented the great powers of French football. In contrast, Paris St Germain and Lyon, who finished first and second, did not lose a game to their main rivals.

At kick-off on a Sunday evening in May, Marseille were fifth, five points behind Monaco and behind on goal difference to Saint-Étienne, who the day before had thrashed Nice 5–0. Within fifty seconds the goal difference had grown. João Moutinho put Monaco one up. Just before the interval, Bernardo Silva struck the post. It was the kind of luck that had largely abandoned Olympique de Marseille since Christmas and this time they profited from it. André Ayew equalised and then, three minutes from the end, Alessandrini met Payet's cross and Marseille were two points behind Monaco with two games remaining. The championship had long gone but hopes can be traded down, exchanged. That night the Vélodrome would settle for a place in the Champions League.

There were two points to make up on Monaco, two games to go. There were, however, no more errors. Marseille finished fourth. They were two places and nine points better off than they had been twelve months before. In terms of raw statistics, Bielsa's first season in Marseille had been one of solid achievement – but it was more than this. A city had been energised, there had been winter dreams of a championship. Marseille had scored more goals than in any season since they won the title in 1972. Two years before Bielsa took charge Marseille had finished second, having scored forty-two goals in thirty-eight games, fewer than Troyes, who were relegated in nineteenth place.

French football was changing, turning from the most open big league in Europe to its most sterile. Between 2008 and 2012 five different clubs – Lyon, Bordeaux, Marseille, Lille and Montpellier – had won the championship. Then came the money from Qatar pouring into the Parc des Princes, which blotted out everything else. Paris St Germain won six of the next seven championships. Monaco were the only club to break that sequence. In those years, Olympique de Marseille did not better the fourth-placed finish they achieved under Bielsa and there were not even that many scraps to pick over. Between 2015 and 2018 Paris St Germain won four consecutive Coupes de France and but for a penalty shoot-out with Rennes in the 2019 final, there would have been a fifth.

Bielsa had an impact on even the most awkward of Marseille's players. For Dimitri Payet this had been one of the seasons of his life. Payet recognised he could be difficult to manage. 'I know how to be a dickhead, it is one of my specialities,' he had remarked after refusing to play for West Ham to force a move back to Marseille in January 2017. 'When I want to piss everyone off, I do it.' Payet's relationship with Marcelo Bielsa did not allow him to be a dickhead. 'He made me do things that nobody else did,' he recalled.

On his first day in charge, he said, 'I am going to keep you on a very tight rein.' He knew my potential and he wanted me to show it in every match, every training session. One day when we were preparing to play Lille in the last game before the winter break, I was a little lax. He took me out of the group and told me I didn't have the right to make a mistake.

What impressed Payet was the way Bielsa talked, the language he used:

Bielsa was mad in the way he operated, in his work, in his emotions, the way he celebrated a goal, the victories. He used strong words but he uttered them with such serenity, such calmness. During a pre-match chat, I looked at Steve Mandanda, pointed at the manager and said: 'I would die for him.' How he managed to motivate us was such a crazy thing. His words could take us very far.

The Art of the Deal

As he approached his second season at Marseille, Marcelo Bielsa was offered a fresh two-year contract. It seemed generous enough, worth €10 million. There was, however, a detail he was unhappy with, a detail that would finish his tenure at the Vélodrome. Although his salary would rise from €300,000 to €415,000 a month, only the first year of the contract was guaranteed. If Marseille did not finish in the top four in 2016, the club could terminate the second year. Bielsa, however, wanted a full two-year contract, without preconditions. If he were to be dismissed after the forthcoming season, he wanted the second year of the contract paid in monthly instalments until its expiry date. He was not unreasonable. It is what most managers with his track record would have asked for.

On Wednesday 5 August a meeting was arranged between

Bielsa and the club's executive director, Philippe Perez, and Igor Levin, a lawyer acting for Marseille's owner, Margarita Louis-Dreyfus. According to a report in *Le Parisien*, there was a marked lack of flexibility in Marseille's approach. Levin, the paper commented, 'acted like an American'. Levin was actually Russian, though he practised in New York and he was not a specialist in football contracts. The meeting ended badly. According to the account Bielsa gave two years later, he was told that if he wanted a guaranteed two-year contract, they would impose a 10 per cent cut in its value. Bielsa said: 'Are you sure about what you're doing? Do you represent the president and the owner?' They replied that they did. 'Very good,' said Bielsa, and left the meeting. He wrote his letter of resignation that evening.

His second summer in Provence had been as difficult as the first and again it concerned the transfer market. Players had left whom Bielsa, along with many others in Marseille, believed should have remained at the Vélodrome. Chief among them was Dimitri Payet, who was sold to West Ham. Florian Thauvin went to Newcastle. Giannelli Imbula was sold to Porto. The sales raised €59.8 million but Olympique de Marseille would begin the new season in a weaker state than they had ended the old one. The club had also suddenly grown suspicious of Bielsa. Eight days before, Mexico had fired their manager, Miguel Herrera. He had just led Mexico to victory in the CONCACAF Gold Cup in the United States, which should have guaranteed him the next two years. It bought him four days. As the team queued for their flight home at Philadelphia airport, Herrera became involved in a public and physical altercation with a television reporter, Christian Martinoli, a persistent critic of the team who had been involved in a Twitter argument with Herrera's daughter. When film of the incident with Martinoli was released, Herrera's fate was sealed. The Mexican FA contacted Bielsa to offer him Herrera's job. Bielsa did not reply to these overtures, although in his resignation statement he made reference to having been offered 'three times' the salary he was being paid by Marseille.

Jan Van Winckel, who worked as the club's fitness co-ordinator and had a strong relationship with Bielsa, believed his manager's situation was precarious enough for him to start looking for work in Saudi Arabia. Three days later on a soggy Saturday night came the opening game of what should have been Bielsa's second season at Marseille, at home to Caen. The game was forgotten sooner than the press conference that followed. Andy Delort, who had disappeared without trace in his one season at Wigan, settled the game for Caen with a shot that cannoned in off Steve Mandanda's bar and into the net. Marseille had much the better of the evening. Benjamin Mendy had already struck the post and Caen's goalkeeper, Rémy Vercoutre, performed exceptionally. At the final whistle, Bielsa, wearing a white Marseille shirt, rose from his plastic cooler box and prepared to face the media. Elodie Malatrait, the club's head of press, found him in his office to take him down to the press room. 'I put my head round the door and saw him deep in thought walking around in circles. He could be like that after a defeat. I became alarmed when I saw that his interpreter, who was there with him, was totally white. I realised something was up.'

In the dressing room, his players were in complete ignorance of what he was about to do. Some thought Bielsa's behaviour in informing the press before his own playing staff was at best disrespectful. In the press room, Bielsa discussed the defeat by Caen for a quarter of an hour before he started to read from a letter of resignation to Labrune.

After a series of meetings, we reached agreement on terms to extend the contract for 2016–17. Over the past few months I have been working and thinking everything was cleared up and that all that remained was for it to be stamped. Last Wednesday I was called in to meet with the CEO and the attorney, Igor Levin, and they informed me they would like to adjust some points of the agreement we have previously reached. It was after this meeting that I reached my decision. I am explaining it and it is definite. I don't know if you approved or ignored it but I know that I rejected some important offers to continue at Marseille because I was very interested in the project. However, today I cannot accept this unstable situation brought on by the move to change the terms of the contract. My position is that I will no longer continue working with you. Working together demands a little bit of trust and now we do not have that.

He had not informed Malatrait of what he was about to do and finished the press conference by announcing: 'I have finished my work here. I am going back to my own country.' He then quoted from the letter. When he saw Vincent Labrune for the last time, the president asked, 'What have you done?'

'I told you I did not want to negotiate with the other two,' the manager replied.

'That's not important. We will sign the contract together. I've already told you that.'

'It's too late.'

The club released a statement suggesting they had thwarted a move to hold the club to ransom:

The board of Olympique de Marseille did everything to offer the club a coach who was up to that responsibility but under no circumstances can OM be held prisoner of someone who places their personal interests well above those of an institution. Marseille is imbued with unique values and possesses a sufficiently rich history to refuse to subject itself to the demands of a single man.

It was a defiant, eloquent statement but rather ignored the fact that Bielsa's principal concern was to ensure his contract was paid up if he were sacked rather than to become the dictator of the Vélodrome. For the second successive summer players were being sold against his will. Marseille's behaviour appeared relentlessly provocative.

The magazine *France Football*, like the *Guardian*, employs a columnist called the Secret Footballer, a current professional whose identity is hidden so they can say what they think. The Secret Footballer thought Marseille's enormous expectations had dragged Bielsa down, as it had suffocated so many others. 'Frankly, it's very complicated if you want to play down there. The whole city carries this weight and it transmits itself to the football club.' He compared Marseille to another club famed for the passion of their fans – Lens in the north-eastern coalfields of France. 'It has a superb atmosphere, magnificent stadium and supporters and a certain party mood when you play there. At the Vélodrome, there's something really heavy and you feel it in the air.'

There were some who had expected Bielsa to have left the Vélodrome long before he did. One of those was his translator, Fabrice Olszewski. 'I knew very well that he was not going to stay,' he said.

Did they want him to stay? I don't know but we couldn't continue like that. I thought it would all come to a head earlier. At one time, everyone thought we would be going halfway through the [first] season. When he got annoyed, he would say: 'Shit, I should never have signed for this club.' I thought he would leave on 31 August [the close of the transfer window] because he would have seen the results with the players that he had. It was not what he wanted. Then there were the players he absolutely wanted to keep who had left – Morel, Fanni, Payet.

There were stories of how Steve Mandanda had offered Bielsa a lift and how throughout the journey he had not looked at, much less talked to, his captain. Mandanda was a man who admired him greatly. When Bielsa left, he said it had felt like being struck over the head with a club. Then there was Lucas Ocampos, who had been signed on loan from Monaco and who had turned down an approach from Fiorentina simply because he wanted to be coached by Marcelo Bielsa. The morning after Bielsa's departure, Ocampos was on the edge of tears. Several days after the spilt, there appeared a long, informed analysis of Bielsa's departure in *Libération*, which quoted several anonymous sources. A member of staff was quoted: 'It was a continuous work in progress. You can't keep doing this forever. Bielsa would threaten to leave every time something annoyed him. You cannot live in constant fear of offending someone.' The member of staff said the club had acceded to all of their manager's demands, including his request to be paid in dollars rather than euros because of the more favourable exchange rate. Then there was one of the Marseille players, also quoted anonymously: 'It wasn't a case of liking or hating Bielsa. With him you know it is going to be hard, that you won't have a life, you won't see your family but we were all convinced we would be on the podium come May.'

The thrust of the article was that Bielsa had been given too much power rather than too little, even though *Libération*'s writer, Mathieu Grégoire, acknowledged the club had changed for the better. He quoted the Lyon president, Jean-Michel Aulas, who noted that if Bielsa had worked for him, 'we wouldn't let him have all the keys. You cannot work like that at Olympique Lyonnais. It is as dangerous if he succeeds as if it's a failure.' As his successor there was talk of Jürgen Klopp, who might have appreciated the passion of the Vélodrome but not its politics. Labrune chose the former Real Madrid midfielder Míchel, who had taken Olympiakos to three successive Greek titles. The move was disastrous. When Míchel was sacked in April 2016, Marseille were fifteenth in Ligue 1. They had not won a league match at the Vélodrome for five months; their last victory anywhere had come in February. Only their run in the Coupe de France had given Míchel a stay of execution. Franck Passi, who had been Bielsa's assistant, was now appointed caretaker and promised 'a commando mission' to take the club to the final. This they managed, but waiting for them at the Stade de France was their nemesis, Paris St Germain.

Vincent Labrune did not long survive. The club was up for sale and he left at the end of the season. Marseille's newspaper *La Provence* was scathing. He was, they said, 'the worst president in the history of Olympique de Marseille'.

Returning to Rosario, Bielsa was true to his word. He took none of the jobs offered to him. He could have managed Mexico, he could have returned to Chile to replace Jorge Sampaoli. Instead, he watched some basketball and saw his elder daughter, Inés, play hockey – he could be seen taking notes during the game. In the midst of all this he oversaw something extraordinary – the building of a hotel at Newell's Old Boys training ground at Bella Vista. Bielsa ploughed around $2.5 million of his own money into a building that would provide accommodation for Newell's players and backroom staff before games, a video analysis room, an auditorium, a games room, a kitchen and canteen. It would be called the Hotel Jorge Griffa, after Bielsa's mentor. One of the requirements Bielsa insisted on was that his involvement in funding the project should not be divulged. There was scarcely a chance of that happening. The idea had been presented to Newell's chairman, Guillermo Lorente, in March 2013 by Marcelo's sister, María Eugenia, herself a professional architect. María Eugenia told Lorente that her brother considered that his years at Newell's had been critical to his career and wanted to give something back.

Lucas Bernardi, Newell's then manager, and Gabriel

Heinze were consulted about the requirements of the hotel. Bielsa wanted the hotel to be 'austere, modern and durable'. The players' accommodation was on one side, the coaching staff on another. The rooms were soundproofed to aid sleep and concentration and were decorated in Newell's colours of red and black. In the corridors and common rooms were motivational slogans and pictures of the men who had brought glory to the Coloso del Parque – Heinze, Batistuta, Martino, Rodríguez and Valdano. There was no mention of Bielsa, although the wall by the car park had twenty-two holes in it, and in the language of betting in Argentina, twenty-two is referred to as 'El Loco'. That, surely, was María Eugenia's work.

In November 2018 the Hotel Jorge Griffa was officially opened. It was two days after Leeds had beaten Wigan, and Bielsa was unable to travel back to Rosario. The Coloso del Parque had by then been renamed the Estadio Marcelo Bielsa, something that provoked pride and a certain embarrassment in the man. Now Bielsa was speaking to the crowd via a video link. The speech he delivered displayed the depth of love he had, would always have, for Newell's and the well of respect he nurtured for Jorge Griffa, the man who made him. 'From 1992 until now, I have had very few opportunities to communicate with Newell's fans,' he said.

The last time this happened was when they gave my name to the Coloso del Parque, a day I remember as the happiest of my career. To feel loved and for this to be expressed by 40,000 people has been an emotion that is hard to explain. There are occasions when you cannot express how you feel because the intensity of it overwhelms you. At that moment I knew I didn't deserve the honour. I have lived in close proximity to the last fifty years of Newell's history and, in my opinion, the most important person in that time has been Jorge Griffa. He deserved the recognition that I received. I don't exaggerate when I say that every day, I relive a moment of the twenty years I spent at the club – players, colleagues, staff members, players who never made it, fans, friends, matches, anecdotes, meetings. An infinite number of memories. Excluding my personal life, nothing makes me more emotional than when I recall Newell's. Griffa taught me how to understand football. He was a visionary and there wasn't an aspect of the game he didn't master.

The words 'Gracias Marcelo Bielsa' were projected onto the side of the building. Jorge Griffa officially opened the hotel and predicted Bielsa would return to manage Newell's Old Boys.

In April 2016, eight months after leaving Marseille, he agreed in principle to go to Serie A to manage Lazio. On the surface it appeared a masterly move; the world's most technically astute coach working in the world's most technical league. The results was a fiasco that would see Bielsa resign two days after his appointment was announced. When the approach came, Lazio had just lost the Rome derby 4–1 to Roma. It was a defeat Lazio's manager, Stefano Pioli, did not survive. Lazio would slide to eighth in Serie A, twenty-six points behind Roma in third and thirty-seven adrift of the champions, Juventus.

From the middle of June there were four weeks of intense negotiations between Rome and Rosario in which Bielsa gave Lazio's president, Claudio Lotito, and his sporting director, Igli Tare, a list of players he expected to be signed by 5 July. By the end of June, it seemed the contract was settled. On 6 July the appointment was announced, which provoked a passionate open letter from the Lazio Supporters' Association. 'We will call you "Il Loco,"' they wrote. 'We love the glorious madness of a romantic hero who rises above the nastiness of the game and stands for spiritual superiority and contempt for mediocrity. We warmly welcome you to Lazio's bench and we will support you without prejudice, guaranteeing you the peace of mind a hard-working man deserves.'

This was the kind of reaction Lotito must have craved. The previous season had seen the Lazio ultras mount a boycott of the club's merchandise in protest against the failure to make real headway in Serie A. It had been sixteen years since Lazio won the Scudetto, thirteen since their president, Sergio Cragnotti, the man who oversaw championships,

Coppa Italias and the last ever Cup-Winners' Cup, was forced out to face fraud charges and, ultimately, jail. Lazio had never recovered from the debts of €91 million he left behind – the borrowed cash that paid for the glory.

Lazio announced that Bielsa was due in Rome on 9 July. He never arrived. The day before, he resigned, forty-eight hours after being appointed, blaming Lotito and Tare for failing to sign any of the players he had asked for. He released a statement:

> After four weeks of work we have not got any of the seven transfer targets who were explicitly approved by president Claudio Lotito. It was agreed that we would purchase at least four players before July 5. By this date no signings had materialised. Despite that, the club made the contract public despite the fact it was not enforceable without those promises being kept.

Given there were still eight weeks of the transfer window remaining, Lazio issued their own statement every bit as aggressive as Marseille's had been the previous summer. 'We note with stupefaction the resignation of Marcelo Bielsa and his team in full violation of the contracts signed and deposited with the league.' Lazio supporters, interviewed by the media, talked of enduring the 'umpteenth humiliation' while Ryanair exploited the crisis with an advert, accompanied by a cartoon of Bielsa, offering tickets for €19.99

for those 'needing a speedy getaway from Rome'. Marcelo's sudden resignation carried echoes of his brother Rafael's decision to resign as Argentina's ambassador to France four days after being appointed in December 2005. In a press conference explaining why he could not resign his seat in Congress to take up the position in Paris, Rafael said he had changed his mind because 'men are not like rivers that cannot turn back'.

Eleven years later, Marcelo chose not to face the cameras, although Lazio did call a press conference at their training centre at Formello. Despite Lotito telling the media he would not speak, they had assembled a powerful top table: the club's lawyer, Gian Michele Gentile, the chief executive, Armando Calveri, and the sporting director, Igli Tare. Curiously, throughout the four weeks of negotiations that produced a thirteen-page contract, there appear to have been no face-to-face negotiations between Bielsa and Lazio. Everything seems to have been conducted over the phone or by email. Gentile confirmed that Bielsa had sent a proposed contract, Lazio had returned it with amendments and it had been agreed and deposited with the league on 1 July. He added that there was not a word in the contract about the proposed signing of players, although it would have been highly unusual if there had been. Gentile told the media the club would be seeking damages from Bielsa, although no legal action was ever prosecuted.

Tare was next to speak, telling the press that they had

made approaches for three of the players Bielsa had asked for – Marcos Llorente from Real Madrid, Emanuel Mammana from River Plate and Jérémy Morel, who had played for Bielsa at Marseille and was now at Lyon. Each was designed to shore up Lazio's defence, which had conceded fifty-two goals, more than any other in Serie A's top ten. Llorente was twenty-one, a defensive midfielder from Bernabéu royalty – his father, Paco, had won La Liga under John Toshack, and his great-uncle, Francisco Gento, had played in eight European Cup finals for Real Madrid. Mammana was a year younger and had won the Copa Libertadores with River Plate. Morel was a battle-hardened, known quantity. Lyon blocked both moves, firstly by refusing to negotiate with Tare over Morel and then by beating Lazio to Mammana's signature. Tare said Bielsa was interested in a fourth player, Rodrigo Caio, a twenty-two-year-old centre-half who was playing for São Paulo.

Lazio had been tracking Caio for a couple of years but negotiations were complicated by the fact that São Paulo were still involved in the Copa Libertadores and that Caio would be playing for Brazil in the Olympics in Rio de Janeiro immediately afterwards. If Lazio had been following Caio for two years, they would also have known that in the summer of 2015 a move to Valencia that would have been worth up to €16.5 million had collapsed. As a fifteen-year-old Caio had shattered his kneecap and now three doctors, including the renowned Barcelona-based Ramón Cugat, had deemed his knees not up to the task.

Bielsa asked about Jean Beausejour, whom he had managed for Chile, and Alexandre Pato. The latter might once have proved a formidable centre-forward. He had scored fifty goals in Serie A in his first four seasons with AC Milan but then the Brazilian's hamstrings had repeatedly given way. He had returned to Brazil with Corinthians but loan spells at São Paulo and Chelsea had not halted the decline. 'Bielsa asked for Pato but I doubted his physical condition,' Tare said.

Bielsa assured me he could train him up. We had a meeting with Pato's agent to formulate a four-year contract which would have been a figure near to what we had paid Miroslav Klose [€2.1 million a year]. I talked to Pato but he told me that, for personal reasons, he didn't want to leave Brazil. I had a talk with Bielsa about the Pato contract. A third person told him that the numbers [we were quoting] were not true. I would have resigned if the figures I had given were not paid.

Lotito was not due to speak to the media at Formello but such was the anger directed towards him by journalists when they were told the president would not be taking questions that, backed into a corner, he faced the microphones. 'We made an act of love to the fans. Everyone said Lazio did not make people dream,' he remarked, confirming that Simone Inzaghi, whose goals had taken Lazio to the

Scudetto under Sven-Göran Eriksson, would step up from youth-team coach to manage the club. 'We want to bring back the Lazio-ness into the dressing room,' Lotito said. It was the kind of remark football club owners deliver when they have nothing else to say. If the only thing Inzaghi brought was the fact he had worn a sky-blue shirt, the club was in serious trouble.

In fact, Inzaghi proved a surprisingly effective manager, taking Lazio to a couple of Coppa Italia finals and some fifth-place finishes, which was probably the limit of their resources. As for Bielsa, he had now left Marseille after one match and Lazio after two days. He was still a coach in demand but the glow of that first season in Bilbao and the opening four months in Marseille were starting to fade on the horizon.

The Gang of Three

Nobody knows how things will turn out. There is a story of two extras running through a cheap papier-mâché set that seems to wobble in time with their footsteps. The camera stops; the extras take off their helmets and lay down their plastic guns. 'Is this the worst film you've ever been involved with?' says one to the other. The film was *Star Wars*. For Marcelo Bielsa, Lille was a *Heaven's Gate*, something that possessed an epic cast, a vast budget and an acclaimed director but which dragged everyone down with it.

The cast assembled by Lille's president, Gerard López, appeared exceptional. Luís Campos, the man whose transfer dealings had allowed Monaco to break Paris St Germain's monopoly of the French League, would be the sporting director. Marc Ingla, the man who had turned Barcelona into a commercial giant, would be the chief executive, while Bielsa would coach the players. The target would be a top-five finish.

Perhaps because each of the three believes he should be in sole charge, triumvirates tend to fall apart. The first one, composed of Rome's two greatest generals, Julius Caesar and Pompey, backed by the empire's wealthiest man, Crassus, saw them all die violent deaths. Bielsa's fate was not nearly so bloody, but he would end up in a restaurant sitting alone on a table by a drinks refrigerator watching his team on a laptop. It would be a death of sorts.

Above them all was López, who had been born in Luxembourg, studied in Miami and become a hugely successful venture capitalist. He had bought the Renault Formula One team and allowed Vladimir Putin to drive one of their cars around an airfield. Given López now has extensive business interests in Russia, this was a shrewd move. López assembled one of the finest car collections in the world, cars that had won Le Mans, Daytona; a Jensen Interceptor here, a 1968 Cadillac Fleetwood there. In January 2017 he bought LOSC Lille and announced he would create something he called LOSC Unlimited.

His money bought López one of the most spectacular stadiums in Europe, the Pierre Mauroy, named after the man who had been mayor of Lille for twenty-eight years and served as François Mitterrand's prime minister. The Stade Pierre Mauroy featured a retractable roof and a pitch that could be raised and slid away to allow the staging of basketball, tennis or concerts. It would form a spectacular stage for López's ambitions.

A month after taking over the club, López made his move for Bielsa, who flew to France in February, taking in Paris St Germain's 4–0 win over Barcelona at the Parc des Princes – a victory that would be spectacularly over-turned in the Nou Camp. It was a result that suggested things should not be taken at face value. Bielsa signed his contract on Valentine's Day and like many romances, this one would end up in court.

López made Bielsa the highest-paid manager in Ligue 1. His salary of €500,000 a month after tax was, according to *L'Équipe*, a third more than Paris St Germain paid Unai Emery. With him were his long-time collaborators: Diego Reyes, Pablo Quiroga, who was in charge of video analysis, Diego Flores and Gabriel Macaya, who would oversee phys-ical conditioning. At their first press conference Bielsa appeared buoyant, prepared to exchange jokes with the reporters. 'My first piece of advice was from my wife,' he said. 'She told me to smile and to look you reporters in the eye. I am trying to do that now. It is definitely a step forward for me in terms of human relations.'

Campos was one of the game's most sought-after indi-viduals. At the age of twenty-seven he moved from being União Leiria's physio to managing the club and went on to coach a series of minor Portuguese sides, including José

Mourinho's hometown team, Vitória Setúbal. Both Mourinho and Carlos Queiroz – men who were to manage Real Madrid – became fans of his methods. When Mourinho arrived in Madrid after taking Inter Milan to the European Cup, he asked Campos to join him. However, Campos's greatest success was to come at Monaco. When he left the Bernabéu with Mourinho in 2013, Monaco had just been promoted back to Ligue 1. The club was the property of the Russian oligarch Dmitry Rybolovlev, who had been brought up in Perm, a city where the ballet impresario Sergei Diaghilev was born. Both men would spend plenty of time on the French Riviera.

At first Rybolovlev did what Russian oligarchs traditionally do. He spent large sums of money on big-name players. Radamel Falcao, James Rodríguez and João Moutinho arrived in the principality. Under Claudio Ranieri, Monaco finished second in Ligue 1. Then Rybolovlev stopped spending. Like many Russian oligarchs, he feared the long, cold reach of Moscow and thought a Monégasque passport would offer additional protection. When the authorities in Monaco refused to grant him one, Rybolovlev asked himself why he should spend any more money on their football team. Then came a very expensive divorce from his wife, Elena, which allegedly led to him dispersing his art collection, which included works by Picasso, Gauguin and Klimt.

Above it all, and directly impacting on AS Monaco, were

Uefa's financial fair play regulations. Monaco, a small club owned by a billionaire that spent big and had relatively few alternative sources of income, was an obvious target. This is when Campos began to shine. He began scouring football for fresh talent and promoting it from within. He created the team of Kylian Mbappé, Bernardo Silva and Benjamin Mendy that was to win the French title and reach the semi-finals of the Champions League in 2017. Mbappé, Silva and Mendy were later sold to Paris St Germain and Manchester City for combined fees of €290 million.

When he left for Lille, Campos warned Monaco that, if they did not follow this programme of scouting and then selling players, 'they will quickly collapse because the other revenues – ticketing, merchandising and television rights – are insufficient'. This was to prove prophetic. Within eighteen months Monaco were floundering in the relegation zone, employing Thierry Henry in a futile attempt to stop the haemorrhaging. Henry lasted 104 days. It cost Monaco around €10 million to fire him.

As he set off for Lille, Campos also remarked, 'I don't want to appear arrogant but I assure you I will create another masterpiece in my career.' This prediction was to prove less accurate. What Bielsa only found out later was that Campos had always been against his appointment as coach. The gang of three would be split from the beginning.

Marc Ingla was the third member of the triumvirate that would supposedly drive Lille towards a championship they had won as recently as 2011. He was close to the two men who were to underpin the Manchester City of Pep Guardiola: Ferran Soriano and Txiki Begiristain. When Ingla joined the board at Barcelona in 2003, they had just finished sixth in La Liga, twenty-two points behind Real Madrid. In the summer Sir Alex Ferguson offered them David Beckham. The world's most famous footballer would publicly snub them for the Bernabéu. Barcelona's motto was 'More than a Club', but commercially they were very much less than they appeared. In terms of income, Barcelona were the thirteenth biggest team in Europe. Within five years, Ingla had overseen the transformation of Barcelona's commercial operations and become vice-president of football affairs, in which capacity he would appoint Guardiola as manager. He and Soriano had brought business techniques unknown even in a club as vast as Barcelona. He told the *Independent*'s Jack Pitt-Brooke: 'We exported it into the world of football, where even in amazing-brand clubs the level of professionalism is very low and the level of amateurism is very high.' Lille, he said, needed to be 'shaken up on all fronts, the sporting front, the economic front and the image-projection front'.

The management front had been a mess for some time. Bielsa was the sixth man to manage Lille in two years – or the seventh if you counted Patrick Collot's two stints as caretaker. They had not had a permanent manager since November 2016 when Frédéric Antonetti, who had salvaged the club from relegation and taken them to a League Cup final, was sacked. Since he had three and a half years of his contract still to run, he was due €840,000 in compensation. Lille were then second bottom. Under the interim management of Collot, who had been the club's reserve-team coach, Lille had risen to fourteenth when López was installed as president in January. They slid back towards the relegation zone. Collot was shunted back to the reserve team and Franck Passi was brought in to lead the club until Bielsa could take over in the summer.

Passi was designed to smooth the way for Bielsa. When Bielsa first arrived at Olympique de Marseille in 2014, Passi had been José Anigo's assistant. Bielsa had little idea who he was until he called him over. 'What would you like to do here?'

'I am a coach. If you have a coaching job for me, that would be good. If you don't have one, then I will go and see the staff and say goodbye.'

'No,' said Bielsa. 'I'll always need a coach.'

So began a relationship that, initially, worked well at Olympique de Marseille and it might have been better for everyone if it had been repeated at Lille. However, after leading the club to eleventh place and safety, Passi resigned and announced he would be leaving. They would have a last, long talk at the training ground at Luchin, which resembled a rural hotel in its own grounds. Bielsa was already making changes. A relaxation room was being installed, and there would be bungalows built for the staff and the players. There was to be a sharp reduction in Lille's playing staff. On 3 July, three days after he officially started work, he went to see a dozen players after they had completed their recovery from training and told them they had no future at the club. One of those told to leave was Éric Bauthéac, a thirty-year-old attacking midfielder signed from Nice two years before. 'I have never met a bloke like him,' Bauthéac reflected. 'He called us together and said in Spanish: "Okay guys, I don't want you. Thank you and goodbye."' The twelve had six weeks before the end of the transfer window on 31 August to find another club. 'It was a little bit like *Big Brother*. At the start there were twelve of us and each week there was one who left,' said Bauthéac. 'On 31 August there were seven of us, if I remember rightly, but five would see their contracts expire at midnight. I made the final two, along with Vincent Enyeama.' The keeper, who had made more than a hundred appearances for Nigeria and played in three World Cups, had just turned thirty-five. He chose to see out the remainder of his contract without appearing in another game for Lille. Bauthéac travelled to Australia to play for Brisbane Roar.

Lille spent €70 million in the summer of 2017, more than any other club save Paris St Germain and Monaco. Bielsa watched a video of every game the twenty-two-year-old forward Nicolas Pépé had played for Angers. The midfielder, Thiago Mendes, arrived from São Paulo; Kévin Malcuit, an attacking full-back, was brought in from Saint-Étienne. When, two years later, Pépé was transferred to Arsenal for €75 million, the whole of that summer was paid for in a single transaction. Mendes and Malcuit earned a further €31 million. This was precisely what the Bielsa–Campos partnership was supposed to do.

Arriving at Luchin, Pépé thought Bielsa's training methods extraordinary. 'Tactically, he was very pernickety. There were no games, just a lot of sessions based on videos. It was something we'd not seen done before. For us it was bizarre and a revelation.' The opening game was at home to Nantes. On each bench sat a miracle worker. Bielsa on one, Ranieri, the man who had taken Leicester to the Premier League title, on the other. Lille won comfortably, 3–0. As dawns go, it was an utterly false sunrise. Lille would not win another game for three months. In that time, they would score three goals.

Lille's second match of the season was a portent of what was to come. They would be at Strasbourg, who were playing their first game in Ligue 1 since 2008. By the time the match was forty minutes gone, Bielsa had made three substitutions. Thiago Mendes and Kévin Malcuit had been lost to injury while Fodé Ballo-Touré was removed for tactical reasons. Nevertheless, the very least Lille might have expected to take away from the Stade de la Meinau was a draw until their goalkeeper, Mike Maignan, decided to throw the ball into an opponent's face. For that he was dismissed and Bielsa, having used his substitutes, ordered his centre-forward, Nicolas de Préville, to go in goal. Once Strasbourg had scored, Bielsa ordered De Préville to hand over the gloves to his captain, Ibrahim Amadou, and go back up front. Strasbourg scored twice more; the last goal was put away by a player called Grimm.

De Préville, who had been Lille's best striker the previous season, started one more match, a 1–1 draw against Angers in which he scored the equaliser before he was sold to Bordeaux for €10 million. There was no logical reason for the club to sell their leading scorer except for an urgent requirement to raise money. The results worsened. The next six matches would see them score two goals and take two points.

Before they played Monaco on 22 September, Bielsa rounded on journalists who thought he might resign and walk away as he had done at Marseille. 'The problem is you don't know anything,' he retorted. 'I am not going to leave; I am not going to resign for any reason. The only possibility of me not being here any more is if I am relieved of my duties – and whether that happens is not up to me.' Monaco won, 4–0.

Worse was to come. A week later, Lille found themselves at newly promoted Amiens. Their stadium, La Licorne, was small but striking. The stands were overhung by clear plastic walls and roofs that gave the impression you were playing between giant bus shelters. In the fifteenth minute,

Lille broke through but as Ballo-Touré ran towards the Lille fans behind the goal and danced in front of them, they surged forward. La Licorne had seats but they had no backs: they were simply bits of plastic bolted to the terraces. A crash barrier gave way and scores of supporters were flung to the ground. Some struck concrete, others the advertising boards. Twenty-nine were injured, seven seriously, and the game was abandoned. Fans of other clubs, including Nice and Marseille, had complained about safety at Amiens. One Lille fan, Georges Penel, a twenty-one-year-old who suffered leg and back injuries, recounted: 'I don't even know who scored. It [the barrier] just suddenly fell on me. I couldn't hear anything; I couldn't see anything and then the emergency workers took me away.' Amiens' chairman, Bernard Joannin, blamed a surge of 'more than 500 Lille fans' against a barrier which he claimed 'was in perfect condition'. After protests from Gerard López, the comments were withdrawn.

In October, Lille, who had fallen to nineteenth in Ligue 1, played Valenciennes in the League Cup and won through only on penalties. RMC Sport, a radio station based in Monaco, quoted an unnamed Lille player who alleged the squad disliked Bielsa's 3-3-1-3 formation, wanted something less rigid and were on the edge of revolt. 'Several players are fed up with not playing in their proper positions. Our aim is clear – to tell the coach we cannot put up with his tactics any more. We have to tell him; otherwise we are going over a cliff.' There were no brakes and there was more than one driver. As the relationship between Bielsa and some of his players began to corrode, so did that between Bielsa and Campos, who felt he should have had far more control and repeated the criticism made by Lyon's president, Jean-Michel Aulas, of Bielsa at Marseille. He had been given the keys to too many rooms.

There were few outright calls for Bielsa to go. At the Stade Pierre Mauroy some supporters unveiled a banner that declared, 'Our Patience is not Unlimited.' As slogans went, it was more like a letter to the *Daily Telegraph* than an explicit threat. At the beginning of November, the club decided to stage an open training session. Bielsa did not attend and those supporters who had come to Luchin expressed their disappointment to the Lille newspaper, *La Voix du Nord*. They would have liked to have seen him put the team through their paces. There was not much training but there were plenty of autographs signed and there was another banner that said, 'Metz Is Your Last Chance.' It was aimed at the players rather than the manager.

The warning was heeded. Metz, bottom of Ligue 1, were beaten 3–0. Another three were put past Saint-Étienne. Nicolas Pépé scored half of those six goals. Three days later came the rearranged match at Amiens. Again, there were three goals. Lille, however, scored none of them. For the first time, supporters on social media began calling for Bielsa's dismissal. They would not have long to wait. News came that Luis Bonini, the man who had worked alongside Bielsa for more than twenty years, was dying of stomach cancer. Bielsa asked the club for permission to fly to Santiago so he could be with him for one last time. The request was refused. Bielsa informed the club that he was going to see his friend and 'they could do what they had to do'.

He flew to Santiago on LATAM, Chile's national airline, on an economy-class ticket. A flight attendant, recognising the man who had been Chile's national manager, offered Bielsa a seat in business class. 'No thank you,' he was reported to have said. 'I paid to go economy and I will travel economy.' Bonini died on 22 November 2017. On the same day, Marcelo Bielsa was 'suspended' as manager of Lille. The news was announced on the club's website at 10.15pm. Lille announced that Luis Campos would take a greater role in the direction of a team that was now deep in the relegation zone.

One of Campos's proteges, João Sacramento, was appointed to run team affairs, alongside Fernando da Cruz, the club's head of recruitment, Benoît Delaval, the conditioning coach, who would join Bielsa at Leeds, and the goalkeeping coach, Franck Mantaux. Sacramento was twenty-eight and had been Lille's video analyst. However, as relations between Campos and Bielsa cooled, Sacramento found himself side-lined. In September, he had asked Bielsa for permission to go on holiday, which Bielsa had refused. In *La Voix du Nord* an unnamed member of Lille's staff said of Sacramento:

'He has a lot of knowledge, is brilliant but also very ambitious. His ambitions could not gel with Bielsa's personality because he felt Sacramento was Campos's eyes and ears.' In November 2019 when Tottenham dismissed Mauricio Pochettino, Sacramento became José Mourinho's assistant.

Lille's first match without Bielsa was at Montpellier. Bielsa was photographed in a modest restaurant watching the game on a laptop with what looked like a bag for life at his feet. He would watch as the 3-3-1-3 formation, which Campos thought far too fragile, was replaced by a more standard 4-2-3-1. There was no change in the result: Montpellier won 3–0. The club had chosen to 'suspend' rather than sack Bielsa because to pay up a contract that ran until June 2019 would cost €14 million and Lille were becoming seriously concerned about money. They were being investigated by the Direction Nationale du Contrôle de Gestion, which oversaw financial fair play and guarded against financial corruption in French football. The DNCC wanted to know the source of Lille's €70 million summer transfer spend. If they thought the money had not come from club funds, Lille faced a fine, a transfer embargo or, in serious cases, demotion. For much of the season it appeared Lille would do the job for them by getting themselves relegated. Lille would be banned from making any signings during the January transfer window.

Five days after his dismissal, Bielsa began an action to recover the balance owing on his contract. He was acting not just for himself but also for his backroom staff. As was his custom, his salary at Lille included those who worked directly for him. The pre-contract that Bielsa had signed in February contained a 'parachute clause', guaranteeing him the full balance of his contract 'whatever the reasons for it being broken'. The full contract, signed on 1 July, contained no such clause. The club responded by making their own legal claim of *faute grave*. By this they meant Bielsa was not due the full balance of his contract because of the serious errors he had made while in office. In this, the post-match press conferences in which Bielsa invariably accepted responsibility for defeat would count against him. In March 2018, an industrial tribunal ruled against Bielsa, attacked the way the contractual dispute had been played out in the media and ordered him to pay €300,000 in damages for bringing a case without due cause, while admitting it did not have the authority to rule on the settlement of his contract.

Lille's lawyer, Bertrand Wambeke, remarked: 'Marcelo Bielsa has tried to play poker with the finances of the club and its employees and he has lost.' If Wambeke and Lille thought this was the end of the matter, they were mistaken. In June 2019, by which time Bielsa had been at Leeds for a year, he announced he would still be pursuing Lille for damages, which would be €19 million for himself and €4 million for his four assistants, three of whom had followed him to Elland Road. The basis of his case was that Bielsa's name had been key to the recruitment of players, like Pépé, whom Lille had then sold on for substantial profits. His lawyer, Benjamin Cabago, said: 'Marcelo's arrival helped the club obtain the necessary contributions to finance a business project based on the principle of player trading with the goal of quick return on investments.' Bielsa said he would be prepared to appear himself before the court.

In his absence, Lille played out the remainder of their season in a pool of poison. Two hundred supporters poured into the directors' box during a game against Nice. Behind the goal a banner was unfurled accusing the players and directors of 'Dirtying Our Club'. Banned from making transfers, Lille attempted to induce their South African striker, Lebo Mothiba, to break his loan arrangement with Ligue 2 Valenciennes by offering him an extended contract and five times his original salary. Valenciennes resisted, accusing Lille of 'holding us to ransom'. Lille made a payment of €1 million to bring Mothiba back to the Pierre Mauroy, which proved value for money. On 28 April Lille, who were second from bottom, exactly where Bielsa left them, faced Metz, who were in last place.

In the past four and a half months, Lille had won a single game. Now Metz were beaten 3–1. Two goals in the last ten minutes overcame Toulouse, 3–2, and then in the final game of a dreadful season at the Pierre Mauroy they beat Dijon 2–1 to ensure their safety. Mothiba scored both goals. The season ended appropriately with a 5–0 thrashing at Saint-Étienne.

Along with Club América, his four months at Lille would count as the most unequivocal failure of Marcelo Bielsa's career. In interviews afterwards, Luis Campos attempted to argue that Bielsa had been given too much power and that his fatal mistake had been to rid the club of its more experienced footballers. When things started to sour, there were few battle-hardened voices in the dressing room to stop the slide. This, and a refusal to alter his tactics to something more flexible, doomed him.

It seems likelier, however, that there were too many loud voices at the Stade Pierre Mauroy rather than too few. López, Campos, Ingla and Bielsa were all powerful men and were possessed of the certainties of powerful men. At times it was difficult to know who was in charge and whether the signings had been made by Campos or Bielsa. Underlying everything was the realisation that López's project, at least initially, did not have the money everyone thought it did. A few months after saving Lille, Mothiba was sold on because the club was in dire need of the €4 million fee.

Asked to sum up Marcelo Bielsa's time in northern France, Gerard López admitted he had made 'a casting error'.

PART THREE:
YORKSHIRE

Room at the Top

They were in a car, the chairman and the director of football. They were discussing who might manage Leeds United. Andrea Radrizzani asked Victor Orta who he would choose if money were no object. Orta nominated Marcelo Bielsa, adding that it would be 'impossible of course'. Radrizzani did not like being told things were impossible and urged Orta to make a call.

Orta knew Bielsa. He had been a journalist who had commentated on the 2004 Olympic football final in Athens. More significantly, at Sevilla he had worked with Ramón Verdejo – better known as Monchi – who, perfecting techniques employed by Bielsa in Rosario and Mexico, had discovered talents such as Sergio Ramos and José Antonio Reyes. The careers of Ivan Rakitić and Freddie Kanouté had been revived while his transfers included Dani Alves and Júlio Baptista. Between 2006 and 2016, Sevilla won the Europa League five times.

From Andalucia, Orta had gone to Zenit St Petersburg where money was not a problem, to Elche where it was. He worked under Aitor Karanka at Middlesbrough, whose chairman, Steve Gibson, praised him for the transfers that saw them promoted to the Premier League and held Orta responsible for the poor deals that resulted in their relegation in 2017. A few weeks later, he found himself at Elland Road. There was something of Bielsa in Orta. As a boy growing up in Madrid, he was obsessive about football, waiting outside the team hotels on the off chance of an autograph or obsessively reading Spain's football newspapers. His first job was with Radio Marca, analysing La Liga.

Orta tried to call Bielsa himself but received no reply to his messages. When he got through, he told his chairman that Bielsa had already watched seven Leeds matches on video. By the time they met Bielsa face to face, in a Buenos Aires hotel, he had watched ten more games and, according to Radrizzani, 'knew the names and characteristics of all our players and the boys in the reserves'. Bielsa was not the only option Radrizzani was considering. The manager he really wanted to bring to Leeds was Antonio Conte, who had just been sacked by Chelsea despite bringing the FA Cup to Stamford Bridge, a year after winning the title. 'I don't deny I made an attempt for Conte,' Radrizzani told *La Gazzetta dello Sport*. 'I have a weakness for him. I would have offered him €20 million. It would have been a shock offer but with him we would have been guaranteed the Premier League.' There was an attempt to persuade Roberto Martínez to return to England after the World Cup, although since he was in charge of a fabulously talented Belgium side that was destined to finish third in Russia, they knew it was a forlorn hope.

Claudio Ranieri – 'an exquisite gentleman' in Radrizzani's words – had got as far as an interview but confessed he would prefer to wait for an opportunity in top-flight football. In November 2018 Ranieri got his wish with Fulham, although they would not be a Premier League club for very long. Ranieri lasted seventeen matches.

There was a second flight to Buenos Aires. This time the Leeds delegation consisted of Victor Orta and the chief executive, Angus Kinnear. There was another marathon meeting – by now Bielsa had examined the plans of the Thorp Arch training ground, which was considerably more modern and impressive than Elland Road. Of all the money Peter Ridsdale had spent in a vain attempt to take Leeds back to the summit of English football at the turn of the century, very little had gone on the stadium. Blackburn and Newcastle may also have fallen back after their challenges to Manchester United were exhausted, but Ewood and St James' Park remained sleek testimony to the investments of Jack Walker and Sir John Hall. With the exception of the towering East Stand, Elland Road still looked much like

Don Revie had left it in 1974. However, £5 million had been spent redeveloping Thorp Arch and when Bielsa met the Leeds delegation in Buenos Aires he possessed a blueprint of the training ground.

In response to the delegation's question as to what Bielsa knew of the Championship, he brought out several sheets of paper detailing how each of Leeds' opponents played. Kinnear would confess that one manager they interviewed could not name a single one of Leeds United's players. Nevertheless, when they returned to Ezeiza airport, Kinnear confessed to being unsure whether they had got their man or not. They would not have long to wait.

Radrizzani and Orta were united by the desire to bring in a major name. It would be cheaper to hire a world-class head coach – Bielsa's salary of €3 million would make him easily the highest-paid manager in the Championship – and revolutionise an existing squad than it would be to buy in a range of players who might not gel. In the world of English second-division football, only Rafa Benítez at Newcastle had ever been paid more.

Their last appointment had been Paul Heckingbottom. His Yorkshire credentials had been impeccable. He was born in Barnsley. He had played for them and, as a manager, had won them promotion to the Championship. He had also played for Bradford and Sheffield Wednesday. Outside the Broad Acres, he was not a name. He had lasted four months. Heckingbottom was the seventeenth full-time manager Leeds had appointed in the sixteen years since David O'Leary was sacked for failing to qualify for the Champions League. Leeds tried men who were close to the chairman (Dennis Wise), men who had been heroes at Elland Road (Gary McAllister), men who were specialists in winning promotion (Neil Warnock), men whom nobody had heard of (Dave Hockaday). Nothing had seemed to work. It was the same in the boardroom, now free of the rented goldfish that had become one of the symbols of Ridsdale's regime where everything had been bought on tick. The goldfish had been rented so somebody from the rental company would be guaranteed to feed them. There was, apparently, nobody at Leeds United who could put fish food into a tank.

Peter Ridsdale was a Leeds fan who as a boy was entranced by the floodlights of Elland Road. He often watched Leeds on his own. In 1965 he took a sleeping bag and spent the night queuing for a ticket to watch them in the FA Cup final against Liverpool. By 1998 he was running the club he adored. Beside him was his executive director, Allan Leighton, whose father had run a local Co-op and who had transformed Asda into a retail giant. In the dug-out was David O'Leary, a young, intelligent Dubliner, who had won the title with Arsenal. On the pitch were the products of Howard Wilkinson's youth policy – Alan Smith, Harry Kewell, Jonathan Woodgate, Stephen McPhail and Paul Robinson – the greatest windfall a Premier League manager would receive since Alex Ferguson inherited the Class of 92 at Old Trafford.

It should have been enough, but it was not. Ridsdale authorised heavy spending on some of the best young British footballers – Rio Ferdinand, Dominic Matteo, Michael Bridges, Seth Johnson. Then Robbie Keane, Mark Viduka and Robbie Fowler were signed from Inter Milan, Celtic and Liverpool. At one time, the club had a roster of six top-class strikers.

In 2000, Leeds United finished third, their highest position since winning the title in 1992. The following year, they reached the semi-finals of the Champions League. They played AC Milan, Barcelona, Lazio and Real Madrid. It was swaggering stuff. All of this was financed by a loan of £60 million, the largest ever raised by an English football club. It was secured on future sales of season tickets and corporate hospitality. All the revenue from their fans was put into a locked account. Every 1 September, the loan was repaid from this account. On the surface it seemed a loan Leeds could manage. In 2001, the year they played Valencia in the semi-finals of the Champions League, their revenue was £86 million. Their profit was £10 million. Ticket sales were up by 33 per cent, merchandising by 40 per cent. Matteo, who had been persuaded to swap Anfield for Elland Road, noted that Leeds used far more luxurious aircraft for their European away games than Liverpool did. When Liverpool won the Champions League in 2005, they returned home from Istanbul in a bog-standard Boeing 737 which had so little room in the cabin that the European Cup had to be strapped into one of the seats.

By then Ridsdale had left Leeds, the club had been relegated and the goldfish had gone back. Elland Road was in the process of being sold. The club was sliding towards administration. Ridsdale's business model relied on regular qualification for the Champions League. They spent only one season in Europe's elite competition and, once the semi-final to Valencia was lost, those revenues would never be regained. In the middle of all this two Leeds players, Woodgate and Lee Bowyer, were facing charges of causing grievous bodily harm with intent after Sarfraz Najeib, a twenty-one-year-old from Rotherham, had been beaten up outside a nightclub. Bowyer was acquitted; Woodgate was convicted of affray. The publicity was appalling: the footballers seemed out of control, and there were desperate denials that there was a racist connotation to the incident. Ridsdale made steadfast public pleas that Leeds United were not on trial. O'Leary published a book called *Leeds United on Trial*. Ridsdale sacked him. The club owed £83 million. Debt repayments were running at £1 million a month.

By Sunday 3 November 2002, Leeds were doomed. They had lost 1–0 at home to Everton. They were thirteenth in the Premier League, and there was no chance of the Champions League football that would rescue them. Ridsdale and his new manager, Terry Venables, loathed each other. There was a fire sale of players, each departure weakening the team. The only question was when it would all collapse. In May 2004, after a 4–1 defeat at Bolton, they were relegated.

Leeds plunged and plunged, they fell and fell. There was administration, there were fifteen-point penalties. Relegation to the third tier of the game; league fixtures with Hartlepool; elimination in the second round of the FA Cup by Histon. There was Ken Bates as chairman and then Massimo Cellino, a convicted Italian fraudster, who retired the number 17 shirt at Leeds because it was 'unlucky' and interfered constantly.

In January 2017, Radrizzani, against all advice, bought a 50 per cent stake in Leeds. By May, he had bought out Cellino entirely. There were some poor decisions, like the one to redesign the Leeds badge which displayed a slightly fascistic emblem of a man punching his heart with his fist. There was the post-season tour to Burma, which was riven by genocidal conflict. However, Radrizzani got the big decisions right. Elland Road, which had been sold following the collapse, was bought back. The women's football team was reincorporated into the club. A world-class manager was signed.

A glance at the balance sheet made you wonder why he bothered. In May 2017, the month Radrizzani took full control, every Championship club but one – Wolverhampton Wanderers – had declared a loss. Sixteen of the clubs had a wages-to-turnover ratio of more than 100 per cent. In other words, they spent more on their staff alone than their total income. Nottingham Forest's wages-to-turnover ratio was 166 per cent. It was the same at Brentford. At Middlesbrough, which Victor Orta had just left, it was 149 per cent. The Championship was an arena in which you could lose a lot of money very quickly. Judged by turnover, Leeds were the fifth-biggest club in the Championship, but largely because of their vast fanbase, they had the lowest wages-to-turnover ratio of any of their opponents – 60 per cent.

A year after Radrizzani assumed control, Leeds had raised their revenue by £11 million to £41 million; but they had dropped to sixth in the Championship's money table – behind Aston Villa, Sunderland, Middlesbrough, Norwich and Hull. However, below the headline figure there were solid grounds for optimism. Leeds' commercial income was, at £22 million, almost double that of the Championship's next biggest clubs, Aston Villa and Norwich. Their average home gate of 31,521 was second behind Aston Villa.

Bringing Marcelo Bielsa to Leeds was the greatest coup achieved by any club outside the top flight since Newcastle persuaded Kevin Keegan to come to St James' Park in 1982, three years after he was voted European Footballer of the Year for the second time. There were emotional ties linking Keegan to the North-East. His grandfather, Frank Keegan, had been a miner in the Durham coalfield and had attempted to rescue his workmates when an explosion tore through the West

Stanley pit in 1909 killing 168 men and boys. On the surface, Leeds had nothing like that kind of emotional attraction for Marcelo Bielsa, except for the fact that at Athletic Bilbao and Marseille, he had gone for big, passionately supported clubs that were in need of an injection of his kind of revivalist football. Leeds is the biggest city in the biggest county in England. It should be a Dallas, a Munich, a Seville, a Turin. Somehow, it was none of these things.

Leeds United possessed an enormous advantage. It was the only professional football club in the biggest city in the biggest county in England. Even in decline this fact alone made Leeds powerful. When Marcelo Bielsa first arrived at Elland Road in the summer of 2018, Leeds was the biggest city in Europe not to have a top-flight football team. The potential had always been obvious. In October 1988, Howard Wilkinson was offered the Leeds United job. He was managing Sheffield Wednesday in the city where he was born. Sheffield Wednesday were fifth in the First Division, above Liverpool, above Manchester United, six points behind the improbable leaders, Norwich. Leeds were twenty-first in the Second Division, sandwiched between Bournemouth and Shrewsbury. Elland Road had bigger crowds than Hillsborough. Wilkinson chose Leeds.

When interviewed by the journalist Anthony Clavane, for his book *A Yorkshire Tragedy*, Wilkinson explained his choice, in terms not just of the football clubs but also the cities themselves: 'Leeds in the mid-to-late eighties had a lot more going for it as a city. It was becoming a big financial and banking centre. There was a lot more wealth than in Sheffield. I dropped down a division to manage them but I felt Leeds had more potential.' Within four years, Wilkinson had made them champions of England. There was talk of Leeds becoming 'the capital of the north'. There was opposition from Newcastle. St James' Park was the most glamorous stadium in the country. The Quayside, which in the opening titles to *Whatever Happened to the Likely Lads* – first broadcast in 1973 – was a place of wharves and warehouses was filled with bars, clubs and hotels. In the event, neither won. The unofficial title, like so many Premier League trophies, went to Manchester but the potential was still there, just below the surface.

This had not been Bielsa's first flirtation with English football. In the summer of 2015, after Sam Allardyce had been sacked for not playing 'the West Ham way', he was targeted by the club's owners, David Sullivan and David Gold. Bielsa had just completed his first, successful season at Marseille. Unai Emery, who had just taken Sevilla to a second successive Europa League trophy, was another candidate. However, Slaven Bilić, whose success in knocking Liverpool out of the Europa League had not been enough to keep his job at Beşiktaş, was the one appointed.

Bielsa gave his first press conference at Elland Road on 25 June. In England there was a heatwave, prompting Radrizzani to welcome reporters to the 'Costa del Yorkshire'.

There were similarities to his arrival in Marseille four years before. It was in the midst of a World Cup. In both cases Argentina would be playing Nigeria the following day and in both matches Argentina's goals would be scored by Lionel Messi and Marcos Rojo.

The World Cup was in Russia. On the banks of the Volga, England had just thrashed Panama 6–1. In St Petersburg, Argentina were facing elimination at the group stages, something they had endured under Bielsa in Japan sixteen years before. The results in Russia had arguably been worse – a draw with Iceland, a crushing 3–0 defeat by Croatia. Bielsa was encouraging: 'From tomorrow, you will see the best of Argentina. I believe in the quality of the players and that Messi's leadership will come to the fore.' He was partially right. In the Krestovsky Stadium, Marcos Rojo would score four minutes from time against Nigeria to send them through to the knockout phase. There Argentina would lose an extraordinary game, 4–3, to France. Unlike Bielsa in 2002, their manager, Jorge Sampaoli, would not survive the debacle.

When asked who had convinced him to come to Leeds, Bielsa replied: 'Nobody had to convince me, I convinced myself. I was convinced by the strength of Leeds as a club and as an institution.' He avoided questions about where he might take Leeds United. 'Making those kinds of statements makes you a demagogue rather than a football coach,' he said.

He had watched all fifty-one games Leeds had played last season and the two matches they had played in Rangoon and Mandalay as part of their tour of Burma. He already knew a lot about his footballers, probably more than any incoming Leeds manager ever had. He wanted a lean squad, not over-encumbered with bit-part players.

The only significant change in personnel was the arrival of Patrick Bamford from Middlesbrough for £7 million, a transfer offset by the sale of the England Under-20 midfielder Ronaldo Vieira to Sampdoria. In January they would sign a goalkeeper, Kiko Casilla, from Real Madrid.

There were interesting questions, one from a journalist from Bilbao, who noted how exact, how precise Bielsa's Spanish was, and wondered how it would translate into an English dressing room. This, on the surface, seemed one of Bielsa's greatest problems. The half-time team talk is one of football's great arts, based not around Churchillian oratory but the simple imparting of information. When Mauricio Pochettino began work at Southampton, he spoke barely a word of English. 'I spoke through hugs, contact, with my facial expressions and my gestures,' he recalled. 'My poor English forced me to find other ways to read people.' Bielsa, who strangely had contacted neither Pochettino nor Pep Guardiola before accepting the Leeds offer, said that while he had great respect for the written and spoken word, 'the biggest fact that gets players playing is emotion. If you struggle in a language, there are ways other than words of getting your point across.' When he left Leeds in the summer of 2019, Pontus Jansson, who had contributed outstandingly at centre-half, cited language as the greatest barrier between himself and his manager. Without a common language there could be no real warmth.

Bielsa brought in Salim Lamrani, the man who had translated for him in his few months at Lille. The questions at Leeds carried far less hostility than they had in Lille and Lamrani became something of a cult hero at Elland Road. He was a specialist on American–Cuban relations, although his presentation to the Axis for Peace Conference in Brussels in 2005 gives an indication to which side of the divide he belonged. It was entitled 'Half a Century of American Terrorism Against Cuba'. He had written a series of books about the beleaguered, blockaded island and a biography of its leader, Fidel Castro. He had come to Bielsa's attention when he wrote a long assessment of his season at Marseille while working at the University of Réunion in the Indian Ocean. Like Bielsa, Lamrani was an intellectual without being a snob. Stuart Dallas, one of the workhorses of this Leeds side, asked him to have Christmas dinner with him when he realised Lamrani would be spending it alone. Lamrani did not reappear for Bielsa's second season.

Much of his conversation with Bielsa revolved around books. Bielsa advised him to read *Eleven Rings*, Phil Jackson's account of how he coached the Chicago Bulls and the Los Angeles Lakers to eleven NBA titles.

Jackson, who grew up in rural Montana the son of two preachers, employed the principles of Zen Buddhism and Native American teaching as part of his techniques to manage the likes of Michael Jordan and Kobe Bryant.

Lamrani also recommended that the Leeds squad be given books to read. 'There are many benefits of reading,' he explained. 'It develops intelligence, aids memory, reinforces concentration, stimulates the imagination and enriches the vocabulary.'

It was not a view that seemed widely shared in English football. During the 2010 World Cup, the England squad were based in an isolated hotel complex in Rustenburg on the South African veld. When Wayne Rooney complained that the squad were bored, Fabio Capello suggested they read a book. The response was portrayed to show how out of touch the England manager was. Lamrani was not so sure.

He drew up a reading list and organised a kind of book club that from September would become as much part of the preparations at Thorp Arch as the video analysis.

Among the books that were put on the players' reading list were; *The Little Prince* by Antoine de Saint-Exupéry, Jack London's *The Call of the Wild* and Victor Hugo's *Les Misérables*. Some choices like *The Secrets of The All Blacks* were aimed more squarely at an audience of sportsmen.

Initially, Leeds had put their new manager up at Rudding Park, a country house hotel near Harrogate that boasts a spa and two golf courses and where rooms cost £320 a night.

It was precisely the kind of hotel guaranteed not to appeal to Marcelo Bielsa. Eventually he moved into a one-bed-roomed flat above a newsagents in Wetherby, although he reportedly haggled over the rent, thinking it too high. There was a nearby Costa Coffee for meetings. He would spend hours there. He shopped in Morrisons, pushing his trolley past the Price Crunch offers in full Leeds training kit. It was like going into a Premier Inn and coming across Daniel Craig dressed as James Bond, drinking a Martini and holding a Walther PPK. José Mourinho had managed Manchester United for two years while living in a suite at the Lowry Hotel that cost £816 a night. Bielsa even wore his grey tracksuit to the black-tie gala that celebrated the centenary of Leeds United in October 2019.

He could be seen walking to the Thorp Arch training ground carrying a backpack with his notes. He regularly had dinner at the Sant'Angelo, an Italian restaurant on the High Street. Bielsa would pose for selfies. The *Yorkshire Evening Post*'s football correspondent, Phil Hay, writing in *Four-Four-Two* magazine, observed:

Leeds were advised when they sat down with Bielsa in Buenos Aires that he wanted changes to the Thorp Arch training ground. To their surprise, he had already acquired blueprints of the property and soon he was recommending modifications to supply beds for his players to rest in between training sessions plus a relaxation room with a pool table, a PlayStation and, bizarrely, a log burner that Bielsa hoped his squad would take turns in maintaining. A complaint by Bielsa that the light switches between the players' beds were off centre delayed work by a week.

Every Wednesday afternoon Bielsa would stage what became known as 'Murderball', a high-intensity eleven-versus-eleven game with no set plays. Adam Forshaw, a midfielder who had worked with Uwe Rösler at Brentford and Aitor Karanka at Middlesbrough, commented: 'The lads call it Murderball because it's tough, it's intense. You replicate a game but with high-intensity moments. It gets you really ready for the game on Saturday. He chops and changes a bit with his team so the lads see it as a chance to impress because it's eleven v. eleven, it's real.'

Craig Brown, the last manager to take Scotland to a World Cup, had long been an admirer of Marcelo Bielsa. He thought the book Bielsa had written while he was managing Chile and Athletic Bilbao – *The Eleven Paths to Goal* – vied with Sir Alex Ferguson's work, *Leading*, as the best he had read on football management. Bielsa's was a strictly technical piece of writing, analysing build-up play, pressing and the use of the pitch. Brown explained:

Andy Roxburgh used video analysis even before Marcelo Bielsa. He took Scotland to victory in the

European Under-18 Championship in 1982 and coached players like Paul McStay and Pat Nevin using videos as a teaching method. What Bielsa did was take it to the next level. Generally speaking, British footballers like to train with a ball. They like five-a-sides which is the sort of thing Bielsa doesn't do. However, when Colin Calderwood moved from Swindon to Tottenham, he said Gerry Francis was the best coach he ever worked with. One of the things Gerry Francis did on the Friday night before a game was to take the players on the pitch and point out where he wanted them to be when they won possession and when they lost possession – 'If the ball is here, I want you to be there' – which strikes me as similar to what Bielsa does. The Tottenham players didn't like it, this shadow play, they wanted their five-a-sides but Gerry Francis shouted at them: 'We don't pay you ten grand a week to be entertained. We pay you to work.' This surprised Calderwood on two grounds. He was only on five grand. I love watching Leeds at set pieces, defending corners and free kicks. Their positional play is superb: a mixture of zonal and man-to-man marking. It's beautifully done.

Out on the pitch at Elland Road, Leeds opened the season with a 3–1 win over Stoke. The game was due to kick off at 4.30pm and the club's fitness coach, Benoit Delaval, aware the forecast was for clear blue skies over

Yorkshire, had charted the progress of the sun over the stadium. Then, Bielsa would know if the goalkeeper would be dazzled by any reflections. 'Lads, it will be hot tomorrow,' Bielsa told his players. 'If it's hotter for our opponents than for us, we will win by two clear goals.' Which, of course, they did.

Unlike at Athletic Bilbao and Olympique Marseille, there was no stuttering start at Leeds United. They sprinted away. Leeds lost one of their opening eleven matches. Bielsa watched, not from an upturned drinks cooler, as he had at the Vélodrome, but an upturned blue bucket. On 25 August they went to Norwich, where the away dressing rooms had been painted pink, a demotivating colour that was supposedly designed to lower testosterone. Leeds won 3–0, and as they prepared to leave Carrow Road, Bielsa asked his players to tidy the dressing room.

The Christmas fixtures were framed by two victories of the kind that champions produce. At Aston Villa, Leeds were two down with thirty-four minutes remaining. They won, 3–2. The next game was on Boxing Day, at home to Blackburn. At Elland Road, they were 2–1 down with only stoppage time to come. Kemar Roofe, who had scored the winner at Villa Park, now found the net twice more. Roofe's football was to come alive under Marcelo Bielsa. He had been brought up at West Bromwich Albion but his career has been a series of loan moves, to Reykjavik, Northampton, Cheltenham and Colchester. In three years, he played twenty-two games and scored two goals, one in the Icelandic Cup, the other against Hartlepool. It was when he went to Oxford that Roofe showed what he was capable of. He was still only twenty-two and reminded himself that Jamie Vardy was three years older when he was transferred to Leicester in the move that would make his career. Roofe was twenty-three when he moved to Elland Road, in the summer of 2016. He enjoyed being coached by Bielsa, comparing it to going to school. He thought Bielsa's genius was making him realise how simple football could be:

> Not only did he give me ideas on how to play, he gave me the game time to be able to show what I can do. Every day would be different. I would be going back to my family and telling them a new story. You would be going off the pitch properly tired. You would be empty. You couldn't go and do any extra finishing. Before every game we would work on five different formations and our individual role would change in each one of these. You might defend in one position and attack in another. We would play eleven versus eleven once a week and that was harder than the actual game. He would be shouting 'Keep going, keep going' and if he saw you walking, he would be onto you. There would be no rest. You learned the body could do so much more than you believed.

The comeback against Aston Villa ensured that Leeds would be leading the Championship on Christmas Day. Of the ten previous clubs to have found themselves top of the league at Christmas, all had been promoted automatically; seven had gone up as champions. Their lead over West Bromwich Albion in third was six points. When Roofe's two stoppage-time goals overcame Blackburn, Leeds were through the fifty-point barrier. They were on course for ninety-eight. At Villa Park, the statistics were reeled out to Marcelo Bielsa. If they were meant to entice some arrogance from him, the figures failed to seduce. 'I hope we won't be the exception. All rules have exceptions. That's why we will take precautions.'

The Spy Who
Coached Me

Derby County's training ground is called Moor Farm and covers 50 acres of land on the northern outskirts of the city. Nearby is a nunnery, the Community of the Holy Name. Opposite Moor Farm is a housing estate, completed in 2001, called Oakwell. It is modern and well tended, the sort of place where people look out for each other. The sort of place where they notice people acting suspiciously.

On Thursday 10 January 2019, someone was seen acting suspiciously around the wire fence that surrounds Moor Farm. Someone from the estate called the police. The suspect, a twenty-year-old intern employed by Marcelo Bielsa, was arrested. The next evening, Derby would be playing Leeds at Elland Road. Suddenly football had its own Watergate.

The twenty-year-old was neither named nor charged with attempting to break into Moor Farm. Although the Derby manager, Frank Lampard, claimed he had been equipped with bolt cutters, he possessed only a pair of secateurs and they were in his car when the police arrived. According to a report in *The Times*, the intern's duties did not end with attempting to watch Derby train. He was expected to chat to fans, assess their mood and read the local press. All potential weaknesses would be reported back. This seems unnecessarily cumbersome and old-fashioned. The *Derby Telegraph* is available online. So, too, is the Derby County Fans' Forum. All this could be done without leaving Thorp Arch. The real prize was the chance to watch the club's final training session before they set off for Leeds. Lampard recalled seeing the same person filming from the road outside Moor Farm in August before Derby had played Leeds at Pride Park. The man with a camera had been confronted and asked to leave. Leeds had crushed Derby, 4–1. Lampard commented that it had never occurred to him the man might have been officially sanctioned by the manager of Leeds United.

The fact you would be spied upon was almost accepted in South America. Before the 2017 Copa Libertadores final, Grêmio used a drone to fly over the training ground of their opponents, Lanús, who were based in the south of Buenos Aires. When the ploy was uncovered, Grêmio's manager, Renato Portaluppi, was unrepentant: 'Every Brazilian club has a spy. The Brazil national team has a spy. The world belongs to those who are sharp,' he remarked. Lanús mounted no sort of official protest. Portaluppi's words proved prescient; Grêmio won.

Bielsa had often employed someone to spy on his opponents. When he was in charge of Chile, it was a seventeen-year-old friend of his daughter, Inés, called Francisco Meneghini, who was put to work on the second floor of Chile's technical centre in Santiago, sometimes providing reports on some of the lesser lights in the Chilean leagues, sometimes carrying out video analysis, sometimes spying on his opponents' closed training sessions. Once Meneghini was spotted halfway up a tree, watching Ecuador being put through their paces.

Meneghini went on to become manager of Unión La Calera in Chile's Primera Division. When asked if he employed spies, he replied, 'No, times have changed a lot. That was ten years ago and now I prefer to analyse opponents through videos.'

Before he came to Chile, when in charge of Argentina, Bielsa had used Gabriel Wainer, a sports radio journalist from Rosario, to gather information on opponents. He had commentated on Newell's Old Boys and, when Bielsa left to manage Atlas Guadalajara, he suggested Wainer take a coaching course. When he returned to Argentina to take charge of Vélez Sarsfield, Bielsa looked up Wainer and put him to work. Wainer would go on to be employed by

Tata Martino when he was manager of Paraguay and by Bielsa's successor with the Argentina national side, José Pékerman. When Pékerman was ousted as Argentina's manager following the 2006 World Cup, Wainer followed him to Colombia. What impressed Martino was Wainer's ability to slip into any given situation and make himself unobtrusively at home. He spoke five languages and had an instinctive understanding of football. His son, Javier, became a professional scout.

When, in October 2000, Bielsa was challenged about his use of Wainer, he retorted:

What do you mean by 'spy'? Gabriel's job is to provide me with information on my opponents. He will continue in his work, which does not seem to us to be either incorrect or underhand. There is one more thing that I want to add. To me this information has little influence on the result but, if it is a case of having it or not having it, I'd prefer to have it.

Nearly nineteen years later, this would be the basis of Bielsa's defence in the eye of the Spygate storm. The information he gained by spying on opponents had little real operational value but he would still prefer to have it. That is one similarity between Watergate and Spygate. There was no real reason for either. In June 1972, when burglars were arrested attempting to plant bugging devices at the headquarters of the Democratic National Committee, Richard Nixon was heading for one of the greatest landslides in the history of American presidential elections. Marcelo Bielsa was taking Leeds to the Premier League at a giddying pace. Both men just wanted to make sure.

The backlash was fierce. Although Andrea Radrizzani thought Derby had made too much of the incident, Leeds issued a formal apology and were fined £200,000. Bielsa paid the fine himself. The massed ranks of English football punditry turned their fire on to Leeds United. Stan Collymore compared it to the actions of the Australian team in South Africa using sandpaper to rough up the ball, actions that had cost Steve Smith, the nation's golden boy, the captaincy. To Martin Keown, 'The moral code of our sport has been severely breached. It's almost a Johnny English moment with bolt cutters, binoculars and a ladder. We are twenty-seven games into the season and what is it that Bielsa doesn't know already about Derby County?' Jermaine Jenas thought Leeds should face a points deduction, although he backtracked to 'a heavy fine'. Michael Owen, who perhaps significantly had played for Real Madrid, said that though Bielsa's actions might have been 'morally wrong', they were hardly a criminal offence.

Derby lost the game at Elland Road 2–0. The post-match press conferences were rather more even. Marcelo Bielsa was astonishingly open. Sir Alex Ferguson would have brushed away the questioning with a glare and a terse 'I'm no' going into that.' Nor did Bielsa insist he would only talk about the match or look to his press officer to shut down the conversation. Bielsa accepted complete responsibility for the affair. It was his idea and his alone. Leeds United had neither known about nor sanctioned the operation.

I am going to explain my behaviour but my intention is not to justify it. I have carried out this practice for many years. I started doing it when I was with Argentina and then with Chile. It is something that is accepted in South America and it is done in England too. In South America when this sort of thing becomes public knowledge it doesn't provoke the same kind of indignation that it does in England. In South America, just like in England, when we find out someone is watching the training session, we ask them to leave but I don't think you should be condemned or punished because you watch a training session. If you watch a training session from a public space, it is not against the law and you don't get arrested by the police. It's the same in this country and in South America. I do not feel I'm cheating for having done that. I didn't get any added advantage from the situation. Then you would ask: 'Why does he do it then?' I do it because it is just an additional source of information. It is something I am used to doing. I understand why Frank Lampard is angry because he thinks I'm someone who's cheating and I understand why he draws this kind of conclusion. I don't feel I cheated because the goal was not to gain an illegal advantage. I'd like to give you an example which reflects my position on the subject. When I was at Athletic Bilbao, we had 280 training sessions and all of them were open to the public and our opponents would come and watch. To me, the information that you get from a training session is not that significant. That's why I was never asked about this subject when I was at Bilbao. Actually, as head coaches we have rather more information than we can actually analyse. You could ask: 'If it's not significant, then why do you collect this kind of information?' The answer is that it provides an additional tool. Regarding the person who was sent to watch the training session, this person was in a public space, he was not arrested and, when he was asked to leave, he left. What we can criticise him for was that, when he was asked if he worked for Leeds United, he gave a negative answer. This is a weak point.

For a man forced on to the back foot, for a man who at some clubs might have been at risk of the sack, this was an impressive performance. One thing Bielsa did not mention was that he almost invariably named his team in his pre-match press conference, which for a Saturday game was held on a Thursday. If Frank Lampard or any other manager in the Championship wished to know the team Bielsa would send out, they only had to log on to the *Yorkshire Evening Post*'s Twitter account.

When it was Lampard's turn to face the press, he seemed disconcerted by the frankness of Bielsa's statement. He admitted that the feebleness of Derby's performance at Elland Road had also undermined his position. Lampard speaks fluent Spanish and was something of an admirer of Marcelo Bielsa. There was a biography of Bielsa on his bookshelves. 'Cheating is a big word,' he said.

If you talk about examining details and gaining advantages, great managers do that. However, this one is over the line and it's not just a toe over the line; it's a hop, skip and a jump over the line. You watch Marcelo Bielsa's career and it's very different – in a good way. He is innovative as a coach and always has been, but this is not the way I do things. I would rather not coach than send people on their hands and knees with pliers and bolt cutters to look at the opposition.

A few days later, Bielsa called a press conference at Thorp Arch. It seemed likely he would be announcing his resignation. Instead, he announced he had spied on every one of Leeds' opponents in the Championship. 'What I have done is not illegal. We can discuss it. It is not seen as a good thing but nor is it a violation of the law. I know that not everything that is legal is right and that the wrong things you do are not done with bad intentions.' For the rest of the press conference, Bielsa delivered two arguments, which were contradictory. He said that he knew that spying was wrong but that it was not illegal. He added that he thought spying on opponents' training grounds brought him no real advantage because he would have watched every game Derby played for the past two seasons but that he did it anyway. He did it because it might bring him some sliver of insight, however small, and his rage for perfection would not let that go. Some in football would understand that thought.

In the 1980s, the last decade before mobile phones, Hugh McIlvanney, regarded as the finest sports journalist of his generation, was on a train to Euston after watching Manchester United at Old Trafford. He and his colleagues began discussing one of the United goals and the sumptuous pass from Bryan Robson that had created it. McIlvanney interjected that the pass had been Frank Stapleton's. By the time the train had pulled into Crewe, everyone else around him, including Patrick Collins of the *Mail on Sunday,* had persuaded McIlvanney that he had been mistaken. McIlvanney pulled the typewriter down from the rack above his head and made to get off the train, saying, 'I'll have to phone the office.' Collins told him that this was the last train back to London and, if he got off, he would be facing a night in a Cheshire railway town without a change of clothes and that nobody reading the next day's *Observer* would realise the error. 'But I would,' said McIlvanney, stepping down on to the platform. Had Marcelo Bielsa gone into football journalism, he, too, would have been in the empty station rather than on the last train to London.

Bielsa then turned on the Powerpoint in the room and up flashed a list of Derby's games. What followed was a masterclass in the art of tactical analysis. 'When you watch an opponent, you are looking for specific information,' he said. 'You want to know the starting eleven, the tactical system they will use and the strategic decisions on set pieces. These are the three main axes the head coach usually analyses. When you watch your opponent, you get this kind of information the day before a game or you confirm the information you already have.' Bielsa said he and his video analysts watched fifty-one games Derby had played in the 2017–18 season when, under Gary Rowett, they had lost in the play-off semi-finals to Fulham and the thirty-one they had played under Frank Lampard. Bielsa asked a journalist in the room to pick a game. He chose number nineteen, Derby's 3–2 defeat at Chelsea in the League Cup. Bielsa then brought up the data for the game, pointing out the chances Derby had created, their half-chances and how the game was broken up into five-minute cycles and how each five minutes was independently analysed.

It was the kind of thing Bielsa had been doing since he became manager of Newell's Old Boys in 1990 but this was the first time it had been set out for public consumption. It was as if Alan Bennett had been giving a lecture on how he wrote *The History Boys*. Then came videos of Derby playing, beginning with them taking a corner. 'We know what the player will do when he raises both hands. I know that and so do all the other head coaches in the Championship.' The video had forty minutes of Derby attacking, culled from the thirty-one games before they had played Leeds, and forty minutes analysing their defensive weaknesses.

The players would be shown eight minutes of Derby defending and eight minutes of Derby attacking. Bielsa commented that an average footballer would not be able to take in more than fifteen minutes of analysis. Derby, under Lampard, used four systems. 'We see who plays in the 4-3-3. In red we have the usual starters and the second group are the subs and the third and fourth group are those who play less.' He went through Derby's formation, their players, where they played, when they played and for how long. By the end it would have been foolish to challenge his assertion that he already possessed all the information he could ever possibly want on Derby County.

'I don't need to watch a training session to know where they play,' he said. 'So why do I go? Because it's not forbidden. I didn't know it would create such a reaction and even though going to watch an opponent is not useful, it allows me to keep my anxiety low.' There were some who did not buy into this argument. While regretting the breach with Radrizzani that Spygate had caused, the Derby chairman, Mel Morris, thought there was a clear and obvious advantage to be gained by looking in on your opponents' training sessions:

> You could see an intricate set-piece routine on the training pitch that could massively change the face of a game. Look at the second leg of the play-off semi-finals [when Leeds fell apart against Derby]. Frank played a diamond formation for the first time. Had someone known, I guarantee Leeds would have set up differently and there might have been a different result.

In September 2019, journalists from *The Times* uncovered evidence that seemed to show that sending a bloke to watch your opponent train was all rather outdated. Six years before, three Manchester City scouts had gone to work for Liverpool. One, Dave Fallows, became Liverpool's head of recruitment, while Julian Ward became the club's European scout for the Iberian peninsula. The newspaper alleged that they, along with Michael Edwards, who is now Liverpool's sporting director, used Manchester City's passwords to access City's scouting database on the Scout 7 system. Scout 7 had data on half a million footballers and possessed millions of minutes of them on video. Manchester City became aware their database had been compromised and speeded up the signings of Fernandinho from Shakhtar

Donetsk and Jesús Navas from Sevilla in case the deals were hijacked. While accepting no liability for what had happened, Liverpool agreed to pay Manchester City £1 million in compensation.

Marcelo Bielsa was elegantly defended by his brother, Rafael, who compared it to the trial of Oscar Wilde, arguing that those who accused the playwright of homosexuality were themselves homosexuals. The storm of anger against his brother was, Rafael argued, an example of the great English tradition of hypocrisy. 'You see the British double standards from corporal punishment to the Profumo affair, when a secretary of state lived a double life. You see it in the spy themes covered by John Le Carré or that wonderful novel by John Banville, *The Untouchable.*' That novel was based on the life of Anthony Blunt, who supplied the Soviet Union with state secrets delivered from the heart of the British establishment – he was Curator of the Queen's Pictures.

Craig Brown was on the side of the Bielsa brothers:

What struck me is the hypocrisy when he admitted to spying on other teams. It has been going on for years. When I worked in Scottish football, scouts would put on a hat, pull up their overcoats and take the dog for a walk somewhere around the opponent's training ground. In sport, knowledge is power. In 1986 I was part of Alex Ferguson's staff when he managed Scotland in the World Cup in Mexico. Our second group game was against West Germany and the big selection dilemma we had was whether Gordon Strachan would play. Alex was paranoid about security. When he was at Manchester United, he wouldn't announce the team until the last possible moment. Scotland were training at the stadium in Querétaro and Franz Beckenbauer, who was managing West Germany, sent his assistant, Berti Vogts, to see what he could discover. As soon as Berti got to the stadium, he was refused entry. He was walking outside when he saw a guy with a trolley selling Coca-Cola. Berti was wearing an official Germany shirt and he went over to the vendor and asked if he could swap shirts. The guy not only gave him his Coca-Cola shirt, he let him have the trolley as well. Berti, wearing the shirt and pushing the barrow, simply walked past security and watched us train. Strachan did play, as it happened, and scored, although West Germany won the game 2–1. After the match, Beckenbauer told us he knew for a fact that Gordon Strachan would play and he told us how he knew. Forever afterwards, Alex Ferguson called Berti Vogts 'the Coca-Cola Man'.

A Very Serious Wound in the Worst Moment

The three managers who contested the two automatic promotion places might have come from differing universes. Marcelo Bielsa had managed in two World Cups, had won championships in Argentina and plaudits from the pantheon of the game. Before arriving at Norwich, Daniel Farke's only managerial job in first-team football had ended with him riding a horse around a small ground in fourth-division Germany. Chris Wilder had come to Sheffield United from football's desolation row – his first two jobs in management had been in the now defunct Meadowhall Sunday League, followed by Halifax, who had gone into liquidation with debts of £2 million. He looked like a football manager: with his face creased, his hair grey, he seemed older than fifty, which was his age at the start of the season. Sheffield

United contrasted with Leeds and Norwich in that their chairman, manager and captain were all from the city they represented. They had a common bond. Only Wilder's voice was a surprise. He had been born and spent most of his life in Yorkshire and had played for Sheffield United but he had passed his boyhood in London, which gave his accent what Wilder termed 'an annoying twang'.

Sheffield United were adrift in League One when Wilder took over from Nigel Adkins, who, in the words of the midfielder Paul Coutts, 'didn't want to upset anyone and ended up annoying everyone'. When asked how he dealt with stress, Adkins recited the poem 'The Guy in the Glass', written in 1934 by the American Dale Wimbrow, about seeing your reflection in the mirror. It concludes with the line: 'Your final reward will be heartache and tears, if you've cheated the man in the glass.' In May 2016, after a 2–0 defeat at home to Scunthorpe guaranteed Sheffield United their lowest finish for thirty-four years, Adkins discovered his reward was the sack. Wilder's first move on taking over was to remove all the motivational messages that festooned Bramall Lane. Within twelve months they were back in the Championship.

Daniel Farke, who steered Norwich to the title, could count as one of the most left-field appointments ever made by a major football club: a man who had barely played the professional game and whose only title as a manager was in the Westphalian Oberliga – the fifth tier of German football. His grandfather, Franz, had won the West German championship with Borussia Dortmund as a player in 1953, but Daniel was far less gifted. He was a striker who spent most of his career in the lower reaches of the game with Paderborn and Lippstadt. In 2009 he became Lippstadt's manager, quickly promoting them two divisions to the fourth tier of the game. 'It was a small club,' he recalled. 'You had to do everything yourself: negotiate with the bus company, do the contracts, all the press and all of the coaching.' After saying farewell to Lippstadt by riding a horse around the pitch, Farke was appointed to manage Borussia Dortmund's second team. Then in the summer of 2017, a time when German managers were making an impact – Jürgen Klopp at Liverpool, David Wagner, the best man at Klopp's wedding, at Huddersfield – Norwich took what proved a wildly successful punt on another. However, Farke's methods proved closer to Guardiola and Bielsa than the 'heavy metal football' played by Jürgen Klopp.

At Carrow Road, Farke had more than halved a wage bill that in 2017 had stood at £63 million. Only Newcastle, of clubs below the top flight, had ever paid their footballers more. Five major players – James Maddison, Alex Pritchard, Josh and Jacob Murphy and Jonny Howson – were sold for £58 million. Their replacements were either free transfers like Tim Krul, who had been part of the Holland side that had come third in the Brazil World Cup under Louis van Gaal, and Teemu Pukki, who finished the season with twenty-nine goals – or they cost a fraction of what had been raised in the transfer market.

For most of the season the question was which of the two would be promoted with Leeds, who were part of the top two for 185 days of the season. In February, Norwich met Leeds at Elland Road and beat them comfortably. Bielsa hurled his water bottle to the ground in a rare public show of frustration, although had Krul been dismissed for bringing down Tyler Roberts outside his area, the result might have been different. Leeds were two down by the interval. Bielsa made two half-time substitutions but, if anything, they played even worse after the break. It was Bielsa's fourth defeat in six matches, the first real sign of the slide that would derail Leeds in the spring. 'It is something we cannot ignore,' he said. 'We cannot say the performance was satisfactory.' He latched onto a statistic that was to become a mantra: how many opportunities Leeds required to score a single goal.

Leeds were no longer top; their time leading the Championship was over. They were still, however, three points clear of Sheffield United. They would play them at Elland Road the following month. In December, Leeds had won at Bramall Lane for the first time since April 1992, the golden spring when they had shaken off Manchester United to become champions of England. It had been a fortuitous victory: the Sheffield United goalkeeper, Dean Henderson, had cleared the ball straight to Jack Clarke, who had presented Pablo Hernández with a tap-in. It had been one of the very few games Leeds would play under Bielsa when they had less possession than their opponents.

Not even Chris Wilder, who was often irritated by the publicity and headlines given to Leeds and Bielsa, claimed Sheffield United had deserved to win the return. Leeds dominated, aiming seventeen shots at Henderson's goal. None was on target. Chris Basham's shot found the net. With seventy-one minutes gone on a sodden afternoon, Billy Sharp and Liam Cooper tussled for possession in the Leeds half. Sharp won it from the Leeds captain and squared the ball for Basham to sweep it home from the edge of the area. Basham may have considered himself lucky to be on the pitch. 'He did well to be the match-winner,' Wilder said afterwards. 'Because he was coming off after twenty-five minutes. He was absolutely useless.'

Elland Road's press facilities were dated and barely fit for purpose. The old press box, where you watched from behind glass in what seemed like cinema seats, had been removed under the chairmanship of Ken Bates, who considered the vantage point could be more profitably used. The post-match press conferences were conducted in a corner of the stand called Howard's Bar, which with its tired wooden furnishings looked like a venue for a low-grade wedding reception. Howard Wilkinson, whose taste was for fine red wine, would probably not have lingered for the Foster's and the packets of Quavers in the bar that bears his name. Bielsa remarked that the defeat would not be decisive – which it would not have been, had Leeds' results then not tailed off disastrously – but as he spoke, the fire alarms began sounding across the stadium. It was an omen of sorts.

Bielsa's players had been angered by the sounds of celebrations coming from the away dressing room. To Patrick Bamford, 'they were celebrating as if they had won the championship'. Sheffield United's victory nudged Leeds into third, and as an early spring came to Yorkshire, and daffodils turned fields and verges into the colours of *Wisden*, Norwich broke away at the top. It became a straight fight between the two Yorkshire clubs. A northern duel.

The doubts about Leeds had come a couple of months before, as the snow smeared the fields around the training ground at Thorp Arch. Bielsa's tactics had refashioned the club, made it into the kind of force it had not been for a generation, but there was something else about Bielsa's game, something that might drag everything down. As Leeds' season neared its climax, the stories grew of how at Athletic Bilbao and Marseille his teams had fallen away, exhausted in the final furlongs. Ander Herrera's pained cry of 'We couldn't move, we couldn't run any more' carried all the way from the San Mamés to Elland Road.

Bielsa knew the argument, and when it was put to him in the press room of Loftus Road after a 1–0 defeat by Queens Park Rangers in late February, he allowed his irritation to show. 'Your question does not have any basis,' he told the *Independent*'s Jack Pitt-Brooke, a journalist who was an admirer of his methods. 'It is clear you don't know what you are talking about because, if it is one thing this team does not lack, it is energy.' As if to prove it, three days later Leeds demolished West Bromwich Albion 4–0 at Elland Road, with Pablo Hernández scoring after sixteen seconds. They then won at Bristol City and Reading without conceding. Leeds were second in the Championship. With nine fixtures remaining they had seventy-three points. They could taste the Premier League; they could smell it. Those nine games yielded ten points.

They needed more. Bielsa's final tally of eighty-three points was twenty-three more than Leeds had achieved the previous season but it would not have been enough to win automatic promotion in any year since 2013 when Hull went up with seventy-nine. The defeat at Loftus Road highlighted another reason why the Bielsa project would fail. Leeds developed a habit of losing both to their nearest rivals and to teams who had almost no expectation of winning. Queens Park Rangers' 1–0 victory would be their only one in Steve McClaren's final fifteen games as the club's manager. They went down at Birmingham, who had lost their last five matches and who appeared to be disintegrating in the face of a nine-point penalty imposed by the Football League for reckless overspending in the days when Gianfranco Zola and Harry Redknapp ran St Andrew's. On Good Friday, at Elland Road, they faced Wigan, a team with the worst away record in the Football League and who found themselves a goal down and reduced to ten men with barely twenty minutes gone. Wigan contrived to win, 2–1. Pontus Jansson was to describe the experience: '[It was] totally devastating to be in front, to have one more player and still lose. It was the worst game of my life.' Bielsa employed more poetry but his verdict was every bit as damning: 'A very serious wound in the worst moment.'

Over the long Easter weekend that became a Calvary for Leeds United, the wound would become fatal. On the Easter Monday, at Brentford, where they had not won since 1950, Leeds were taken apart, demolished in a way they had almost never been under Bielsa. In the little press room at Griffin Park, Bielsa admitted that his team had for long periods of the season 'played above their limitations'. Now those limitations were being exposed. To those listening, this seemed an accurate reflection of the collapse. Leeds had nowhere near the talent of a Marseille or an Athletic Bilbao, and theirs had been a longer season in a far more uncertain division. It was perhaps only a surprise that the reckoning had been this long delayed.

They would finish the league programme at Ipswich. The result was, more or less, an irrelevance. Derby's 3–1 win over West Brom guaranteed Leeds would finish third whatever the result at Portman Road. However, the result was dreadful. Having jettisoned Mick McCarthy in search of more attractive football overseen by a younger manager, Ipswich had been relegated with nearly two months of the season still remaining. They were nearing £100 million in debt. They had not beaten anyone outside the relegation zone since December and they had not scored three goals at home for seventeen months. Leeds ensured both those statistics would be supplanted and managed to miss their third successive penalty. They seemed like an exhausted, disintegrating mess. Bielsa's analysis did not dwell on tiredness. He concluded that Leeds had failed to gain automatic promotion not because they were weary, but because they had not taken their chances.

By his own relentless calculations, Leeds had fashioned at least a hundred scoring opportunities more than the two clubs that did go up, Norwich and Sheffield United. Of the top six in the Championship only Derby had scored fewer than Leeds' seventy-three goals. Norwich had scored twenty more. Both Leeds and Sheffield United had a morbid, ingrained fear of the play-offs. Between them they had entered this end-of-season lottery ten times and had never been promoted. There was a symmetry to the fixtures. Over the final eight games they would each play Millwall, Birmingham, Preston and Ipswich. There would, however, be a difference in timing. Leeds were the bigger club, Bielsa was the bigger story and for Sky Television they were the greater attraction – more than half of Leeds' forty-six games would be screened live. Generally, they would play after Sheffield United.

When one of the great title races, between Manchester

United and Newcastle, unfolded in the spring of 1996, something similar happened. Newcastle were the fresher, sexier team with the more immediately charismatic manager in Kevin Keegan. They were almost invariably selected for television coverage, generally playing after Manchester United, who, spearheaded by Eric Cantona, ran off a string of 1–0 wins, usually on the Saturday. On the Sunday afternoons and Monday nights, Newcastle – of whom only David Batty had experienced winning a league title – became infected by nerves.

Something similar may have happened to Leeds. It may not be coincidence that the best performance Leeds delivered over those final eight matches came against Sheffield Wednesday immediately after Sheffield United had fouled up a home game with Millwall. At Bramall Lane, Sheffield United had been leading Millwall by a single goal that would have put them two points clear of Leeds. Then everything had swung wildly out of control. Two of Sheffield United's most precious assets, Basham and Sharp, had gone off with hamstring injuries. A third, John Egan, was dismissed for handling on the line. Ben Marshall had missed the subsequent penalty and then, in the ninety-fifth minute, Millwall equalised. The news crackled around Elland Road. This was their chance.

They took it beautifully. The scoreline registered a bare 1–0 victory but the margins ran much wider. The goal was scored by Jack Harrison, a young winger who had spent four years playing in the United States before being signed by Manchester City. Explaining his decision to loan him out to play for Marcelo Bielsa, Pep Guardiola said that what awaited Harrison at Leeds 'would be challenging but would be good'. The celebrations when Harrison broke through were so intense that one supporter broke his ankle.

Sheffield Wednesday were the eighth different club Steve Bruce had managed at Elland Road and he could not recall being as outclassed with any of them as he had been here. The pace, movement and intensity of the play rose with the noise of the crowd. Scarves were being swung rhythmically aloft; the effect was like an orchestra reaching a crescendo. The conductor stood with his hands behind his back, seemingly disengaged from it all. 'There has been a lot written about Marcelo Bielsa, how he is this, how he is that,' said Bruce afterwards.

But when you look at this team, you can see what he has done. The transformation – with similar players – to where they were twelve months ago is remarkable. We found the intensity they played at a struggle. The way the crowd are reminded me of what it was twenty years ago. You'd fancy them to go up with the four games they've got.

It would have amazed Bruce to learn that Leeds would fail to win any of them.

As the season faded out, support for Bielsa was unwavering. A racehorse named Bielsa won the Sheffield Novice Stakes at Doncaster Racecourse. Just before what he called the 'very serious wound' of the defeat by Wigan, a plane flew over Elland Road trailing a banner behind it that proclaimed: 'Bielsa is God'.

One of the worst defeats in April had been a 1–0 reverse at Birmingham. It was a flat, mundane performance. With the stadium set among decaying light industry that has not changed since the days of British Leyland, losing at St Andrew's does not encourage fantasy. On the train back from Birmingham New Street, the first-class carriage was full of Leeds fans. On one table was piled cans of lager and a bottle of Sancerre. The conversation was loud, the laughter louder. The speakers agreed that, at its core, this Leeds team was ordinary. The conversation moved on to making up a team of the best players they had watched; and given most were in their late forties, they had watched an awful lot. Nigel Martyn would play in goal and there was unanimous agreement that Gary Speed and Gordon Strachan, whose name drew a chorus of 'the Ginger Wizard', would feature in midfield. There was agreement too about who would manage this Leeds fantasy team. They were too young to remember Don Revie's triumphs but they were not too young for Howard Wilkinson, who led Leeds to the title two years after promoting them. They could have gone for David O'Leary, who had taken Leeds to within one game of a European Cup final. Instead they opted for the man who had overseen that dreary defeat. They went for Marcelo Bielsa.

Managers are rarely the subjects of songs. In his twenty-seven years at Old Trafford, it is hard to recall anything memorable sung or chanted about Sir Alex Ferguson. You could say the same for Bill Shankly or Arsène Wenger. In 1996, a group of Sunderland supporters adapted the Monkees' 'Daydream Believer' into a song about their manager called 'Cheer Up Peter Reid'. Sunderland were then on course for promotion to the Premier League and, as with Leeds under Bielsa, there was a mood of awakening. The song made number forty-one in the charts. Just before Christmas 2018, Marcelo Bielsa became the subject of a song that would reach number five in the iTunes charts. It was based on Queen's 'Bohemian Rhapsody' and was called 'Bielsa Rhapsody'. Its opening line – 'Open your eyes, look up to the skies, we're Leeds' – came to Micky P. Kerr at seven in the morning. Kerr is a shock of black hair and beard, who mixes being a primary school teacher with stand-up musical comedy. That year he had reached the final of *Britain's Got Talent*, which with its audience of fifteen million generated an astonishing degree of fame. In a single, mile-long walk to the pub, he was flagged down by half a dozen cars. 'Once the series stopped, that sort of thing stopped with it,' he said at a bar on the edge of Roundhay Park.

The problem with going on *Britain's Got Talent* as a comedian is that you can only use the material once and you use your best material to get to the final. For the final I had a routine which I believe could have won it. The problem was that it had some Bee Gees' lyrics in it and I was told we couldn't use it for copyright reasons. It was suggested I do another song which is called 'I'm not Arrogant I'm Just Better than Everybody Else'. It's a good song to play if you've already won the crowd over but you can't do it at the start of a set. It was just not suitable and went terribly. I fell at the last. How very Leeds United. In my formative years Leeds were the best team in the country. I would have been ten or eleven when they won the championship in 1992. My team was the best in the league. Then, around the turn of the century, it was a young, exciting team, playing in Europe and challenging Manchester United. Then the rug was pulled and we went from the Champions League to the old Third Division, down there with a lot of nobodies. It has been that way for fifteen years. I did a podcast just before Bielsa came. We had Paul Heckingbottom in charge, we had finished thirteenth. We could not see where we were heading. Then Bielsa comes and everything changes. People are talking about us in a way they haven't done for years. We have been out of the top flight for so long that getting back into the Premier League has become to us what winning it is to Liverpool fans. I am told Bielsa is a Queen fan. Adam Pope, who commentates for BBC Radio Leeds, asked him about it and so did Phil Hay of the *Yorkshire Evening Post*. He said he had heard it and loved it. That made my life.

Kerr wrote another song about Bielsa, called 'Bucket Man', based on his propensity to watch games on an upturned bit of plastic – at Marseille it had been a drinks cooler. It was a reworking of Elton John's 'Rocket Man'. The original had been released in 1972, the same year as Les Reed and Barry Mason had written 'Marching on Together', which had become the club's battle hymn. 'Marching on Together' was unusual. Unlike 'You'll Never Walk Alone', 'I'm Forever Blowing Bubbles' and 'Blue Moon', it had been specially written for the club that was to sing it. Like 'Unchained Melody' by the Righteous Brothers it was a B-side that eclipsed the song it was supposed to support, which in its case was a song written for the 1972 FA Cup final imaginatively titled 'Leeds United'. 'Bucket Man' was a high-end production, recorded at the Nave Studios in Pudsey. Its lyrics were probably better than 'Bielsa Rhapsody' – 'Don't think it's gonna be a long, long time before we win promotion, don't resign. You aren't the man they think you are at home – El Loco, no.' It did not, however, sell as well. 'It just bombed,' said Kerr.

'Bielsa Rhapsody' got into the charts because it came out when Leeds were flying. 'Bucket Man' came out when the season was starting to tail off and nobody seemed interested. I don't blame Bielsa for Leeds not winning promotion. If Liverpool had not won the European Cup last season, their fans would still have thought it something special to have gone to Anfield, see their team batter the opposition and end up with ninety-seven points. I felt like that about Leeds. I have never encountered an atmosphere like I did at Elland Road last season. There's an arrogance to Bielsa, a feeling that he does not need to make these marquee signings, that he does not need to adapt his style. He goes against the grain. He is strong-willed and stubborn. There's a Shakespearean quality to him. He's a romantic, a tragic romantic, someone who should win but doesn't. Leeds are like that. They are a good fit.

Twenty Minutes

Don Revie left Elland Road in 1974. They were league champions, one of the finest sides in Europe. To some they were something else. They were Dirty Leeds, the Damned United. Just like Olympique de Marseille under Bernard Tapie, glory seemed to be mixed in with the grime. Revie, like Tapie, gave his club days they sensed they might never have again: League championships, Wembley appearances, European finals. He was loved by his dressing room. Adored. They were among the best-paid players in England. In 1963 John Giles had won the FA Cup with Manchester United but had fallen out with Matt Busby, who allowed him to join Leeds, then in the Second Division. Giles was on £30 a week at Old Trafford (around £617 in today's terms). Revie trebled it. It says something for Revie's attention to detail that Leeds also had the best pensions. He created an atmosphere of a tight, tough family with himself as its godfather. The night before a game there would be quizzes with the players, games of carpet bowls and impossibly thick dossiers on the opposition compiled by his chief scout, Tony Collins, who as the first black manager in the Football League had taken Rochdale to the League Cup final in 1962. The quizzes would later be employed by Alex Ferguson at Manchester United. The dossiers were the forerunners of the video analysis Marcelo Bielsa perfected. The carpet bowls never took off anywhere else.

There was, however, another side to Revie and Leeds. There was the thuggery, epitomised by the Battle of Goodison Park in November 1964 in which Everton's Derek Temple had been so badly tackled his team-mates initially thought he had been killed. There were the people in Jack Charlton's little black book, where names deserving of retribution were entered. There was something darker, too. In April 1962 there was a danger that Revie's first season at Elland Road would end in relegation to the Third Division. Bob Stokoe, then manager of Bury, claimed Revie had offered him money to 'go easy on Leeds'. The match finished in a goalless draw. Leeds survived by beating Newcastle 3–0. Stokoe never spoke to Revie again, not even on the Wembley day in 1973 when Sunderland, then in the Second Division, overthrew the great Leeds machine. There was the ice of revenge running through that fairy tale.

Gary Sprake was Leeds' goalkeeper that night against Bury and when Revie's career as England manager was in its final throes, he went to the *Daily Mirror*, accusing him of match fixing. It says something that Revie had saved Sprake from prison. In 1971, the Welshman had gone for a night out, drunk too much and crashed his car. The woman in the passenger seat was injured; Sprake abandoned her and fled. When the police came to Elland Road to arrest the goalkeeper, Revie persuaded them to drop the charges and report that the car had been stolen. In the words of Brian Clough, 'Don Revie's so-called family had more to do with the mafia than Mothercare'. The reputation of Dirty Leeds lingered, and when Bielsa confessed to spying on every club in the Championship they were dirty again. Then came the events of 28 April 2019. They were playing Aston Villa. What happened next made headlines worldwide. Five months later, Bielsa and Leeds were invited to Milan to be presented with the Fifa Fair Play Award.

It was still possible that Leeds could be promoted automatically but it would have needed them to win both their remaining fixtures and for Sheffield United to lose their final match of the season, at Stoke. There would also need to be a swing of around ten goals to Leeds. It was possible in the same way a Liberal Democrat government was possible.

The game reflected Leeds' changed circumstances after the disastrous long Easter weekend. It was drab – the mood was subdued. Under Dean Smith, managing the club he supported when growing up in the Black Country, Aston Villa had won ten in a row, breaking a club record that had stood since 1910. They were the kind of team everyone wanted to avoid in the play-offs, the one in form. However, at Elland Road they too seemed subdued and listless, as if killing time until the play-offs began. Then pandemonium broke loose. Liam Cooper clattered Jonathan Kodjia in the centre circle. The Aston Villa striker stayed down. The ball was at Tyler Roberts' feet on the Leeds left. Roberts seemed not to know what to do. There were calls to put the ball out of play and Roberts delivered a nondescript pass down the byline, aimed at nobody in particular. Mateusz Klich seized it, cut into the Villa area and scored.

It triggered a brawl. Klich was grabbed by Conor Hourihane. Patrick Bamford went for Anwar El Ghazi, who had played for Bielsa at Lille. El Ghazi made as if to punch the Leeds forward. There was no contact, although Bamford went down as if struck in the face. El Ghazi was dismissed; Bamford received a yellow card and, when the video analysis was done, a two-match ban for simulation. On the touchline, John Terry, Aston Villa's assistant manager, began squaring up to Bielsa. Smith shouted that Leeds should let Villa score to even things up. He had no expectation the suggestion would be carried out. Then as Villa kicked off, amid shrugged shoulders and gestures, Bielsa shouted at his players and implored them to 'give a goal, give a goal'. As Aston Villa played the ball forward, the white shirts parted. Only Pontus Jansson, who seemed to disagree profoundly with the order, tried to put in a tackle. Albert Adomah passed the ball into the net for what would be his last goal for Aston Villa. The match finished 1–1. Sheffield United were formally promoted to the Premier League.

'Everything happened so fast,' said Jansson.

I was the first one over to the Aston Villa bench to apologise when we scored. They were saying: 'Why don't you let us score one?' I told them, 'We can't do that. I can't just let you score. That's not how I work.' It took me a while to understand that our bench was screaming at us to let them score. In the end, I let them do it but I wanted to show I didn't accept the decision. There and then, I thought I was right but, in hindsight, it was the right thing to let them score.

As praise rained down upon him, making headlines in Spain and Argentina where it became known as El Gesto (the Gesture), Bielsa appeared indifferent to it all, almost unwilling to discuss it. 'We just gave the goal back,' he said. 'The facts are what everybody saw. We expressed our interpretations of the fact by what we did. English football is known for its sportsmanship so I don't have to comment on it.' Aston Villa's sporting director, Jesús García Pitarch, who had worked with Rafa Benítez at Valencia, overheard Bielsa's discussion with his players. 'The game took more than ten minutes to resume,' Pitarch said. 'I was listening to Bielsa telling his players not to do anything to stop us scoring after we kicked off. I was thinking to myself: "Will he be capable of carrying this out?" He was. After the game, I went down to the Leeds dressing room to congratulate him. He is a football character in capital letters.'

While praising Bielsa's sportsmanship, Arsène Wenger pointed out that, technically, there had been no reason for Leeds to stop playing. 'The players should watch a video of it because, if there is no head injury, only the referee can stop the game,' he said. 'Aston Villa should not have stopped. Leeds took advantage of that. We should say thank you to Marcelo Bielsa. It is a remarkable gesture. They are playing to come up to the Premier League. There is something at stake. The whole world has to watch that.'

Not everyone was enthused by Bielsa's gesture. Luis Chilavert, his goalkeeper at Vélez Sarsfield, brought up an old wound inflicted when Bielsa was manager of Argentina: 'El Loco Bielsa teaches fair play in England but why did he allow Pochettino to score with his hand against Paraguay in Asunción?' He then quoted a song by Mercedes Sosa, the Argentine folk singer who became a symbol of opposition to the junta. 'Mercedes Sosa's song really suits him. "Everything Changes" in such a contaminated environment. To hell with lies in football.'

There was a scramble to find comparisons to what Bielsa had done. There was Stan Cullis's refusal to bring down Albert Stubbins as the Liverpool striker sprinted away on the final day of the season at Molineux to ensure the

1947 league title would go to Anfield rather than Cullis's own club, Wolverhampton Wanderers. The closest parallel involved Wenger, who in February 1999 had offered to replay Arsenal's fifth-round FA Cup tie with Sheffield United. Then, when both teams had expected him to put the ball out so one of Steve Bruce's players could receive treatment, Nwankwo Kanu had crossed for Marc Overmars to score. The tie was replayed ten days later, with the same result, a 2–1 win to Arsenal.

Bielsa did not travel to Milan to accept the Fair Play Award. He sent the Leeds fitness coach, Benoît Delaval, whom he said had 'significantly influenced' his decision to allow Aston Villa to score, and the Leeds captain, Liam Cooper, to represent the players 'who had the uncomfortable task of following my instructions'. His letter of acceptance had the usual thanks – to his club, his family and the fans of Leeds United – but it was aimed at the hidden masses, those who watch football but from a distance, those who may not go to a game but look to sport to give them some kind of moral bearing. 'I want to thank Leeds United and its fans, who did not question my actions,' Bielsa wrote.

They could have claimed that I had to respect the ruling of the official but instead they accepted my particular interpretation of differentiating between something that is legal with something that is fair. I want to mention my mother who always knew what was right and what was wrong. I also want to mention Newell's Old Boys of Rosario, a club to which I belong, where for twenty years I learned to live football in a particular way. There are permanent presences in my life such as my wife, my sister and some friends who remind me of values that should not be forgotten. Football, due to its enormous impact, at times operates on some aspect of public morals and it is especially involved in moulding the lives of those who have less or who are the weakest. However, I think that most of those who have less still choose to do the right thing. With great effort, they remain worthy and retain decency. The recognition that Fifa gives us includes them, because it rewards the same behaviour that they anonymously live every day.

There were more than a few raised eyebrows when Cooper, wearing a dinner jacket, and Delaval, his tie loosened, stepped up to take the award. The most archly raised belonged to Frank Lampard, who – although Derby had lost the play-off final to Aston Villa – had done enough to be offered a return to Stamford Bridge as manager of Chelsea. 'I did smile; I don't know who votes for it,' said Lampard. 'What happened with Spygate was well documented. The rules changed slightly because of it and they were fined. I felt it was improper. To get an award on the back of that, I thought it was irony at first.'

Bielsa's generosity may have done more than anything else to consign 'Dirty Leeds' to history but it guaranteed Sheffield United the Premier League and Leeds the play-offs. Among teams in the Championship, Leeds had come first in terms of shots at goal, chances created and possession. They had come third in terms of league position.

The following day, Chris Wilder gave an interview in which he crystallised the reasons why he had won this Yorkshire duel, which would see him voted Manager of the Year:

Leeds got beaten seven times since Christmas and we have been beaten once. We set it up from Christmas to be in the race and we have steamrollered it. After the international break, in March, we averaged two points a game. That's promotion form right the way through the pressure part of the season. Listen, don't mention anything about bottle or bollocks or about us dipping out. The way we have gone about it has gone under the radar. It's not got enough credit in terms of media coverage. Everybody wanted Leeds to go up and we have come steaming through.

Leeds had participated in the Football League's first ever play-offs, in 1987. Then the third-, fourth- and fifth-placed clubs in the Second Division joined the side that had finished fourth from bottom in the top flight, which was Charlton. Having beaten Oldham over two legs in the semi-finals, Billy Bremner's side, already worn down by a run to the FA Cup semi-finals, faced Charlton in a two-legged final. Both games finished 1–0 to the home team and since the Football League had made no provision for a penalty shoot-out, a replay was ordered at St Andrew's in Birmingham. A dreadful game, watched by an over-whelmingly Yorkshire crowd amid swathes of dark, empty terracing, had staggered goallessly into extra time. Then came a free kick from John Sheridan that seemed to have ended Leeds' five-year exile from top-flight football. There were twenty-one minutes left, time enough for Charlton's centre-back, the Sheffield-born Peter Shirtliff, to score twice. Bremner's men collapsed to the turf, some in tears. Much the same would happen to Bielsa's team.

They would face Derby in the semi-finals. Spygate and its aftermath had created the kind of tension between the two clubs not seen since the bitter rivalry between Revie and Clough. At Moor Farm, where Frank Lampard explained that Derby did not have the money to do anything more than put up a few extra sheets of tarpaulin around the perimeter to keep out prying eyes, there was an attempt to diffuse the tensions. Lampard said he respected Bielsa when he came to England and respected him still. Spygate, he said, had not exerted a significant effect on Leeds' win in January. For his part, Bielsa said that if there was a similar incident to the one against Aston Villa, they would play to the referee's whistle and not feel obliged to stop the game.

There were reasons to suspect Leeds would not go through the play-offs. There was their history in the competition, Bielsa's end-of-season record and their wretched recent form, which had culminated in defeat at the bottom club, Ipswich. There was plenty of talk that the third-placed clubs, the ones who had just missed out on automatic promotion, were at a disadvantage. There was, in fact, no 'curse of the third-placed team'. Over the previous thirty years, third-placed teams were more likely than any other to win through, though clubs who finished fifth did better than those who were fourth.

As if to prove it, Leeds delivered a commanding, controlled performance in the first leg at Pride Park. It was a classic managerial contest between a great footballer – and at Chelsea Lampard had won every available honour – and a great analyst of the game. The analyst had won the first two games and Bielsa would win the third.

Lampard's contacts had enabled him to bring a couple of talented young footballers to Derby on loan – Mason Mount from Chelsea and Harry Wilson from Liverpool – who were neutralised by Bielsa's tactics. Kemar Roofe, standing in for the suspended Bamford, scored a well-worked goal. Leeds might have won by more than 1–0 but statistically it was crushing. No team had ever won a Championship play-off semi-final after losing the first leg at home. Standing in a patch of sunshine in a corner of Pride Park, the Leeds fans taunted Lampard, whom they thought had overplayed Spygate, with a version of Oasis's 'Stop Crying Your Eyes

Out'. It was a tune that in a few days' time would be played back to them.

April 2019 had, however, been a month in which first-leg leads had ceased to matter. In the Champions League semi-finals, Liverpool and Tottenham had wrested seemingly overwhelming advantages from Barcelona and Ajax. The sight of Mauricio Pochettino breaking down in tears on the touchline in Amsterdam and claiming that he 'owed everything to Marcelo Bielsa' would, however, have touched Leeds hearts more than those at Derby. Afterwards, Lampard wondered if he could use this as motivation at Elland Road, though he later admitted he did not really believe it would happen. It was a passing straw to cling to. However, what happened at Leeds on the Wednesday night was as dramatic as anything seen at Anfield or the Johan Cruyff Arena.

Before the first leg, as for every home game, over the tannoys at Pride Park there had been read out a poem by Jamie Thrasivoulou, a fan living in London, called 'We are Derby'. It had powerful lines: 'We're engineers with dirty fingernails. Graft and sweat pump through our veins. We're Rolls-Royce engines, Belper nails, Toyota motors, Bombardier trains.' Elland Road went for something more visceral. Scarves had been placed on every seat and, as they were held up, to create a white wall, the noise became a crescendo mixed in with aggressive choruses of 'Marching on Together'. It was the kind of noise Bielsa would have recognised from the biggest nights at the Coloso del Parque, the San Mamés or the Vélodrome: aggressive, masculine, confident.

Leeds were almost three-quarters of the way through their play-off semi-final with Derby. They had won the first leg 1–0. After forty-four minutes they were 1–0 up at Elland Road. Two clear goals. The crowd was loud, noisy, triumphant.

Then in twenty minutes, a twenty minutes Bielsa would never quite come to terms with, Leeds lost control, panicked and seized up completely. Derby, who had scored one goal in almost five and a half hours of football against Bielsa's Leeds, scored four times in forty minutes. Just before the interval, Liam Cooper tried to shield a routine ball back to his goalkeeper, Kiko Casilla, who was out of his area. The two men collided and Jack Marriott, a Derby substitute who had been on the pitch a matter of seconds, rolled the ball into an empty net. Casilla had been signed from Real Madrid, where he had been understudy to Keylor Navas. He had played in the Champions League. He was thirty-two. He was not a kid. Now he played like a ball boy who had been thrown a pair of gloves and been told to go in goal. Sprake had once thrown the ball into his own net at Anfield in 1967 and been forever serenaded with choruses of 'Careless Hands'. Casilla's errors were far costlier. Within seconds of the restart, Mount beat him from just inside the area, chipping his shot delicately as he fell. Then Cooper gave away a penalty with a needless tug on a shirt. Stuart Dallas, who had opened the scoring for Leeds, broke through improbably again. It was 3–3 on aggregate – away goals did not count. The tie yearned for a few minutes of balance, a breathing space. None came.

Cooper's central defensive partner, Gaetano Berardi, who had kept his place ahead of Pontus Jansson, promptly got himself sent off for two needless challenges within a few minutes of each other and left the pitch punching the polythene wall of the tunnel. Leeds' defence was disintegrating and a path to a goalkeeper who was enduring a meltdown was open. Harry Wilson should have scored. Marriott, like Wilson, advancing through the dead centre of the Leeds area, did.

The last few minutes were chaos: wildly aimed drives, shots blocked by desperate, tired bodies. It was this that Bielsa would have been unable to comprehend. All his methods were about preparation, anticipation, the use of space, the treating of football as a science. He had planned for an assassination through telescopic sights. Instead it had come down to a bar-room brawl. Watching from the sidelines, Pontus Jansson thought the pattern of the match 'absurd'.

At the final whistle Bielsa's team lay on the spring turf, all in white, exhausted, broken men, much like Bremner's had been at St Andrew's, thirty-two years before. Away to one side they could hear the chants and the songs. Midlands voices. The other three-quarters of Elland Road was filled with a kind of astonished silence. The season was over. It had closed like a door caught by a gust of wind might close, with a loud, unexpected and entirely final bang.

Afterwards it was more than usually difficult to reach Howard's Bar. You had to make your way through a throng of Derby supporters who were in no mood to leave. 'Stop Crying Your Heart Out' was being sung back to the Leeds fans as Lampard's players walked around the pitch making binocular shapes with their hands, mimicking Bielsa's attempts to spy on their training ground. You could hear the singing as Bielsa padded into the room. It was certain he would take responsibility for the defeat; it was possible he would do so by resigning. The first question was always put to him by Radio Leeds. He was asked how Leeds could so totally have lost control for twenty minutes. He answered it and then later in the press conference returned to the point:

We had twenty minutes of disorder. I could not find a solution to it. When an attacking team fades or disappoints, we ask whether that team should have been more conservative but, if you look at the game, the worst moments for us were when we tried to be conservative. The best moments were when we imposed ourselves. However, when it comes to explaining defeats and disappointments, it's hard to have any authority.

Later he made it clearer: 'The gentleman said something that I won't forget about this game. He said the team had lost control for twenty minutes. I said I could not find a solution to it. My job is to find solutions to problems.' Nobody in the room doubted Bielsa's assertion that this was not the time to discuss his future but for those looking for clues there was contradictory evidence. His deal with Leeds was in effect a series of three one-year contracts. Bielsa said he was prepared to listen to any offers the club put to him. However, he delivered a long, thoughtful answer that suggested there might be no more of him in Yorkshire. 'We had so many difficulties that mentioning them would look like making excuses because we could not reach our goal,' he said.

At the same time, we had the ability to finish first or second and we had the ability to show we were the best team in the play-offs. We couldn't finish first or second and we couldn't reach the play-off final. The fact we couldn't reach something that was reachable always places doubt around the head coach. If you have the resources to win something and you don't, you have to assume responsibility.

Lampard, meanwhile, took his entire squad and backroom staff to the King's Head, a pub in Duffield, a well-to-do town on the banks of the Derwent just north of Derby. The bar bill, published by the landlord, revealed they consumed five bottles of prosecco, seventy-five Jägermeisters, sixty-five shots of Grey Goose vodka, fifty-four sambucas, thirty-eight tequilas, twenty-nine glasses of Canadian whisky and twenty-five amoretti. There was one Diet Coke.

The Tyranny
of Trophies

It is May 2004. Leeds United are playing the final game of a season that was the story of a relegation long foretold. They are losing 1–0 to Chelsea, a club that is preparing to fire Claudio Ranieri. He will be replaced by José Mourinho, who has just taken Porto to a European Cup final, a trophy he will win. The Leeds fans at Stamford Bridge begin singing 'We'll meet again, don't know where, don't know when'. In the next fifteen years Chelsea would win the championship four times, the European Cup, the Europa League twice, five FA Cups and three League Cups. Leeds would behave like Vera Lynn might have done had she taken to gin and cigarettes before breakfast rather than raising money for veterans and cancer research.

In the intervening years those Leeds supporters would see

their club make a mess of their lives. There would be one more meeting with Chelsea, in the League Cup in December 2012 at Elland Road. Leeds went into the interval a goal up through Luciano Becchio. In the second half they would concede a goal every nine minutes. Whenever Leeds were relegated they tended to stay down. They were not the kind of club that leapt back up. They suffered.

It had taken Leeds nine years to return to the top flight after their relegation in 1947, four after 1960, eight after Allan Clarke had taken them down in 1982. When an uneasy dawn broke over Elland Road on 16 May 2019, there was the realisation that it would now be at least sixteen years before they returned to a division where Watford, Burnley and Bournemouth had become regular members.

The three managers who had promoted Leeds since the Second World War were remarkable men – Howard Wilkinson, Don Revie and Raich Carter, who had taken them up alongside Sheffield Wednesday in 1956. Carter was a dazzlingly famous footballer, the only man to have won the FA Cup before and after the Second World War. His likeness was on display at Madame Tussauds; a weekly football magazine carried his name. He played cricket for Durham and Derbyshire. When he managed Hull, he signed Revie. At Leeds he built his side around the formidable frame of John Charles.

If Leeds were to be promoted, it seemed essential that Marcelo Bielsa remained. There had long been talk in Rosario that he would return to take charge of Newell's Old Boys.

There was a lucrative offer to manage Girona, who may have been in the Segunda División in Spain but who were owned and funded by the Abu Dhabi football conglomerate that ran Manchester City. In April, just as the season at Elland Road was starting to fall apart, Rafael Bielsa gave an interview to *La Nación*. He spoke to Marcelo every day and the subject was usually Newell's, who were undergoing an agonising time. For Bielsa to return to rescue them in the stadium that now bore his name appeared a wonderfully romantic idea. His contract with Leeds was one Rafael had drawn up. If Leeds had won promotion to the Premier League, the second year of the contract would have been mandatory. In the unlikely event that he did not wish to manage in the Premier League, Marcelo would have to buy himself out of it. When he had gone to manage Espanyol in 1998, there had been a break clause allowing him to leave the Montjuïc if he were offered the job of coaching Argentina. There was nothing of that kind in his contract at Leeds.

As the grandchildren of the most esteemed lawyer in Argentina's history, the Bielsas had a horror of breaking contracts. When he had resigned from Marseille and Lazio, Marcelo could argue that promises made to him had not been kept. Marseille had tried to change the contract, and therefore he was perfectly within his rights to walk away from it. Rafael pointed out that when Marcelo had been sacked by Club América, he had sued and won. He was in the process of doing the same with Lille. 'Nobody more than me would like to see Marcelo back at Newell's,' said Rafael, 'but it can't be done this way. The Bielsa family does not break the rules. These are values that you learn as a child, from your mother, from your grandfather and from the whole family.'

The squad changed subtly. Pontus Jansson left. He had played in thirty-nine of Leeds' forty-six Championship matches and had been selected in the Championship Team of the Season. 'Being chosen by "experts" is one thing but being selected by opposition players and coaches is quite another,' he said. 'It was bloody flattering, the best prize I have ever received.' Jansson had enjoyed Bielsa's coaching but the relationship with his manager had become abrasive. He found Bielsa distant, a fact not helped by the language barrier. At Malmö in his native Sweden he had enjoyed a close relationship with Roland Nilsson and Rikard Norling but there had not been the same warmth at Leeds. Bielsa first described Jansson as his best player and then informed him he should find another club.

Brentford seemed a strange choice. Jansson's stated ambition was the Premier League and Griffin Park had not staged top-flight football since 1947. However, he had told his agent, Martin Dahlin, that he would prefer to remain in England, and Thomas Frank, the Brentford manager, had promised him considerable responsibility and the captaincy. Frank, who is Danish, was also far easier to talk to. 'Marcelo does not want that close relationship with footballers,' Jansson said. 'One reason is the language barrier because he doesn't speak English very well, but with

Marcelo Bielsa you get so much for free and, as a player, you just have to show him some respect. He has achieved so much that you just have to accept it and do everything he says. You can't go against him.'

Kemar Roofe, who had scored fourteen league goals, left Yorkshire for Brussels, a destination that was more unlikely than Brentford. Vincent Kompany, who would rival Tony Book as the finest captain in Manchester City's history, had returned to Belgium to become player-manager of Anderlecht. He phoned Roofe, who was slightly surprised Kompany knew who he was. A fee of £7 million was agreed. Another fee, this time of around £10 million, was arranged to take Jack Clarke to Tottenham. Clarke was eighteen, born in York, a graduate of the Leeds Academy. He had been voted the club's young player of the year.

In the course of a summer, Leeds had lost their best defender, their leading goalscorer and their best young footballer. Clarke was loaned back to Leeds by Mauricio Pochettino but in the event he barely played. In December, when Pochettino had been sacked six months after taking Spurs to the first European Cup final in their history, José Mourinho recalled him.

This was the first time since 2012 that Bielsa had a full second season with a club and there were uncanny parallels with Athletic Bilbao, when the first campaign had ended exhaustingly close to glory. Then Javi Martínez had been sold and Fernando Llorente had agitated to leave the San

Mamés. That season in Spain had dribbled away. Bielsa's second season in Yorkshire did nothing of the sort. In many ways, it was more impressive. The core of the squad was thinner. There was the immense disappointment of the play-off defeat to be scrubbed out from under the fingernails of the team. There was an absurdly distant pre-season tour of Australia, which Bielsa attended for the briefest possible time – to take charge of a game against Manchester United in Perth, followed by West Sydney Wanderers. There was every excuse for Leeds to falter.

Instead, they shone. Bristol City were beaten 3–1 at Ashton Gate on the opening weekend. There were seven straight wins between November and December. Ben White, a beautifully balanced ball-playing centre-half, arrived on loan from Brighton. In January 2018 he had been part of the Newport side that had knocked Leeds out of the FA Cup. Michael Flynn, the Newport manager, described White, then twenty, as the best loan signing the club had ever made. At Leeds he ensured Jansson was barely missed.

Bielsa was by now heavily reliant on loan players. Pep Guardiola agreed a second season for Jack Harrison. A loan deal for Arsenal's twenty-year-old forward, Eddie Nketiah, produced three league goals but after a barren two months he returned to London following the New Year's Day match at West Bromwich Albion. Hélder Costa was the most interesting of the loanees. Born in Angola, he had been part of the same Benfica youth side as Bernardo Silva, who was now a pivotal member of Guardiola's squad at Manchester City. Paul Lambert had made him Wolverhampton Wanderers' record signing but Lambert's successor at Molineux, Nuno Espírito Santo, was not one for wingers. Bielsa was, and Costa was signed on a season-long loan with a view to a £15 million permanent transfer in June. Initially he struggled to adapt to Bielsa's high-pressing game. He scored only his third goal on 29 December, the opener in a remarkable 5–4 victory at Birmingham, the kind of slugfest all too reminiscent of the play-off decider against Derby.

It was a victory that ensured Leeds United would finish the decade on top of their league, just as they had in 1989, 1999 and 2009. The identity of those leagues was a guide to the club's progress: the old Second Division, the Premier League, League One. The first and last of those seasons would see Leeds win promotion. As the nation celebrated the new century with the Queen and Tony Blair joining hands in the Millennium Dome for an uneasy rendition of 'Auld Lang Syne', it appeared Leeds might end up as champions eight years after Wilkinson's boys had done it. However, in the words of their young striker, Michael Bridges, 'We shit our pants.' They finished twenty-two points adrift of Manchester United.

There was always the danger of Bielsa's teams suffering a collective nervous or physical breakdown. Even on Boxing Day, when the statue of Billy Bremner was swathed in scarves to keep out the cold while nearby there was a swirl of the bagpipes playing 'Amazing Grace', there was a small scent of fear mixed in with the smell of the Lynx Africa gift sets. Leeds were comfortably in an automatic promotion position, but they had squandered a three-goal lead to Cardiff, lost to Fulham and seen Pablo Hernández, one of the pivots of their team, suffer a hamstring injury.

Preston had won once at Elland Road since 1961 and that was a game in which they had been 4–1 down and recovered to win 6–4. They came within a minute of a second victory until Stuart Dallas, who at Leeds had played on the wing, as a wing-back and as a conventional full-back and was now employed as a midfielder, scored a deflected equaliser. Dallas was one of those footballers who was prepared to play anywhere and, as a result, received much less than his due, except in Cookstown in Ulster, where he grew up. There Dallas's face appeared on a mural alongside two other Cookstown boys who had represented Northern Ireland – Aaron Hughes, who had played 112 internationals, and Ray McCoy, a milkman who while playing for Coleraine was voted Ulster's Footballer of the Year in 1987.

Until Dallas scored, as Leeds pressed and pressed, the mood had been edgy, frantic. When Patrick Bamford was replaced by Nketiah, there was a certain incomprehension. Elland Road was not a place to question Marcelo Bielsa but Leeds needed a goal from somewhere and surely they were more likely to score one with two strikers on the pitch. If Bielsa had refused to play two strikers against Sweden in the dying moments of Argentina's World Cup campaign, he was not going to start against Preston North End. Dallas's equaliser was a vindication of sorts.

The result at St Andrew's was the only vindication. To have won 5–4 was something but it smacked of the loss of control, the lost twenty minutes, against Derby. Bielsa's opening comments in the post-match press conference were to acknowledge that he was still alive. Then came New Year's Day at West Bromwich Albion, a contest between the two likeliest teams to make it to the Premier League. Like Leeds, Slaven Bilić's side had stumbled, winning one of their last five – and that, too, was a narrow, high-scoring victory at Birmingham. It was, nevertheless, billed as a title decider, a contest between the two best teams the Football League had to offer. At the Hawthorns, the floodlights burned and the pitchside banners billowed. The loudspeakers blared out 'O Fortuna' from *Carmina Burana*. The music has an epic, gladiatorial quality that would have appealed to Old Spice when they looked for a theme to advertise their aftershave. However, like the bride and groom who choose 'Every Breath You Take' for their first dance, they never presumably examined the lyrics, which are admittedly in Latin. The first verse ends with the line 'Power melts like ice'; the last verse climaxes with 'Fate strikes down the strong. Everyone weep with me.' At the Hawthorns, the dramatic effect was slightly lessened by the sight of the teams being welcomed onto the pitch by a bloke dressed as a boiler, in deference to West Brom's sponsors.

The two sides were eight points clear of the chasing pack, a pack that seemed weaker than it had twelve months ago. Then Leeds and Norwich were being pursued by West Brom, Sheffield United, Middlesbrough and Derby. Aston Villa, the club that would end the season in the Premier League, were ninth, fourteen points off the lead. Somehow, they seemed an altogether more formidable group than Fulham, Brentford, Nottingham Forest and Sheffield Wednesday, who formed this year's pack, one with blunter teeth and more questionable stamina. Or so Bilić and Bielsa would have hoped.

The evening finished as a 1–1 draw and a long embrace between the two managers. When asked why, Bilić replied: 'I rate myself. I am a confident guy but Bielsa is Bielsa and to compete with him is a great privilege.' Bilić had read Bielsa's book *The Eleven Paths to Goal* and referred to it whenever he wanted to do specific training on pressing or high-intensity football. Bielsa, he said, was comparable to Rinus Michels, the inventor of Total Football. It was a reminder of what Bielsa still meant to other football men, even though there would be some who would glance through the statistics and ask what precisely Marcelo Bielsa had achieved.

On Monday 6 January Bielsa took Leeds to Arsenal for an FA Cup tie, a fixture that pricked memories of the 1972 final, of Allan Clarke's header, of the banner that proclaimed 'Norman Bites Your Legs', of Mick Jones receiving his medal with a dislocated elbow, of the time when Leeds United cast their longest shadows. Mikel Arteta, who had taken over from the wreckage left behind by Unai Emery, had compared playing against Bielsa's Leeds to 'a trip to the dentist'. Having been assistant to Pep Guardiola at Manchester City, he knew first-hand what playing against one of Bielsa's teams would be like.

In the event, Arsenal had their molars loosened without having them extracted. Had Patrick Bamford, Jack Harrison or Ezgjan Alioski converted one of the many chances Leeds fashioned in the first half, Arsenal might have needed anaesthetic. In many ways, despite the 1–0 defeat, it was a perfect night for Leeds. No lower-division club since Preston in 1964 had reached an FA Cup final and been promoted and, at the Emirates Stadium, while Leeds had given an indication of their quality, they would not be sucked into a draining run in the competition. They looked like what they were: a side ready for the Premier League.

You could create a brief history of Leeds United around their FA Cup ties with Arsenal. In 1972 they had been masters of their universe. In 1991, the year they took the Arsenal machine fashioned by George Graham to three replays, Leeds had given notice they possessed the resilience to win the title the following year. In 2004, as Leeds careered towards relegation and insolvency, they had been shot to pieces inside their own stadium by Arsène Wenger's 'Invincibles'. It says something for their long march through the wilderness that the Emirates Stadium was in its fourteenth year and Leeds had yet to play a league game there. In January 2012, on another Monday night, in another FA Cup third-round tie at Arsenal, Leeds had been a dozen minutes from forcing a replay. Then Thierry Henry, now thirty-four and back at the Emirates Stadium for the first time in five years and on loan from the New York Red Bulls, ran through to score. It was his 227th goal for Arsenal and there would be only one more. For Leeds, and their manager Simon Grayson, it had been defeat with honour. It took a month for Ken Bates to fire him. That was how they treated managers at Elland Road and they were to become ever more disposable.

Now, during that compelling forty-five minutes Bielsa engineered in north London, the 8,000 who had come from Yorkshire sang their song about 'Dominic Matteo scoring a fucking great goal in the San Siro'. David O'Leary, who had fashioned the side that had played AC Milan, Lazio and Real Madrid in a single, mesmerising Champions League campaign, was at the Emirates Stadium and he would have recognised a side that was, after so many barren years, starting to turn a corner towards at least an echo of those nights.

Around the inner perimeter of the Emirates Stadium there are depictions of every trophy won by Arsenal, starting with the FA Cup of 1930 and finishing with the one lifted in 2017. Ten were won by Wenger alone. Early on in his time at Elland Road, Bielsa had conducted a post-match television interview and been asked how 'someone who has won so much' would judge the game. Bielsa gave a little laugh and explained that, in reality, he had not won that much. Three Argentine league titles and an Olympic gold medal do not constitute much of a return for the best coach in the world, which is what Guardiola claims him to be.

Bielsa has always rejected judging a manager or a club by what they have won: he does not allow himself to be measured by what he once called 'the tyranny of trophies'. Sir Alex Ferguson won thirty-eight major pieces of silverware at Aberdeen and Manchester United, more than four times the number Brian Clough won at Derby and Nottingham Forest. Roy Keane, who was managed by Clough for three years and by Ferguson for twelve, will tell you that the three shaped him more than the twelve. If you judge only by trophies, then Bing Crosby's performance as Father Chuck O'Malley in *Going My Way* was superior to Humphrey Bogart's in *Casablanca*, because Crosby won the Oscar for Best Actor and Bogart did not. Influence is more difficult to measure. Brian Eno, who co-founded Roxy Music and produced albums for David Bowie, Talking Heads and U2, nominated the Velvet Underground as the greatest influence on modern music. Their record sales were pitiful but, as Eno remarked, 'Everyone who went to see them formed a band.'

You could say much the same of Marcelo Bielsa. After the long night in Máximo Paz, Pep Guardiola went out and became a football manager. Bielsa directly influenced Mauricio Pochettino, Gabriel Heinze, Diego Simeone and virtually every footballer he encountered. What stands out about Bielsa is the variety of the relationships he has forged with his footballers. When Steve McClaren began his brief, disastrous term with England, he would refer to the men he coached as 'Becks', 'Lamps' and 'Stevie G', as if he were one of the lads who just happened to be team manager. Bielsa was never one of the lads, not even at the University of Buenos Aires, when he was just a few years older than those he trained. There has always been a distance and an aloofness between the coach and the coached. Yet he was able to forge a deep relationship with footballers as diverse as Patrick Bamford, who was offered a scholarship to Harvard University, and Carlos Tévez, whose family scrabbled a living from the absolute poverty and lawlessness of Fort Apache.

The football Bielsa directed thirty years earlier in the stadium in Rosario that now bears his name was not so very different from the *Gegenpressing* with which Jürgen Klopp stormed the heights, first at Borussia Dortmund and now at Liverpool. The video analysis – the carving of a match into five-minute segments where every kick would be dissected, which three decades ago was thought unnecessarily obsessive and slightly weird – is now standard practice: so much so that the nickname of El Loco has begun to fade away. The madness of 1990 became the normality of 2020. That, rather than silverware, is the extent of Bielsa's triumph. His ideas have become the mainstream and, as he once observed, 'Everyone with new ideas is thought mad until they work.'

The Redeemer

Marcelo Bielsa was dressed in white robes, his arms outstretched. He looked into the middle distance and above his head was the slogan 'Marchando Juntos'. Below his feet, which were entirely obscured by the hem of his robes, was a date, also written in Spanish: 'Dos Mil Veinte'. In Rosario, Bielsa had a stadium named after him, and they had left letters and gifts outside his hotel in Bilbao, but this was the first time he had been depicted as Christ the Redeemer.

The mural was on the side wall of a pet shop in Wortley, a drab, functional district in west Leeds. It was painted by Nicolas Dixon, an artist whose work can also be found in New York, Melbourne, Ibiza and Tanzania. He painted it shortly after Bielsa had led Leeds back to the Premier League.

'He made a pretty average side into champions,' Dixon said. 'He is not just a football man, he is a philosopher, he is a teacher. He is your dad; he is your grandad. I started crying when I saw him celebrating. I have seen pictures of him winning his first title with Newell's and he looks like Pablo Escobar being carried through the streets. This was so very different.'

There is one part of Wortley that has always encouraged fantasy. Not far from Nicolas Dixon's mural are the overgrown remains of the T.V. Harrison Ground. It was where Leeds City Boys used to play; where Paul Madeley, David Batty, Noel Whelan and Brian Deane fashioned their talent. It was opened in 1931, the year Leeds and Manchester United were both relegated from top-flight football. It was abandoned in 2004, the year Leeds fell out of the Premier League, and now it has been earmarked for housing. There were some who thought that 2020, the year of Leeds' return, might be time to save the fields where so many dreams had been born. The mural was commissioned to highlight the fight.

'Doing a mural of Marcelo Bielsa just seemed the right thing to do,' said Dixon. 'He is our redeemer and our saviour and he would mean more to ordinary people in the city than the footballers who played for Leeds City Boys, however great they became.'

Nicolas Dixon had begun supporting Leeds just as the club was enduring relegation under Allan Clarke, part of a triumvirate of Don Revie's lieutenants – Eddie Gray and Billy Bremner were the others – whom the club imagined could rekindle the old master's magic.

'It was a volatile time full of violent, terrifying experiences,' he said. 'In 1987 we went to Hillsborough for the FA Cup semi-final against Coventry. It was two years before the Hillsborough semi-final that everybody remembers and we were in the same Leppings Lane End as the Liverpool fans. It was a crush then and they began pulling people out because they couldn't move, couldn't breathe. I went with my friend, Jimmy Carroll, and after the game I spent forty minutes in tears, and not just because Leeds had lost. It was an awful experience. I was a teenager in secondary school. A month or so later, I persuaded my mum to let me go to Birmingham to see the play-off final replay between Charlton and Leeds. It was a midweek night, St Andrew's looked awful, there seemed to be trees growing out of the terraces, but Leeds were one up, there were only a few minutes left and we were all doing the conga. Then Peter Shirtliff, who probably hadn't scored a goal in a decade, got two. Those were my memories of growing up supporting Leeds United.'

Then, in the warm, blossom-filled spring of the coronavirus, it seemed there might be a disappointment to eclipse the body blows of 1987. It was 7 March. Leeds were playing Huddersfield at Elland Road. In his account of the season, *Covid Interruptus!*, the Leeds fan David Watkins recalls going for his usual pre-match pint at the Old White Hart in nearby Beeston. The coming pandemic was a major topic of conversation among those preparing to set off for the game. For the first time Watkins could remember, there was a queue to wash your hands in the toilets.

It was not a game to arrive late to. Within three minutes Leeds had scored one of the goals of their season, something that Bielsa might have sketched out on the training pitches at Thorp Arch. A back-heel from Mateusz Klich finds Pablo Hernández, who funnels the ball out to Jack Harrison on the left flank. Harrison looks up as he runs, delays his pass. Just when you think he has delayed too long, he sends over a deep cross that Luke Ayling meets on the volley to send crashing into the net from the bottom of the crossbar. It was a goal that was both violent and beautiful.

This Yorkshire derby might have been won by a greater margin than two goals. Harrison shot against the intersection of crossbar and post and when Jonas Lössl had saved Ben White's header with every sinew of his body stretched to its maximum, Patrick Bamford clipped the rebound home. Point blank.

'If you are going to be outmanaged, then be outmanaged by a genius,' reflected the Huddersfield manager, Danny Cowley. 'I am not sure we've ever got to that level of performance that Leeds did today. You look at the energy and intensity. He must be relentless in his demands of them to play with that physical output. I'll be interested to see how the Premier League copes with them when they go up.'

To Cowley, whose success in steering Huddersfield clear of a second successive relegation would be rewarded with the sack, there seemed little question Leeds would make the Premier League. They were top of the Championship, seven points clear of Fulham in third with nine matches remaining. Then everything stopped. There would not be another game for three and a half months.

Leeds' path to the summit had not been smooth. The narrow FA Cup defeat at Arsenal in January may have announced to a wider world what a Leeds United driven by Marcelo Bielsa might offer the Premier League, but it triggered a sharp downturn. Once more, it appeared a season would unravel in mid flow. Leeds lost four of their next five games – at home to Sheffield Wednesday and Wigan and away to Queens Park Rangers and Nottingham Forest. In those four games Leeds did not manage so much as a goal.

The match they did win was against Millwall, where they had gone into the Elland Road dressing rooms two goals down at the interval. It was a sign of the overflowing tension that Leeds' director of football, Victor Orta, and their director of communications, James Mooney, confronted the referee, Darren England, in the tunnel. Their actions earned them a stadium ban and £2,700 worth of fines. They ought to have had more faith in their footballers. Goals from Patrick Bamford and Hernández snatched Leeds a 3–2 win.

However, it seemed that once more Bielsa's history was repeating. Leeds were seizing up as they had seized up the season before. As Athletic Bilbao and Marseille had. The feeling extended to the dressing room. Mateusz Klich, the pivot of Bielsa's midfield, began to think that once more Leeds would fall short.

'We had made a great start to the season but then came the shortness of breath,' he said. 'We fell into a hole and the whispering began in the corners: "It is starting again. It won't work again." The atmosphere was such that I feared there would be no promotion.'

It was during these weeks that Andrea Radrizzani approached both Zlatan Ibrahimović and Edinson Cavani. The former was thirty-eight and playing for Los Angeles Galaxy, Cavani was about to turn thirty-three and was running down his contract at Paris St Germain. Bringing either man to Yorkshire would have been a coup akin to Bielsa's arrival nineteen months before. A short-term deal to the end of the season would have been an electrifying statement of intent. However, it would be extremely expensive. Ibrahimović's salary in Los Angeles was £5.5 million. In the summer of 2020, Cavani's proposed move to Benfica collapsed over the Uruguayan striker's demands he be paid £8.8 million a season.

There would have been more than a financial risk. Radrizzani did not inform Bielsa of these approaches. He was skiing off-piste, trying to energise a faltering campaign on his own initiative. However, as Vincent Labrune had discovered at Marseille, there were few things more certain to upset Marcelo Bielsa than having footballers imposed on him from the boardroom. When, two months later, Bielsa learnt of these approaches, after Radrizzani had given an interview to the Italian media, he said he was 'surprised'.

Radrizzani confessed that working with Bielsa, whom he described as 'a singular man with strict rules, a philosopher, a great connoisseur of football', was 'sometimes not easy'. This could only have increased the degree of difficulty. Radrizzani argued he would only have put the deal to his manager once he had a statement of intent. Ibrahimović, said Radrizzani, 'was very honest but he understood that English football may not be ideal for him at this stage of his career'. He rejoined AC Milan. Bielsa would reinvigorate Leeds' campaign without Zlatan's assistance.

On 11 February, Leeds travelled to Griffin Park, the mood black and despairing. Their record at Brentford was atrocious, and in two months their lead over the chasing pack had been cut from eleven points to zero. Their only protection was now goal difference and they were no longer scoring goals.

Brentford were one of five clubs, from Bristol City in seventh to Fulham in third, who were within five points of Leeds. This was Brentford's third successive match against Yorkshire opposition. Thomas Frank's team had put five past Hull, three past Middlesbrough. Their three-pronged attack of Benrahma, Mbeumo and Watkins went under the epithet of BMW. Brentford were accelerating like a 7 Series on an Autobahn. It would not be long before Leeds fell behind to a car crash of a goal. Kiko Casilla allowed a straightforward back-pass to roll under his boot and Saïd

Benrahma was presented with an empty net. Benrahma's father had died less than a fortnight before and the boy who grew up amid the vineyards and orchards of northern Algeria grieved fiercely. He had scored three against Hull and now he lifted his shirt to reveal a message: 'Je t'aime, Papa'. For the ninth time in ten games, Leeds had fallen behind. Mauricio Pochettino was among the crowd, looking at the kind of inexplicable, unforced error that had cost him his job at Tottenham.

Griffin Park echoed to the chant of 'Leeds are falling apart again'. They were bent and buckled but they did not break, and by the end they were the better side. Liam Cooper's equaliser, his first goal of the season, was the minimum Leeds deserved. In retrospect, this was the decisive night of Leeds' second season under Bielsa. Had they lost, they would have fallen out of the automatic promotion positions and might never have regained them. They held on, they turned the tide and won their next five without conceding a goal. Then everything stopped.

The coronavirus pandemic brought European football to a halt more completely even than the Second World War. On 22 June 1941, Rapid Vienna, who were deemed part of the Third Reich, came from three down to beat Schalke 4–3 in the final of the German Championship in front of 95,000 in Berlin's Olympic Stadium. Hours before, as dawn broke over the forests, lakes and flatlands that marked the borders of the Soviet Union, three million German, Finnish and Romanian troops, supported by four Panzer armies and virtually the entire Luftwaffe, had launched Operation Barbarossa.

The Covid-19 pandemic left football nothing except the Belarussian League, which carried on in defiance of all science. Suddenly you were being offered odds on the Minsk derby or BATE Borisov against Torpedo Zhodino. As the virus swept west, one by one the European leagues shut down: the Bundesliga on 11 March, Ligue 1 two days later. Serie A, which in 1973 had carried on through a cholera epidemic that killed 170 in Naples alone, had already succumbed.

As a nation retreated deeper into its homes, the great threat to Leeds was that the season would be declared void. It had happened in the Netherlands. No league title would be awarded and there would be no promotion to the Eredivisie. Cambuur and De Graafschap, the two leading clubs in the second division, found their way up barred and bolted.

For Radrizzani, voiding the season would be cruel and financially ruinous, and would put his ownership of the club in question. 'To be competitive, a club like ours loses £8–10 million every year and nobody wants to carry on a business that loses money every year. Not having five home games means we would lose £2.5 million.'

Marcelo Bielsa's first season at Elland Road may have transformed Leeds as a club but it came at a price. The accounts for the 2018–19 season showed a loss of £21.4 million. The wages-to-turnover ratio, once a comfortable 60 per cent, was now 94 per cent. The average for the Championship was

107 per cent, and compared with Reading – who spent an insane £2.26 on wages for every pound they earned – it was manageable, especially if Leeds were promoted.

As someone who made his money in the selling of television rights, what especially irked Radrizzani was how little the extensive coverage on Sky had made Leeds United. Under Bielsa, they were the Championship's greatest attraction and had been selected nineteen times for live coverage. The timing of those broadcasts, often making Leeds play after Sheffield United, had arguably contributed to their downfall in 2019. They had been paid £7.7 million. Huddersfield, who finished bottom of the Premier League with sixteen points, were paid £12.3 million for their eight televised games.

Leeds employed 272 people either full- or part-time. Most of those jobs were now under threat. There was never any question that Bielsa, who had been known to gather his squad in a room and tell them how long a litter picker would have to work to afford a ticket to Elland Road, would feel a sense of responsibility. He and his squad agreed a wage deferral to avoid redundancies.

For players like Mateusz Klich, who had grown up in the elegant market town of Tarnów in southern Poland, it was now a matter of waiting it out. He was not signed by Marcelo Bielsa but his career had been transformed by him. When he was twenty-one, Klich had been given what seemed his big break: he was signed by Wolfsburg, who under the management of Felix Magath had won the Bundesliga two years before. Like Bielsa, Magath was often thought mad, although his madness contained a thick seam of sadism. One of his tricks was to send his players on gruelling summer runs. When they returned, exhausted and bathed in sweat, he would have hidden their water bottles. Refusing to believe Klich was injured, Magath once sent him on a 100 km bike ride. There were loan spells in Holland before a return to Wolfsburg, where he overslept and missed the team briefing. The bus went without him. At Kaiserslautern in the German second division he was thought too slow to fit into the 4-4-2 system on the wing.

Carsten Schroeter, a journalist with the German football magazine *Kicker,* said: 'It was obvious Klich was a very good player but he needed a coach who would give him confidence, who would build a team around him and allow him to take some risks, which would include making mistakes.' That man was Bielsa.

'I never thought I would come here and play like this,' Klich said. 'I don't know the words in English to describe how happy I am. I have been at a few clubs across Europe and never felt pressure like this.'

There was perhaps more pressure in being confined to his home in a village on the outskirts of Harrogate during the pandemic. There were two bike rides a week, plus daily runs, with his weight being sent back to the club each day.

'I realised how sad my life would be when I stopped playing football,' he said. 'I don't have normal training sessions; I don't go to the club. I don't see the boys in the dressing room. I get up and I am a dad twenty-four hours a day. My wife, Magda, can confirm I go around the house and kick everything.'

When he took his dog for a walk, Klich could see the Harrogate Convention Centre being turned into a Nightingale hospital that would take the overflow when the NHS was overwhelmed by the epidemic. Beds and oxygen bottles were being shipped in. 'The English are preparing for the worst-case scenario,' he told the Polish publication *Przeglad Sportowy*. There have been more than 43,000 deaths in the UK from Covid-19 at the time of writing, but the worst case did not come to pass. The NHS did not break. Harrogate's Nightingale hospital did not treat a single coronavirus patient.

In another hospital, they were treating Norman Hunter, who succumbed to coronavirus in April. More than anyone bar Billy Bremner, he epitomised the Leeds of Don Revie. He tackled ferociously and uncompromisingly; he bit legs. However, Hunter was the first man to be voted Footballer of the Year by his fellow players in the Professional Footballers' Association. There was skill and timing mixed in with the grit.

Watching from the broadcast gantry at Elland Road in recent years, Hunter was still passionate about the club. He was desperate to see Leeds return to the Premier League in his lifetime. It was a wish that was so very nearly granted. His coffin was taken into Elland Road and laid, for a moment, by the touchline.

In July 2020 there were thousands in the streets of Ashington, a Northumberland town known for its mines and its football. One local family alone, the Milburns, had produced seven professional footballers. Two of them had won the World Cup. One, Jackie Milburn, was reckoned the greatest footballer in Newcastle's history. Three had played for Leeds. Ashington had come to say farewell to Jack Charlton. With Billy Bremner he held the club appearance record – 773 matches – but his passing felt less specific to Leeds than Hunter's, who had played 726. As one of the Boys of 66, Jack Charlton also belonged to England. As their greatest manager he belonged to Ireland. He belonged to the rivers and fields of the British Isles, where he fished and hunted.

In between the passing of Hunter and Charlton, Trevor Cherry, who had been part of Leeds' Championship-winning side of 1974, died of a heart attack. One by one, the giants of another era were taking their leave.

On 16 May, football returned to Germany, the one major European nation that appeared to have controlled the virus. The highlight of the opening day was the *Revierderby* between Borussia Dortmund and Schalke. Theirs was a rivalry forged in the coal mines, the furnaces and the chemical works of the Ruhr. The 2020 version was literally and figuratively antiseptic. The teams arrived on multiple buses to maintain social distancing; everyone wore masks and had their temperatures checked. Goals were celebrated with elbow bumps. The footballs were disinfected by ball boys at half-time. There were 213 people, including the playing staff, inside Germany's biggest arena, the Westfalenstadion. After a 4–0 win, the Dortmund players ran to the vast stand where 25,000 of their most passionate supporters would have formed the famed Yellow Wall and applauded the empty seats.

In England, League Two and League One had abandoned their seasons. Clubs would be promoted on a points-per-game basis, although the play-offs would go ahead. Points-per-game would have suited Leeds very well. They would have been promoted as champions. The top two leagues, however, were to be played to a finish. The odds were entirely in Leeds' favour. They were facing what was in effect a nine-game season and Bielsa's teams had always begun seasons with a sprint start. They were seven points clear of the play-off places. Only one of those games, at home to Fulham on 27 June, looked potentially decisive.

The only drawback was that there would be no crowd. The passion and menace of Elland Road would be missing. In their place were 15,000 cut-outs of spectators, strategically placed to make it look as if someone were watching. This would be a triumph played out in a vacuum.

Leeds would take twenty-two points – more than any other club – from those nine fixtures but there was no sprint start. There was a stumble, a 2–0 defeat at Cardiff and two points dropped at home to Luton. In between came a convincing 3–0 dismissal of Fulham in the most important of the nine fixtures.

The stands may have been empty but Brentford were saying an astonishing goodbye in their final season at Griffin Park. There were eight straight wins and after a 1–0 victory over Preston on 15 July they were third, one point behind West Bromwich Albion, three behind Leeds, who owed their lead to Pablo Hernández's late, icily finished winner at Swansea. Both clubs could feel Brentford's breath on their shoulder. They could also see the finish line. The games were running out.

The following evening, Leeds played Barnsley. They did not play particularly well. Their goal was an own goal. There was plenty of tinkering from Bielsa. Hernández came on, Hélder Costa came off. Four at the back became three at the back and then four again. However, Leeds endured. On the final whistle, they needed a point from their final two games to end their exile.

The point was not even required. The following evening, in another part of Yorkshire, Huddersfield beat West Bromich Albion. Only one club, Brentford, could now catch them. They were up.

The Leeds squad had gathered at Elland Road to watch the game and they were filmed counting down to the final whistle at Huddersfield. Below them was a vast crowd that had poured down Lowfields Road and was pooling in front of the stadium. They carried banners, some of which stated 'Viva Bielsa' or proclaimed him the King of Elland Road. It was mid-July; it was still light and the blue and yellow smoke from the flares gushed into the grey skies above. The statue of Billy Bremner was festooned with scarves.

The obvious question was how this compared with the triumphs of 1974 or 1992, but this was a young crowd for whom the run to the 2001 Champions League semi-final would have been a hazy memory, if it were a memory at all. This was their team. These were their memories.

'I went to City Square, or Millennium Square as it is now,' said Nicolas Dixon. 'It felt like a scene from another time. There was an old Leeds United Union Jack, which might have been from the 1970s, draped from the City Museum. There were four or five young kids, who couldn't have been more than twelve, with their shirts off, hanging off lampposts while the smoke from the flares drifted across.'

It was thirty years since Bielsa had taken charge of his first match for Newell's Old Boys. It would have been a lovely piece of symmetry had he flung himself into the crowd shouting: 'Leeds *carajo!*' Bielsa was, however, almost sixty-five and he was at home in Wetherby. There was a small crowd by the dry-stone wall outside his flat. He came out to thank them, apologised for not speaking English, bumped elbows and posed for selfies. He was the picture of modesty and self-effacement. He was told he was God.

Things were moving giddyingly fast. The following day,

Brentford lost at Stoke. Leeds United were champions. By one of those ironies football revels in, Leeds were at Derby, facing the club that last season had inflicted such pain upon them. Had spectators been allowed into Pride Park, there would have been plenty of gloating, plenty of hands making binocular shapes as a nod to Spygate. Victor Orta did just that, although others' actions showed a little more class.

After the game, which Leeds won 3–1, Bielsa was driving away from Pride Park when he spotted a severely disabled fan in an electric wheelchair. He stopped the car and went over to embrace her. There are those who would argue that Bielsa is from a family of politicians; he knows a photo opportunity when he sees it. However, that afternoon in Derby there were no professional photographers around.

Led by Wayne Rooney, the Derby players had lined up to give Leeds a guard of honour. The Derby chairman, Mel Morris, presented the club with a bottle of Dom Pérignon. The vintage had been carefully chosen – 2004, the year Leeds United had last been part of the elite. It was, coincidentally, the year Marcelo Bielsa had last won a trophy.

One of Tony Benn's favourite quotations when he was jostling to lead the Labour Party was from Lao Tzu, the Chinese philosopher who wrote a manual on strategy called *The Art of War*. 'As for the best leaders, people do not notice their existence. When the best leader's work is done, the people say: "We did it ourselves."' There was something of that in the way Bielsa spoke afterwards. As Leeds' season reached a triumphant climax, he seemed to retreat into himself, to push others into the limelight. He made no great speech, said nothing memorable. When asked to explain Leeds' success, he remarked that the players had done it themselves.

The final game was at home to Charlton. In Leeds' last season in the Premier League, their final game at Elland Road had been a frantic 3–3 draw with Charlton that saw Alan Smith's farewell to the club. Leeds had already been relegated and some 38,000 had come to Elland Road for a farewell party laced with plenty of gallows humour. At the end, Smith, the boy from Rothwell who had fought so hard to keep the season alive, was chaired off the pitch in tears. The supporters who carried him on their shoulders accepted Smith could not stay, although they might not have been so accepting of his decision to leave had they known his destination was Old Trafford. One supporter carried a banner that proclaimed: 'Leeds First Division 2005: Champions Elect'. He would have to wait sixteen years for the prediction to be fulfilled.

Now there was no crowd at Elland Road to see Charlton, managed by Lee Bowyer, be shot to pieces and relegated. Ben White scored his first and – since Brighton had no intention of extending his loan – last goal for Leeds. It was a majestic drive from the edge of the area and behind the net was a giant number six shirt with Norman Hunter's name on the back. Radrizzani brought out the Championship trophy for Liam Cooper to lift.

Next season, he estimated, Leeds United would have a turnover of £180 million, roughly the same as AC Milan. His gamble on Marcelo Bielsa, who had been persuaded to don a white shirt and join in the celebrations, had been spectacularly vindicated. When Cooper raised the trophy above his head, Bielsa took a step backwards.

Mateusz Klich was not a fan of footballers using Instagram. 'When I see players hire a private plane for a lot of money basically just to upload a photo on Instagram it hurts me,' he said. 'I read an article that most robberies against footballers happen through Instagram. Well, if a guy uploads a video of himself driving a £200,000 car while wearing a £200,000 watch, it is no wonder footballers become victims of robberies.' When Leeds were promoted as champions, Klich uploaded a photo on his Instagram account. It showed him with a beer bottle in one hand and large cigar in the other, wearing a shirt that said: 'The Damned United Are Back'.

Jorge Griffa was not one for Instagram or Cuban cigars. He now lived in Recoleta, a stylish, middle-class district of Buenos Aires. Recoleta is a place of restaurants, bars, galleries and museums. It is most famous for its cemetery, which contains the overblown tombs of Argentina's presidents, poets and generals in tree-lined avenues. From Roman to Art Deco and Gothic, all styles are on display here. Surprisingly, the tomb of Eva Perón is among the most modest. Like Griffa's flat, full of mementos of a career that began in 1954 at Newell's Old Boys, Recoleta is a place of memories.

As someone who first met Marcelo Bielsa more than forty years before and who had helped launch him on what had become an extraordinary journey, it was a good time to ask Griffa, now eighty-five, what he made of the latest twist in the road.

'He asked the question of this English team and they answered him,' he said. 'Naturally, after all these years I am delighted. It seems so long ago that we were searching through the interior for players like Pochettino. I was not surprised Marcelo went to a club like Leeds who were not in the top division. That is his style, that is his way. He knew it was an opportunity and he knew how to make the most of it. Of course, the fans in Leeds appreciate him. Fans want to see the simple things, there is no need to go deeper. They want hard work. Marcelo is a very hard worker and it shows. When you are a coach or a manager, you unconsciously forget to live a life outside football. As a coach, he has never changed. It has always depended on the players. First and foremost, they have to have character. Footballers who win have character inbred into them. Only once did he come close to failing.'

Then Griffa tells the story of the 6–0 home defeat by San Lorenzo in 1992 and the breakdown that followed. 'He came to me and said: "Jorge, I am going to quit. I cannot carry on as manager." I told him: "You are going to go to Santa Fe, you are going to win and you are going to carry on." From that moment on, he learnt something about being a successful coach. He always wanted boys with character, boys who could express themselves. All he wanted was the space to develop his vision.'

When Kevin Keegan took Newcastle to the top flight in 1984, he did not stay. There was an end-of-season testimonial against Liverpool and then a helicopter took him from the centre circle and into retirement. The idea of walking into the sunset – he was never one for helicopters – might appeal to Marcelo Bielsa.

There was a brief flurry of headlines that Bielsa would go to Barcelona, where in the wake of their humiliation in the Champions League by Bayern Munich, the relationship between Lionel Messi and the president Josep Bartomeu had broken down completely. When Messi made his abortive attempt to force himself out of a club he had helped turn into the most glamorous sporting institution in the world, fans of Newell's Old Boys marched through the streets of Rosario with black and red flags demanding that he come home. They wanted the same for Bielsa.

'Many people in Rosario hope Marcelo will take charge of Newell's once more. It would be a lovely final touch with which to end your career,' said Griffa. 'Recently, Newell's were looking for a manager and I said to the president: "You can call Marcelo but he won't come. If I call him, I think he will come." However, I didn't call him. There was too much going on around him. Other things got in the way. It is all about opportunity and luck. It could still happen. I still think of him as young and life is about coincidences and opportunities. You know that in Rosario we lived in apartments that were fifty metres apart without realising it?'

There were some managers, particularly in South America, who thought that the praise for Marcelo Bielsa was wildly over the top. There were some like Alfio Basile, a manager with two Copas América to his name as manager of Argentina, who had always thought him overrated.

'Bielsa is the most overhyped coach in the world – more than Guardiola and Mourinho put together,' he had announced in 2018, the year Bielsa came to Leeds. 'He manages mediocre teams who don't have the pressure on them to become champions.'

Amazon had commissioned a film, narrated by Russell Crowe, who – growing up in Sydney just as Revie's side was dominating the English game half a world away – had fallen in love with Leeds United. *Take Us Home* had ended amid the wreckage of Leeds' defeat to Derby in the play-offs. Now, two more episodes were filmed to cover the club's promotion. Over in Uruguay, Martín Lasarte was unimpressed: 'I was in charge of Real Sociedad in the second division of La Liga. I won them promotion in my first season and they didn't make a film about me,' he said. 'I say this with respect. Bielsa has just won a second-division title after two years in charge.'

Another Uruguayan manager, Gerardo Pelusso, who had won championships in three South American countries, was even more scathing. 'They are talking about Leeds as if they had won the World Cup,' he said. 'Bielsa has not won a title for sixteen years. Zidane wins them every six months.'

And yet there was a fierce pride in Argentina, where Leeds United were back-page headlines. By now, Rafael Bielsa was Argentina's ambassador to Chile, although as he confessed in an article for *Clarín*, it had not prevented him from watching every one of Leeds' fixtures, sometimes from unlikely places. Under the headline 'He Is Our Robinson Crusoe', Rafael went into remarkable detail about how Marcelo had subtly adapted his tactics for Leeds' second season in the Championship. Pablo Hernández had been given more freedom, told to look for gaps and to venture deeper into the opponents' area.

Hernández's winner at Swansea was a subject of particular fascination in the embassy in Santiago. Rafael pointed out that the goal had been made not just by Luke Ayling's athleticism, which saw him begin the move in his own penalty area and keep running to provide the fatal cross, but by the way Ayling read the game, even when he would have been drained by the summer heat. Marcelo, he said, adapted rather than changed his style and he would not change it for the Premier League. 'An adventure writer narrates adventures, he does not change genre,' Rafael wrote. 'However, in his latest instalment, he modified the length of the chapters, the style and some of the characters.'

Now there would be a new story by the man he compared

to Robinson Crusoe, not just because he was thousands of miles from home but because he did all his writing, all his work, alone. As Rafael Bielsa pointed out with a flourish, Robinson Crusoe was also from Yorkshire.

A Time of Gifts

Like Leeds, Liverpool had ended a long march through a wilderness under a manager who was both charismatic and tactically innovative. Jürgen Klopp, too, had seen his achievements celebrated in art. In the city's Baltic Triangle, where warehouses had become artisan bakeries, craft beer bars and publishing houses, Klopp could be seen twice. He had made Liverpool world and European champions but, most importantly, he had made them league champions for the first time since 1990, the year Leeds had been promoted to the old First Division.

Then as now, Leeds would return to the top flight on Merseyside. Thirty years before, Howard Wilkinson's men had won, 3–2, at Everton. Now, Marcelo Bielsa would begin at Liverpool. All three of Leeds' Championship triumphs had in some way involved Anfield.

On 28 April 1969 they had won their first title with a goalless draw against their nearest challengers, Liverpool. Jack Charlton thought it a more moving occasion than winning the World Cup with England. He had been part of the England set-up for a little over a year when Bobby Moore wiped his muddied hands on a tablecloth before accepting the Jules Rimet trophy from the Queen. Charlton had signed his first professional contract with Leeds when he was seventeen. In a few days he would be thirty-five. Anfield was the end of a very long journey. He would always recall the generosity of the Kop in defeat.

On 24 April 1974 Liverpool lost to Arsenal to guarantee they could no longer catch a Leeds side that had led from the off. Don Revie thought it a greater achievement than the triumph five years before. At the beginning there had been some breath-taking football, among the best they had played under Revie. They had won in the teeth of a three-day week, power shortages and a sixteen-week miners' strike that had paralysed the great Yorkshire coalfield. Leeds United, like the miners, had won.

Eighteen years later, it was Manchester United's 2–0 defeat at Liverpool that confirmed Howard Wilkinson's side as champions. That night, the Leeds squad met up at the Flying Pizza in Roundhay. David Batty, a man whose eyes would glaze over during Wilkinson's intricate team talks, stood upright in Steve Hodge's Mercedes, his head and shoulders protruding through the sunroof, as it drove around City

Square. Later, as the team celebrated on the steps of Leeds Town Hall, Eric Cantona addressed the crowd: 'Why I love you, I don't know, but I love you.' Leeds were to find that love is a transferable emotion.

This time, Anfield represented a free hit. The last Premier League manager to come away from Anfield with three points was Sam Allardyce, then at the helm of Crystal Palace. That was in April 2017. If Leeds lost, nobody would draw any conclusions from the defeat. They lost, brilliantly and heroically, 4–3. In the Sky Television studio, Graeme Souness remarked he could not recall the last time the opposition had enjoyed more possession than Liverpool at Anfield. Jack Harrison's equaliser was a thing of beauty and athleticism; he took down a long pass from Kalvin Phillips with one foot and swept it past Trent Alexander-Arnold with the other before the ball had touched the turf. Patrick Bamford pounced on an error from Virgil van Dijk in a way he might not have done twelve months before.

Most managers in Bielsa's position would have seized on these positives, cradled and polished them in front of the television cameras. Jürgen Klopp's reaction – 'What a game, what an opponent, what a performance from both teams. A proper spectacle' – would have been built upon and embellished. However, to Marcelo Bielsa there was no such thing as heroic defeat. 'It was just a defeat,' he said. 'In the second half we struggled to get the ball from defence to attack.' He was critical of some shoddy defending. Leeds had conceded two penalties and given Van Dijk a free header.

The cast changed. Despite a fierce campaign on social media from Leeds fans, Ben White returned to Brighton. Just as White had replaced Pontus Jansson, so Robin Koch became Liam Cooper's latest partner in central defence. Koch, who played for Freiburg, had pedigree. He was already an international and his father, Harry, famed for his long, permed locks, had been part of one of German football's most romantic stories when the newly promoted Kaiserslautern won the Bundesliga in 1998.

Twenty-two years on and the romance had been squeezed out. Bayern Munich had won the Bundesliga for eight consecutive years. If, at the start of the season, you bet £10 that they would make it nine, your winnings would amount to £1.30. There had been interest from Leipzig and a meeting with Hertha Berlin's manager, Bruno Labbadia, but Leeds offered the twenty-four-year-old a rather more competitive league than he would find in Germany. They could also offer him Bielsa.

'I spoke to a lot of people who are fascinated by Bielsa,' said Koch. 'When I went to Leeds some of my team-mates at Freiburg got in touch to ask what training there was like. I tried to get as many impressions about Bielsa and his style of play as I could but it was Mateusz Klich, who had been a team-mate at Kaiserslautern, who gave me the most vivid picture. I watched *Take Us Home* but it was only when my name was linked with Leeds on social media that I realised it is no ordinary club.'

The way Robin Koch worked out whether he would be a good fit for Leeds was peculiarly modern. He watched videos of their games and cut in clips of himself playing for Freiburg to see how far he would have to adapt. The answer was not much.

There were other signings. Rodrigo Moreno Machado did not seem like a typical Bielsa player. In March, the forward would turn thirty. A season with Bolton had produced a single goal – against Wigan. His last season with Valencia had yielded just four in La Liga. Yet in the Champions League, Rodrigo had scored the winners at Chelsea and Ajax and had been part of the Valencia side that had beaten Barcelona to win the Copa del Rey in 2019. Five years before, he had taken part in an extraordinary season with Benfica. Had they not lost to Sevilla on penalties in the final of the Europa League, they would have won four trophies in a season. Rodrigo was one of those who saw his penalty saved.

On balance, it seemed a transfer that might work and it was welcomed by those Leeds fans who had tired of the amount of chances Patrick Bamford needed to score a goal.

The nadir had been against Derby in September 2019 when Bamford had missed several opportunities from close range and struck the post from perhaps a yard out. It was the first time Derby had come to Elland Road since the debacle of the play-offs. There was a vivid desire for some kind of revenge.

Leeds had dominated and Derby had snatched an equaliser in stoppage time. Bamford had been blamed for the loss of two points, although had Klich not rolled his penalty wide – a penalty that Bamford had won – Leeds would have had their victory.

He was still fresh-faced and good looking but at twenty-seven, he could no longer be classed as promising. He was also posh, born in Grantham, a product of Nottingham High School for Boys, where fees in 2020 were £5,148 a term and the traditional sport of choice was rugby. In sport, when you struggle, your background tends to be mentioned.

He had scored sixteen goals in Leeds' promotion season, the only member of Bielsa's squad to reach double figures but it had taken him 121 chances.

Yet, as Leeds returned to the Premier League, playing against better defences, Bamford would score in each of the opening three matches. Against Fulham and Sheffield United, those goals would be decisive.

Perhaps something had clicked in his game, perhaps the pressure of knowing Leeds had spent £27 million on Rodrigo spurred him on or perhaps it was the absence of a crowd.

Whenever Bamford struggled, his team-mates would point out how well he played in training. The stunning volley he scored on the practice pitches at Thorp Arch in November 2018 which saw Bielsa running over to embrace him is evidence of that.

Put another way, Bamford performed better without an

audience and without the pressure of a crowd he was suddenly and maybe coincidentally playing with real confidence.

In empty stadiums the dynamics of the game had changed. The Chelsea striker, Olivier Giroud, noted: 'The pitch feels bigger with no fans in the stadium. It's crazy to say it because it is the same pitch but it feels bigger because the bearings and the points of reference are not the same.' He added that you could now hear every instruction from the bench.

Perhaps because there had barely been a pre-season, perhaps because Premier League matches now felt like friendlies, perhaps because defences no longer had the sound of the crowd to warn them about an overlap or an opponent behind them, strikers ran riot.

When the Premier League paused for its first international break in October, the opening thirty-eight matches had produced 144 goals or 3.78 per game. The last two had seen Manchester United beaten 6-1 by Tottenham at Old Trafford while Liverpool had conceded seven at Aston Villa.

Not since 1929-30 had English top-flight football seen defences breached so often. Then Sheffield Wednesday had won the title scoring 105 times while Sheffield United had scored ninety-one and avoided relegation on goal average.

The return of Premier League football to Elland Road should have been an occasion of unfettered celebration; of noise, of chants, of pints being drunk in The Old Peacock. Instead, top-flight football came to Leeds in silence.

Bielsa's achievement in promoting a thin and sometimes

ordinary squad had not just returned the glory to Elland Road, it had protected the club against a cold, dark financial tide that was threatening to engulf English football.

In the Championship, matchday revenue had earned Leeds around £500,000 for every league game they staged at Elland Road. It was on a par with the money taken at Molineux, Villa Park or Craven Cottage; double the revenues at The Hawthorns, Turf Moor or Bramall Lane.

The sale of tickets, food, programmes and corporate hospitality accounted for 28 per cent of the club's revenue. That money had now disappeared entirely.

In the Premier League, with its vast television revenues, it was a problem that could be managed; even at Manchester United and Tottenham who were losing more than £4 million a game. In the Championship it could be fatal. At the beginning of October 2020, the *Northern Echo* reported that Middlesbrough, a large, well-run Championship club with running costs of £32 million and revenues reduced to £8 million, would run out of money by the end of November.

Fulham and Leeds must have been more than usually grateful to have escaped the Championship. When they met in September 2020, once more seven goals were shared. This time it was Leeds who scored the four.

When Jorge Valdano was sporting director at Real Madrid, he told the president, Florentino Pérez, that, statistically, three in every five transfers failed. It triggered the policy of the *galáctico*. Footballers such as Luís Figo, Zinedine

Zidane and David Beckham – so good they could not possibly fail – would be brought to the Bernabéu. The gaps would be filled in by academy graduates. At Leeds, Victor Orta and Marcelo Bielsa could claim a record better than two in five. However, the goalkeeper remained a problem. Kiko Casilla's pedigree as a product of the Real Madrid academy was undermined by some dreadful errors in the cauldron of the play-off semi-final against Derby and the 1–1 draw at Brentford just before football shut down.

Casilla had become a liability in other ways, too. In September 2019, he was accused of racially abusing the Charlton striker Jonathan Leko, in the most offensive terms. In February 2020, he was banned for eight games and fined £60,000. Leeds did not commit the crass errors Liverpool had when attempting to defend Luis Suárez against charges he had racially abused Patrice Evra. Unlike Kenny Dalglish, Bielsa did not order his squad to parade in T-shirts backing a man whose evidence the FA panel would describe as 'unreliable' and 'inconsistent'. However, nor did Leeds handle the issue well. Casilla's evidence was as unimpressive as Suárez's had been in 2011. The FA panel did not believe the goalkeeper had never heard the word 'nigger' before. They handed down the same ban Suárez had received.

Leko claimed that he received no apology from either the club or Casilla. Leeds had issued a statement noting that Casilla had been convicted on 'the balance of probability' rather than the criminal test of 'beyond reasonable doubt'.

Given the 'balance of probability' is good enough for the General Medical Council to determine negligence claims, eyebrows were raised. In response to the statement from Elland Road, the FA briefed that the verdict had not been a close one.

When, a year after the incident, Bielsa made Casilla captain for Leeds' League Cup tie against Hull, eyebrows arched still further. This was a rare misstep by Bielsa, one of the few times since his arrival in Yorkshire that his decision had been openly questioned by a section of the club's supporters. Bielsa retorted that the players had wanted Casilla to lead the team and they surely knew him better than those on social media.

'I interpreted the feelings of his team-mates,' Bielsa said. 'They thought he deserved to be captain and we have to listen to those messages. The players see in their captain someone who can represent them. Surely, those who judge Kiko ignore a lot of the things his team-mates see in him. The opinion of the masses should always be heard but I don't know if you guys know what percentage of fans that is. The public won't have all the information that his team-mates have.'

However, the emergence of the twenty-year-old Illan Meslier had already pushed Casilla into the shadows. Meslier was from Morbihan, on Brittany's wild Atlantic coast, a last stronghold of the Breton language. Across the bay from his village was Lorient, a club that had emerged from almost permanent obscurity to win promotion and, in 2002, the

Coupe de France. Meslier was nine when he started playing for the club's academy. Then came the under-17 World Cup in India and appearances for France at under-21 level. Leeds had paid £5.8 million for him and he had made his debut amid the grandeur of their FA Cup tie at Arsenal. Meslier replaced Casilla during his ban and kept his place.

Leeds were facing a Sheffield United side that had finished ninth in the Premier League in 2020 but had failed to score in its opening two matches of the new 2020–21 season.

It would have been a worthy first goal. Ben Osborn breaking down the left, sending over a low cross that David McGoldrick deflected into the path of John Lundstram with a back-flick. It was not point-blank range but it was close enough. Meslier produced a save worthy of his hero, Manuel Neuer. Bamford snatched the win at the death, becoming the first Leeds player since Mick Jones in 1968 to score in the opening three games of a top-flight season. The fourth game would be at home to Manchester City.

It sparked the stories of the meeting between Bielsa and Pep Guardiola in Máximo Paz fourteen years before. They were fourteen years in which Guardiola had become acknowledged as the greatest coach in world football while telling anyone who would listen that Bielsa was better. The question posed at the end of that evening – 'Do you like blood so much?' – was replayed, along with Guardiola's riposte: 'I need that blood.'

Before the match, Bielsa played down his influence on a

man who as a manager had won eight league titles in three countries. 'I don't feel like a mentor to him,' he said. 'If there is a manager who has fashioned his own ideas, it is Guardiola; his teams play like no other. Many believe Guardiola's Barcelona is the best club side ever created.'

In Manchester, Guardiola was effusive. 'He is probably the man I admire most in world football – as a manager and as a person,' he said. 'He is the most authentic manager in terms of how he conducts his teams. He is unique; nobody can imitate him. I don't see him quite as often as I would like but when I spend time with him, it's always inspirational. The value of a manager does not depend on how many titles you have won. My teams won more titles than his but, in terms of knowledge of the game and many other things including training sessions, I am still a way off him.'

The match lived up to its billing and echoed the meeting between Athletic Bilbao and Barcelona at the San Mamés in 2011, not just because it was played in fierce driving rain and not just because it was drawn. It was the same relentless, punishing, beautiful football. Manchester City, playing without a recognised striker, attacked from the off. Kevin De Bruyne clanged a free kick against the post. Raheem Sterling, cutting in from the left, opened the Leeds defence up with fatal results. Stuart Dallas cleared off the line.

In defence and attack, Leeds were tireless. They flooded forward and they funnelled back in numbers to defend. Rodrigo struck the outside of the bar and when Ederson fumbled the subsequent corner he had his second goal in Premier League football, in a game that would be remembered more vividly than Bolton vs. Wigan.

At the final whistle, Marcelo Bielsa remained crouched in the downpour before getting up and asking Pep Guardiola what he thought of the game. 'I am not able to analyse the game after one second,' came the reply. 'I am not able to process it.'

Then the Premier League paused for breath and an international break. When Bielsa took over at Leeds, he had told the players he could not guarantee he would promote them but he would make them better footballers. He had made Kalvin Phillips, who like James Milner had grown up in Wortley, into an England international, dubbed 'the Yorkshire Pirlo' by Leeds supporters. Before the season began, Phillips was called up for games against Iceland and Denmark. He was the first Leeds player since 2004 to be selected for England. Bielsa asked Phillips to come up to his office at Thorp Arch. There he handed the midfielder an old-fashioned, collared T-shirt with red and black halves. There was also a note for Phillips's mother and grandmother. It was a Newell's Old Boys' shirt, one that Bielsa had worn during his brief playing career at the Coloso del Parque. There were few things more precious to Bielsa than his mementos of Newell's. It was, Phillips thought, quite a gift. He had been given other gifts by Marcelo Bielsa, but this was the only one he could touch.

Acknowledgements

Special thanks to: Esteban Bekerman, Ben Brock, Craig Brown, Daniel Gabin, Raul Gámez, Jorge Griffa, Simon Hart, Micky P. Kerr, Ally McKay, Harold Mayne-Nicholls, David Luxton, Richard Milner, Joel Richards, Santiago Segurola, Phil Shaw, Rory Smith, Henry Winter.

Bibliography

Guillem Balague, *Brave New World* (Weidenfeld and Nicolson, 2017)

Anthony Clavane, *A Yorkshire Tragedy* (Quercus, 2016)

Thomas Goubin, *El Loco Unchained* (Hugo Sport, 2015)

Danny Hall, *He's One of our Own* (Vertical Editions, 2018)

Roman Iucht, *La vida por el futbol* (Sudamericana, 2012)

Romain Laplanche, *Le mystère Bielsa* (Solar Editions, 2017)

Sergio Maffei, *El lado V* (Sudamericana, 2011)

Luis Gaston Mora Obregon, *Marcelo Bielsa*: *El día que todo cambió* (Editorial Forja, 2018)

Ariel Senosiain, *Lo Suficientemente Loco* (Corregidor, 2004)

Jonathan Wilson, *Angels with Dirty Faces* (Weidenfeld and Nicolson, 2016)

Newspapers and websites: *The Big Interview with Graham Hunter, The Bleacher Report, El Mercurio, These Football Times, Guardian, New York Times, Clarín, La Nación, Olé, Sun, Daily Mail, Four-Four-Two, Yorkshire Evening Post, La Capital, L'Equipe, La Provence, La Voix du Nord.*

Index